Elaine Culbertson has almost no sacred objects from her ancestors: no Star of David pendant from a grandmother; no tallis worn by a great-uncle as he swayed in shul. What she has instead are the stories that her parents, both Holocaust survivors, told from the time Culbertson was a child hiding under the dining room table. In Mamaleh, she deftly weaves those stories—including excerpts from her mother's anguished, poignant writing—with her own memories of growing up Jewish in Northeast Philadelphia, a childhood shadowed by the Holocaust. The result is a 20th century saga that is frank, bitter, drenched in grief and yet inspired by her parents' fierce will to survive and Culbertson's commitment to telling the truth of all their lives.

Anndee Hochman
Writer, teacher, storyteller

I0458395

Tursulowe Press

Philadelphia, Pennsylvania
www.phillybookshop.com
www.mamalehthebook.com

Library of Congress Control Number 2025915091

ISBN 978-1-957057-22-4

Printed in the United States of America

Elaine Culbertson's *Mamaleh* is a powerful and poignant memoir, painfully honest, deeply warm and uniquely original. It tells the story of a child of Holocaust survivors who is blessed and burdened with the memories of the past. She recounts the story of her parents' experience with insight and integrity and then reflects on the life they built for themselves and the community they created in the United States with respect and charm. Like the truthteller I know her to be, she does not gloss over the tensions between mother and daughter, the losses her parents had suffered and the transmission of those losses directly, knowingly and inadvertently to the next generation (s). She speaks for herself bravely and boldly and also speaks for her generation who bore the scars of the past as they created their own distinct paths forward as Americans and Jews. I have known Elaine as a dedicated and skillful Holocaust educator for more than three decades, but I learned so much more about her. As I read chapter after chapter my respect for her grew, so it will be with her readers.

Michael Berenbaum
Distinguished Professor of Jewish Studies
Director, the Sigi Ziering Institute
American Jewish University
Los Angeles, CA

In the growing landscape of Holocaust memoirs, *Mamaleh* by Elaine Culbertson stands out as a luminous, moving achievement. Why this memoir, among so many? First, because Culbertson succeeds in blending a child's hidden vantage with an adult's fierce clarity, rendering scenes of Holocaust aftermath not only from survivor perspectives inside the camps, but from a little girl's perspective beneath a Brooklyn dinner table, among shoes and whispered grief. Second, the memoir's dual authorship, woven from Elaine's narrative and the haunting, eloquent writings of her mother, Dora Freilich, imbues the book with a rare combination of emotional resonance and historical authenticity, where the voices of survivor and daughter echo and deepen each other. Third, Culbertson's prose is at once intimate and unflinching, building a portrait of memory, humor, affection, and a longing for connection over the generations.

This is a memoir about what was lost. It is also the story of how a survivor and her daughter shared, shaped, and questioned the ramifications of that loss. In *Mamaleh*, remembrance is an act of both past and future, preservation and perpetuation. It is also an act of love, an urgent plea for understanding, and a daughter's reckoning with the quiet truths buried in her mother's cries.

Mamaleh does more than commemorate the past; it catapults readers into the immediacy of a past that refuses to go away. Highly recommended.

Joshua M. Greene
New York Times Bestselling author of *Unstoppable*

Elaine Culbertson has been a pillar in the field of Holocaust education for decades. Now, she's turned her great talents to literary memoir. From the first pages of her book *Mamaleh*, she excavates with heart and soul her own family's past, bringing to the work a rare and necessary combination of unflinching honesty and profound compassion. As in all great memoir, Culbertson's personal story becomes a lens through which readers encounter a broader story, in this case, the complexity of Holocaust survivors' post-war experiences which reverberated not only through their families but across American society as a whole.

This book is not just for Jewish readers or those who are interested in the Holocaust. It's for anyone who has grappled with family legacies and how the past shapes the present. In other words, it is a story for all of us.

Alexandra Zapruder
Author of *Salvaged Pages*

Few people have so consistently and accurately tended to the teaching and understanding of the Holocaust as Elaine Culbertson, daughter of two remarkable Holocaust survivors. In *Mamaleh*, Culbertson wisely reflects upon the many stories her parents related about their experiences and upon her mother's personal writings. With compassion, insight, and tenderness, she also makes astute observations upon what it was like to grow up in a household filled with the trauma and determination of two concentration camp survivors. This book should be read by all those who want a more complete picture of the Holocaust.

Stephen Feinberg
Former educator,
United States Holocaust Memorial Museum and
Holocaust and Jewish Resistance
Teachers Program of the American
Gathering of Jewish Holocaust Survivors

Midway through *Mamaleh*, Elaine Culbertson's deeply moving memoir, she writes that "My family had no heirlooms to pass down to me as I came into adulthood. Everything our family had owned had been destroyed or looted during the Holocaust." Everything, that is, except for the inheritance of memories and memory that she absorbed into her consciousness and has now brought to life in this outstanding volume. Brilliantly and sensitively written, *Mamaleh* is an important addition to the core curriculum of Holocaust literature.

Menachem Z. Rosensaft
Adjunct professor, Cornell Law School
Founding chair, International Network
of Children of Jewish Holocaust Survivors

Mamaleh

A Legacy of Loss and Love

Elaine Culbertson

with excerpts from the writings
of her mother Dora Freilich

And how shall I mourn for you on this memorial day
There are too few candles and not enough prayers
Perhaps from the sky I will gather the stars
And they will become your memorial candles
For you and for your burned communities
For what remains after war but candles and prayers

A poem written by
Dora Freilich
in Yiddish and English

Mamaleh

A Legacy of Loss and Love

The Storyteller

Under the kitchen table, made larger by the leaves we keep in the closet to accommodate the guests, I inspect each set of shoes—my mother's summer wedgies, my father's ripple soled oxfords, the multicolored heels and flats of the lady card players and coffee drinkers, the loafers of their male companions. We are a shoe family. My father's father owned a small shoe factory in Poland, and my father labors now in a shop that provides handcrafted shoes for victims of polio. From an early age I am familiar with the smell and the feel of the leather that my father brings home for the work he completes to make an extra bit of cash.

The shoes under the table serve as a compass to let me know where my father sits and where my mother will eventually settle once the food has been served. I must be careful not to let either of them know I am lurking in forbidden territory. I am supposed to be in the other room, watching television with the children who accompany their parents on every visit. No one can afford a babysitter; who would leave their children at home alone? Too much can happen when parents are not there to protect their children; too much has already happened to all these guests.

The Brooklyn apartment, made more affordable because we share it with the elderly landlord, is still warm from the preparation of marinated herring and unpeeled boiled potatoes—a Litvak delicacy. The aromas seek and find every corner of the rooms. The company has relished this familiar meal as a reminder of their youth, and a simpler time, the "before time" and so the talk has been about their childhoods. Now, as the plates are cleared to make room for the coffee and cake, the stories of the war will begin.

The flowered tablecloth obscures my view somewhat, but it provides a haven from their eyes, and I can listen to their stories without being told to leave the room. New to America, this group of Polish refugees speaks to one another in Yiddish. The men boast of their wartime exploits, and the women lament the difficulties of their adjustments to this new country. Had they known I was in the room they would have switched to Polish, because we children have not been taught Polish. That is the secret language used for topics too adult for us, or when they are talking about us in secret. Because no one realizes I am there, their stories are vivid with details **that are** too graphic for my four-year-old ears. As each person recounts a tale of wartime escape and miraculous survival, I try to understand what they are talking about. Most of it is well beyond me. Still, the tone of each voice conveys the need to be the one who must be heard this time, the one whose story will not shock the group but rather, will confirm the right to membership in this society of Holocaust survivors.

My father's voice is always the loudest, the most insistent, the most filled with anger and resentment against his Nazi tormentors and their Polish and Ukrainian collaborators. I can hear my mother trying to calm him down, insisting that this is a social gathering, asking him to temper his words or lower his voice, but to little avail.

"Bernie, stop. Not now. We are here to have a good time. Let's be happy! Can we have a moment without all of that?" Her words fail to keep him quiet. His stories recount how he foiled the enemy, while hers, whenever she chooses to speak, are wrought with anguish and mourning. My mother rarely shares in this large group. When she talks about what happened to her it is with one or two of her women friends who have endured similar circumstances, those for whom very little explanation is necessary. In this larger group, my mother listens and consoles. I can hear her sigh as the stories unfold around her. I am sitting near her and watch as she twists and untwists her legs. I want to reach out and touch her, to comfort her, but if I do, she will know that I am here. So, I maintain my hiding place by remaining silent and still.

My father is trying to teach the world a lesson with every story he tells, the same lessons he drills into me at every opportunity. "Be alert, watch out for those who want to hurt you. Don't let them bully you. Fight back." I am too young to understand exactly what he wants me to do, but I know there is an enemy I should be wary of, and that I should stand strong against it. My mother, on the other hand, is seeking someone with whom she can commiserate, someone who will understand without too many words. She has much more from which to heal; her war experiences dwarf those of my father, but she does not engage in a battle of words or a contest of suffering, and she cannot tell the stories without crying. For my father, anger brings a temporary catharsis; for my mother something else is at work. She is the one who will scream in the night. Hers is the voice I will hear as I lie in bed—the shouts that turn to sobs.

From my hiding place, I hear words in Yiddish that are not part of my vocabulary. They are the words like *milchama* (war) *lager*, (concentration camp), crematoria, and barrack. There are proper names as well, names like Hitler, Roosevelt, Stalin, Mengele, and then there are family names like Fradel, Simcha and Velvel. Sometimes when the conversation is lighter, I hear about the towns, the schools, the holidays and the food, especially the food, the likes of which they swear they will never taste again. The summer raspberries so juicy and sweet, the pierogies that my father could never get enough of or the potato latkes that my paternal grandmother fried for Chanukah, the challah bread from my maternal grandfather's bakery from which my mother would steal the tip and run before her father realized what she had done. Nothing here in America can rival what they remember. When they talk of food, their voices lose their anger and heavy emotion. A lightness falls around the table as the sweet memories of the before times are brought back in their stories.

When I am finally discovered under the table, perhaps because I start to fall asleep and my toes slip out from under the tablecloth, or perhaps because my hand lands on top of my mother's foot as I try to stretch out, I am shooed away. My mother asks the company whether I might have heard something I shouldn't have. She worries that the stories are too grim, too frightening for a girl of four.

"She'll have to learn about this sooner or later. Don't worry so much," my father insists. "The sooner she understands, the sooner she will be able to protect herself against our enemies."

"Bernie don't steal her childhood," my mother laments. She knows even more about losing one's childhood than he does.

What I know is there is something different about my parents and their friends and that there was something called "war." I know that bad things can happen. I am not sure if those bad things can happen to me, but I am already being warned about "them." Them is other people, but I am not sure how to distinguish between the good people and the enemies. My father can tell instantly, and so I assume I, too, will learn how to do this as I grow up.

When I grow too big to hide myself under the table, I lurk in the doorways of the rooms where the adults are talking. When the other children leave to go outside or tussle over which television show to watch, I find a way to edge towards the table. Sometimes my mother will halt the conversation, insisting that I leave, but as I grow older, she will allow me to stay. She will call me an *alte kop*, an old head, old before my time, and I will eventually blend into the group's conversations. I will be allowed to ask questions all the while reassuring my mother and the others **that** I do understand what they are talking about. I promise if I hear something that upsets me too much, I will walk away. I don't walk away often.

The words I did not understand when I was four slowly become part of my vocabulary. I understand that somehow, all the good in the before times vanished, that all the joy evaporated into memories that would have to sustain my parents and their friends all through the war and into the future.

As the years go by, I am no longer shielded at all from the horror. Even my mother stops holding her tongue. She will tell me about her family and of her "camp sisters," those women who banded together to provide moral support to each other in the concentration camp, somehow mitigating the horror through their concern for each other, reminding each other that good times will come again.

My father's stories will grow more horrifying, the brutality more vivid in its detail, and his anger more evident. He will speak of his family but all talk of them will always end in betrayal and death. Sometimes he will bite his lip in a characteristic grimace that will let me know he is thinking about what happened and cursing his inability to save the people he loved, his mother, his brother, his sisters. If he had only been in the right place at the right time! I can see the frustration that afflicts him, the rage that he channels into strength, the way he bends a metal rod into a hook with his bare hands when hoodlums steal part of the awning over his shoe store window. He will never be powerless again.

In the *before time* stories my grandparents and the people who would have been my aunts and uncles are still alive. I am part of what was a large family on both my mother's and father's side— grandparents, aunts, uncles and cousins, names upon names, many carrying the same names as those of my distant great grandparents, a whole dictionary of names. Now there is just the four of us, my mother and father, my little brother and me. My father's brother is the only other immediate family member who

4

remains, and he and his family are all we have. The grandparents and aunts and uncles and cousins are all gone, each one murdered by the Nazis. Sometimes the storyteller knows the details of their fates, the year, the place, and how death was inflicted, sometimes one must imagine. I am not sure which is easier to take, knowing actual details or allowing my imagination to fill them in.

I am taught to hate the Germans and everything that is German. We cannot pass a Volkswagen car or hear a German word without some sort of negative response from my father.

"They were the most civilized country in Europe, those murdering bastards. They killed children. Innocent children! And now, they are our best friends. Even in Israel they drive German cars! I would sooner crawl than drive a German car. How soon we forget. They are all still Nazis," he proclaims.

Even years after the war, he continues to warn us to stay alert. His anger never lessens. Anything that doesn't go his way he deems antisemitic, from being waited on poorly in a restaurant by an unfriendly waiter who Dad is sure has recognized him as a Jew, to buying a defective product that somehow works for everybody else but not for him. It is *all* antisemitism, and Dad is always both the victim and the one whose purpose it is to warn the rest of us about it. If Easter dawns sunny and bright, my father calls it the *goyishe mazel*, the luck of the gentiles. The cards are always stacked against him, but even so, he continues to resist. His successes come despite the odds. He will not let *them* win.

My father is a brilliant man whose education has been cut short by the circumstances of the Second World War—first by the Soviet takeover of his part of Poland in 1939, and then by the subsequent Nazi invasion in 1941. He would have been something other than the owner of a shoe store had his education not been snatched from him by his tormentors. His sharp mind is matched by his incredible manual dexterity, both of which saved him in the camps. He can envision and build anything; it is antisemitism alone that has kept him from his dreams and consigned him to making a living doing something that does not challenge his intellect or skill. He is dutybound to provide for his family, and he bears the daily frustration of not becoming the engineer he might have been.

For my mother, the losses cut in a more personal way. The only survivor of her immediate family, she was a typical girl of that time

5

who had no dreams of professional success. She was a teenager who lost everyone she loved, some deaths happening right before her eyes. As I mature and decode the stories, I wonder how she survived at all. What mechanism inside a teenage girl breaks when she witnesses her sister's murder? When my mother asks the veteran inmates of the camp on her first day in Auschwitz where her mother might be, they point to the smoke issuing from the crematorium and tell her to look for her mother there. How can she continue living after that? Knowing what she endured, I marvel that my mother can go on about her daily life. In my teenage years I wonder how she had the courage to bear children at all.

There is not a family meal, holiday or event that goes by that is not in some way comparable to something that occurred before or during the War. Every part of life calls up the Holocaust, from the most mundane aspects of daily living to the most crucial. My mother tells my father in Polish *psheistein*, "be silent," hoping that my brother and I don't understand that she is trying to censor the horrific details that are part of each of his stories. It becomes an inside joke; my brother and I learn the Polish word and when my father goes on a rant, we laugh and say *psheistein* to him, to protect ourselves from what is unbearable. Even my husband Jim picks up on it many years later offering the Polish word to my father as a kind way of asking for a bit of peace. The stories are so familiar that we short-circuit my father at times and as a chorus, we cut straight to the ending. "Yeah, Dad. We know. And then you outsmarted them once again." This doesn't anger him; he has become aware of his habits and knows that he is going on a bit too long and too furiously, but he is on a mission, at first with me and my brother, then with my husband, and then with our son Joshua. Eventually, he will tell anyone who will listen.

The people in the stories, the ones whose faces I have never seen, are as present in my life as those people who have survived and who populate the survivor card table that my parents or another one of their group hosts each week. The dead grandmothers and grandfathers for whom my brother and I are named loom large in our lives. My parents mourn them, but what differentiates us from our born-in-America friends and neighbors who may have lost an elder is that my parents have the added sorrow of mourning for their murdered brothers and sisters as well.

I mourn for them although I never knew them. Theirs are the stories that break my heart, the stories of the way the family is decimated, the inescapable curse of being a Jew in eastern Europe at that time. Even as a child I know it may be normal to have lost a grandparent, but there is something unique about having lost all but one of the aunts and uncles in what was once a large family

Not a single picture exists of my father's family. They are not only ghosts; they are faceless ghosts as well. The photos we have from my mother's side stop suddenly in 1939, the year the war began, the year my mother's uncles in America lost contact with their sister, my grandmother, the year my family's life was changed forever. The pictures freeze her family in time, a grandmother who never ages, children who never grow up. When my mother opens the photo album, her fingers caress the pictures tenderly as if she is touching actual faces. For my father, memories will have to suffice. He paints their portraits in words, an odd tidbit of information emerging sometimes to flesh out the specter—his sister Bronia had beautiful long red hair, his little brother Feivel was the smartest boy in the school, his father had a sensitive stomach and would never eat freshly baked bread. From these scattered pieces I weave a memory blanket not big enough to comfort me, but enough of a remnant of this lost world to wrap partially around me.

I wonder if I look like them. I ask my father's brother, but he never answers directly. His pain silences him. Unlike my father, he does not speak about those times unless my father goads him into it. How different these two brothers are, one who avoids the stories and one whose very existence is driven by them.

These little details that bring the ghosts to life motivate me to want in turn to tell anyone who will listen, and I grow up to become the living repository of these stories. I am my father's daughter. His warnings took hold; his work is done. It's my turn now.

Who is Mamaleh?

The Yiddish word *Mamaleh* is a diminutive of the word *mama* or mother. It is not the name I called my mother. It is the name my mother called me. I was named for her mother, a Jewish tradition to name a child for a dead parent, but there was much more to it than that. My mother was sixteen when her mother was murdered in Auschwitz. Of course, I would be named for this beloved and deeply missed person lost so early in my mother's life, but the fact that my mother addressed me as "little mother" sits at the core of this story. I was the replacement mother, the replacement sister she watched die, as well as a replacement for every childhood friend that she lost as the Nazi hold tightened on her small town. In her old age my mother would call everyone working in her care facility "mamaleh," but even her nursing aides knew that I was the real Mamaleh, the one whose attention she craved and whose love she demanded.

I did not really know my mother as a person. I knew her as my mother, but not in the way others perceived her, how she seemed to her friends, or what my father saw in her that made him want to marry her. Even when I became an adult, and especially when my mother aged into that time in her life when she needed me more than I needed her (and I say this knowing everyone who is reading this has probably thought or will think the same thing about an aging parent), I could not have a relationship with my mother anything like the relationship I might have with any other older woman. We could never be equals. We could never be friends.

I could not, as her daughter, ever understand her. I might find out things about her past, about her childhood, about the horrors she endured during the Holocaust, even little snippets about what it was like for her to be married to my father, but I would never really have the true sum of who she was. And that is why I set out to write down what I *did* know, and to reflect on her past, and how that colored and continues to color my life.

My mother was married at nineteen and was twenty-two when I was born. Just recently my brother and I were reminiscing about the two of them, and he mentioned that our parents could not have known each other very long before they married. I had never thought about it, but he was right. Who was my mother at that young age? What could she have known about life? Her circumstances could not have been more different from mine. Her choices were based on the experiences that went on to resonate throughout both of our lives.

My mother had gone back to her hometown in Poland after the end of the war, after the death camps and the forced marches, after she had recuperated a bit. It was sometime in the early fall of 1945. Finding nothing and no one and feeling threatened by her former non-Jewish neighbors who indicated they would not return any of the family possessions they had seized after the town's Jews were deported to Auschwitz, she left brokenhearted, realizing she was the sole survivor of her immediate family. She left what she had known for somewhere else, because what she had known was no longer what it had been.

Dor and Bernie in Lodz, Poland, 1946

My parents had not known each other before the War. Theirs is not a story of sweethearts being reunited, or of people from the same town who suddenly realize they were meant for each other all along. They would never have met if not for the upheaval all of Europe was undergoing. They met because my father's older brother Sam was courting my mother's friend Basha, a fellow survivor from my mother's hometown. Somehow the dating couple convinced the unattached two to meet, and they became a couple as well. My dad was only twenty-two. But these ages are only chronological; the experiences of these people made them both older and younger than their years. What my mother had experienced by the time she was married was an overwhelming number of crushing events that left her both battle-weary and naïve.

The couples married in February of 1946, in a triple ceremony that included another friend and his bride; the joke was they did not have money to pay a rabbi and to buy cake and wine for three separate celebrations, so they economized. The third couple's marriage fell apart very quickly, but the two brothers and their wives were married until the deaths of the brothers many years later, a very long time indeed. But the relevant question, the one that has always puzzled me, is whether my parents loved each other, or whether they married out of loneliness and because everyone else was getting married, just something that one did.

My father had one remaining family member, his brother Sam, so he was determined to build a family of his own. The two brothers were devoted to each other, and they had, throughout their lives during and after the war, several opportunities to prove the love their parents had instilled in them. But I am getting ahead of myself, as is so easy to do when one starts to weave or perhaps more accurately unravel a family story.

My father likely married my mother because she was the kind of woman he should marry. She was alone in the world and had only three male cousins who had also survived the war. Like my father, she was willing to work hard to make a life. She was also willing to be a partner in his lifelong dream of going to what was then Palestine. She was intelligent, learned in Hebrew and Yiddish. More importantly, she understood the magnitude of the terrible things my father had endured, for the things she had endured were in many ways worse. She was also indisputably beautiful, and she grew more beautiful through the years. Mostly, my mother was *familiar*; she was the kind of woman my father thought could make a home that resembled what he remembered of home.

What he didn't know was how deep those war wounds were for my mother. Not only had she lost her immediate family, but she had suffered more than her outward appearance and disposition suggested. She had spent two grueling years in Auschwitz Birkenau, had witnessed the murder of her sister, and had endured relentless hunger, disease, and heartbreak. Her nightmares punctuated their nights together. I remember that even in my childhood she would wake screaming and sobbing. It would take hours for her to calm down after one of her bad dreams; hours to realize she was no longer at the mercy of the Nazis.

My mother's fears would haunt her for the rest of her life. There would never be enough makeup to cover the sadness that lived under her public smile. And the large brown eyes that had seen unspeakable acts of violence were never quite at rest. Would my father have married her had he known how deeply she had been affected by the war? I can't know. Dad often said he could not understand how Mom had survived the war, since she had no instinct for danger, no ability to protect herself, no sense of self-preservation. How had she survived?

Who was she? Dora Golubowicz, my mother, was the second daughter of Itzhak and Chava Tenenbaum Golubowicz, born on December 25, 1926. Her older sister Fradel was the beauty of the family. Dora was, in her own telling, the playful younger brat. Her early years, according to what she told me, were wonderful. The small town of Pruzana, in northern Poland (now Belarus) was a haven for Yiddishkeit. I was told that it fostered a Hebrew high school (called a gymnasium) and a Yiddish paper, a rarity especially in such a small town. My grandfather owned a bakery where my grandmother worked as a part time cashier. My mother used to say of her father, he "didn't go to the ovens," which I took to mean that he did not actually do the baking.

The Golubowicz family was prominent in the town. The family owned a forest tract from which they procured wood for the bakery ovens, and the bakery provided a good living. My grandfather's older brother Yankel owned a grocery store. Their older sister Czarna owned a smaller grocery store in another part of the town.

Fradel and Dora in Pruzana around 1929

She was a widow with four young sons to raise. My grandfather bought his groceries from his sister, not his brother. This brought about some tension in the family, but he was performing an act of charity, helping to keep his sister and her family alive in a way that did not make her lose her dignity. From an early age my mother understood familial ties and obligations by the example her father set. Everyone in Pruzana knew the family; even in my childhood years after the war, survivors from my mother's hometown would remark about the Golubowicz family, their wealth, their tall stature, their wavy hair, the full figures of the women which was the much-admired look of that time. It was a compliment to say that you looked like a Golubowicz.

My mother told me that her father, the youngest of all the Golubowicz siblings, was the favorite of his nieces and nephews. He loved to play cards with them, to wrestle with the boys and to tease the girls. He was tall and handsome, a kind and loving father to Fradel and Dora, and then to his young son Velvel, about two or three years younger than Dora.

Dora and Fradel in Pruzana, 1929

The girls went to Polish public school, but they were tutored in Yiddish and Hebrew and were starting French lessons when the war broke out. They even went to summer camp. One of my mother's favorite memories of her father was the time he rode out to the camp on his bicycle, carrying baskets of rolls fresh from the bakery to share with all the children. The Golubowicz girls gloried in their father's care and attention. They were loved and protected by a strong and caring man with a great sense of fun.

There are no remaining photos of my grandfather. I can only imagine what he might have looked like. At the end of her life my mother lamented that she could no longer remember his face. It was hardly surprising. The last time she saw him she was sixteen years old.

Chava Golubowicz, my grandmother, was a bit stricter with her daughters. Chava was the second of four in the Tenenbaum family. She had an older sister Bryna, who was married and lived in the big city of Lodz. Bryna's husband was the manager of a textile factory owned by the Poznanski family, one of the richest Jewish families in Europe. Each year at the end of the summer Chava would take her daughters to Lodz to outfit them with the knitted goods they would need for the winter. My mother remembered the train ride, visiting their aunt's apartment, and getting the new underwear and thick woolen stockings. She loved seeing her older cousin Lola, who often came to visit the family in Pruzana because their grandmother Zlateh Bayleh Tenenbaum lived in Chava and Yitzhak's house. Chava's two younger brothers, Abe and Eli, had emigrated to America in the 1930's. Chava kept in touch with them through letters and sent photos of her children as they grew. These photos, surviving in American albums and stuffed into boxes of memories stored in closets in New York by Abe and Eli, were the only pictures my mother had of her family, the few images that survived the war. They are the only pictures I have of my grandmother today.

Chava was a tall and imposing woman. She was dark-haired and well-endowed. In the photo I have of her she is wearing a dark coat with a fur collar and a cloche hat. She doesn't smile but perhaps this was the way one posed for formal portraits at the photography studio. I can see my mother's face and stature in my grandmother. My mother said she never saw her mother without her lace-up corset; she thinks her mother suffered from back

Chava Golubowicz(Dora's mother) with her brother Eli, Fradel and Dora.

troubles and that the corset was supposed to provide support. Or perhaps it was the other way around, and the back troubles were the result of years of trying to rein in her full figure, which was characteristic of the women in the family.

Chava had domestic workers in the house to help with the cooking and cleaning. Her children were dressed in clothing made especially for them by a seamstress who would come to the house in fall and spring. My mother often told the story of the time **that** she and her sister left the house wearing the new dresses **that** the seamstress had sewn for them for Passover. The girls wanted to show their father their new frocks and they ran down the street and found their father standing in the window of the bakery. When they saw him, they began to spin and twirl, showing off their finery. He laughed and applauded as he came out of the store, calling them his beautiful princesses while the girls held a finger to their lips, swearing him to secrecy. They feared their mother would not approve of their little escapade. My mother called her father *Papa* and whenever she said the word when telling me a story about him, a smile and a look of unfathomable sadness and longing would come across her face.

Why do I retell this story and begin to tear up even as I write it now? Is it because my grandfather, someone whose face I have never seen, becomes human, if only for an instant? Is it because I can imagine him standing in the doorway of the bakery and admiring his lovely daughters? What I see are the carefree days of my mother's amputated childhood. The characters who will soon disappear in this story, are still vividly alive in them—two twirling girls in lovely dresses, two girls being cherished and admired by their father who adores them.

I once told my mother that she had known a childhood without the Holocaust in it, but that I never had the same. The Holocaust was a constant presence in my childhood, like a relative you have known from birth and who will play a part in your life until you die. It was a cruel remark I realize now, but it was true.

Dora adored her big sister, Fradel. Though everyone complimented Fradel on her beauty and her pleasant nature, Dora insisted she was never jealous. She wanted to be like her and watched closely as her sister matured into a lovely young woman. I am not sure of the difference in their ages, and although I asked my mother many

Dora (wearing light sweater) with friends around 1939

times how much older Fradel was, she never gave me an exact answer. It was as if the date had never cemented itself in her mind, or perhaps her subconscious was protecting her from a memory too painful to bear. From the few photos we have, Fradel seems to be about two or three years older than my mother. Dora remembered that when they were in the ghetto in the early 1940's, Fradel, who had big blue eyes, was already old enough to be fussing with her eyebrows, a habit that kept her standing in front of the mirror for extended periods of time. It seems boys were paying attention to Fradel and she to them, but for Dora, who was just turning fourteen, this was not yet a concern.

Both sisters had the thick dark hair that was a family trait. As was the custom, their hair was worn in braids, sometimes wound around their heads like a crown, sometimes hanging down their backs. In the early photos, when they are about four and six respectively, they are dressed alike in sailor dresses or knit outfits with matching caps; their hair is still cut short in a pixie style with bangs. Mom told me that later Fradel had started pin-curling her bangs to look older and more sophisticated as she reached her teens. They both loved to look at movie magazines and knew the names of Hollywood stars, particularly Shirley Temple, whose name my mother pronounced "*Templeh*," no silent *e*.

Poland seemed centuries away to me and somehow not of this earth, so it always surprised me when my mother made a reference from her childhood that I could recognize. In one case, I found it shocking my mother had had a movie star crush on Tyrone Power. Certainly, he had been a star during my childhood, and it made my mother's life seem far less exotic if she could know the same celebrity I knew. Somehow the distance between her early existence and mine was shortened by something so familiar and mundane— perhaps because our childhoods, and particularly our adolescent years, were more different than one could ever imagine.

Mom had a little brother who was about three years younger than she was. His name was Velvel or William. All the first-born boys in the family Golubowicz seemed to be named Velvel after a certain grandfather. Velvel is present in some of the photos we have that were sent to America. He is a round little boy in short pants. His hair is cut very close, and he has that sturdy Golubowicz stature. My mother never spoke much about him. In fact, in her Shoah interview she calls him "the boy," but this may just have been attributable to her nervousness at being filmed. There was also a baby sister, Yehudit, who was born in 1939 or 1940. The repercussions of her sad story would be felt in our family for generations.

When the war broke out in 1939, Pruzana was in the part of Poland ceded to Russia under the Ribbentrop-Molotov pact, and life for my mother and her family started changing. My grandfather's bakery was nationalized. He became a worker and no longer an entrepreneur, although the family still had a steady income. At school, my mother could not join the Red Scouts and wear the red neckerchief so prized by her now Communist classmates because her father had been the owner of a business and therefore a capitalist. She felt left out, and pouted at the dining table, lamenting the fact that other girls in her class were sporting the neckerchief and attending meetings from which she was barred. What seemed like an unfair fate at the time became trivial compared to what she would eventually endure, but she could not have known that yet. She was a teenager who wanted to fit in with the crowd.

Our parents come to us full grown and yet, for my mother, this instinctive need to fit in never left her. I can still hear her urging me to go to dances and to begin dating at what for me was far too young. It was as if her own aborted teenage life could somehow be relived through mine. The pressure she placed on me to be socially active was fueled by her own disappointment at missing out on those years. I understand this now, but then I could not. Then, I only knew my mother was far too invested in my social life and popularity, so much so that even when I was only eight or nine, she would snatch my glasses from my face and warn me that no one would ever marry me if I insisted on wearing them. Her belief that everything a young girl did was practice for her dating life was an immovable barrier she placed between us. Everything in life was determined by how one looked, how easily one could mingle. My mother's intense focus on these things alienated us from each other in ways she could not possibly have anticipated.

Many of her notions about America and American life came from her obsession with magazines like *True Confessions* and *Modern Romance*, which were filled with stories about love won and lost and won back again. (This was also the reading material that taught her to be fluent in English.) Their illustrations were in keeping with the kind of bodice ripper covers on romance novels today—handsome and swarthy men leaning over delicate, scantily-clad maidens. I have memories of trying and failing to understand these stories when I was first learning to read, and even when I was older, they were not to my taste. But I do understand her fascination with them. Here were the tales of love and loss, of losing and finding. She was intimately acquainted with the theme of loss in these stories, and so I imagine she read them for the finding, for the eventual reconciliation, the happy reunion sort of ending she never experienced.

Dora

My mother Dora loved literature and poetry but was not very interested in math or science. Sometime during her schooling, when the Russians had occupied her part of Poland after 1939, she was given the assignment of reassembling a small motor from its parts. It was a test of both dexterity and the ability to follow directions, and Dora was stymied by it. No matter what she tried she could not get the machine parts to fit. She asked a friend, a boy in her class, to help her complete the assignment. He gave her a series of small pieces of paper she was to use in the exact order needed to successfully reassemble the apparatus. Dora whisked through the reassembly but forgot to remove some of the small slips of paper as she secured the parts. When the teacher called her up to his desk, he showed her the damning evidence. Dora turned red, stammered something unintelligible, and ran from the classroom. When she would retell the story, she would insist she could not understand the purpose of the assignment, that she did not think it was important for a girl to know how to assemble a machine. She did admit she had done something wrong by asking for answers from the boy and using the crib sheets rather than figuring it out for herself, but she did not accept total responsibility. If the assignment was a faulty one, then clearly, she should not be held accountable for her actions. This stance epitomized her life philosophy. It was the way she drove a car, the way she balanced a checkbook, the way she raised her children. She was a victim, an actor in a play she had not written, and one in which she was unable to change even a line.

The Russians were antisemitic, but they had no plans to kill all the Jews. In 1941, when the Nazis reneged on their pact with Russia and began the assault on western Poland under Operation Barbarossa, life became much more precarious. Dora and her family were faced with the ever-increasing restrictions that accompanied the takeover of their town. They were required to give up their single-family home and move into an apartment in the ghetto that they shared with one of my grandfather's brothers and his family. My grandfather could no longer work, and as their activities and possessions were stripped from them, life became harsher. Still, the family creed was that if they were together, they could endure. And it is here where Yehudit's story becomes a part of our legacy. Much of what happens next can best be described by

Dora with her brother Velvel and sister Fradel, circa 1933

the term "choiceless choices"— no matter what choices one is presented with, there is no good option.

Dora's baby sister, who was born in 1939, was a blond and blue-eyed cherub. Being a girl made the possibility of escape from the ghetto a reality, since she could not be recognized as a Jew by a circumcision that marked every Jewish boy. The fact that she, a toddler, did not yet speak Polish with a Yiddish inflection, a stigma for Jews in Poland, was also an asset. Those who were able to pass as non-Jews during the war were those who were able to overcome this dialect, or who had never learned to speak this way at all.

The family had a confidante in Wally, the head baker in my grandfather's bakery. Wally had worked for my grandfather for many years and was trusted with all things. He was extraordinarily adept at icing the cakes and making fancy desserts and was likely one of the reasons the bakery was the financial success it was. When my grandfather was forced to work in the bakery, Wally helped him, covering for his inadequacies.

Wally lived in a small farming village outside of Pruzana, and since my grandfather Itzhak had been a kind and generous employer, Wally wanted to help in any way he could. He offered to take Yehudit to his home, to remove her from the ghetto and to keep her with his children and grandchildren. Her blond hair would fit in easily with his own family, and if anyone asked, he could say she was his brother's granddaughter, there on a visit to ease the financial burdens of her family during wartime deprivation.

Itzhak and Chava, my grandparents, debated what to do. They knew Fradel and Dora could not be rescued. People in the town knew who they were, and they would be easily identified as Jews and captured or given up by the neighbors in exchange for favors from the Nazis. Velvel could not be a part of any of these activities. He was circumcised and could be easily found out. It was not uncommon for Jewish boys to have to pull down their pants, even on the street, if ordered to do so. And identity could mean death. Yehudit was the only one who could be saved, so she was smuggled out of the ghetto and taken by Wally to his home.

I don't know what life was like for her there, what confusion and dislocation she might have felt, and whether she cried for her family. I only know what went on in the apartment where my mother remained with the rest of the family. My grandmother was inconsolable, and the girls were as well. For three days the family agonized, and then the decision was made to bring Yehudit back. Wally warned my grandfather that it was not a good idea, but my grandfather and grandmother had decided it was better to suffer the consequences together, whatever they might be. Was it the right thing to do? It was a choiceless choice.

Their time in the ghetto could not prepare them for what was to come. Though they suffered terrible deprivation and though they realized they were trapped, there was no information coming in from the outside world that could have warned them of their eventual fate. I have often wondered about this. My grandfather had been a wealthy man. He had two brothers-in-law in America to whom he could have turned for help in getting out of Poland. I am not sure they could have helped him financially, but they could have helped with the paperwork necessary for emigration if he had pursued it. Why did he choose to stay in a Europe that was showing signs of shattering under Nazi domination? I can never know what he knew or when he knew it. What my mother told me was that he loved Poland, he loved his small town, and he felt relatively safe. Why leave? The hatred for Jews was nothing new, although according to my mother this was not a phenomenon she witnessed as a child. And perhaps she was right. Perhaps there was just enough of a feeling of relative safety that Itzhak did not feel compelled to leave. His sister Czarna's husband had gone to America years before with the intention of making enough money to have his wife and four sons join him. He had died before anyone in his family could follow him, and was buried in New York, his whole family thousands of miles away. Having seen how hard the separation had been for his sister's family, my grandfather did not want to repeat that mistake, even if it meant possibly saving them. They would stay together, and whatever happened to one of them would happen to them all.

How many of this large family died at the hands of the Nazis? I can never get an accurate count. When I would ask my mother, she would always forget someone and either a name or a whole group would escape her memory. She could not remember and so I will never know.

Deportation

Sometimes my brother will ask me how I know some arcane bit of information about our parents, to which I answer that when he was outside playing ball, I was inside listening. I was under the table even when I was very small, hearing my parents' stories being told in my first language, Yiddish. Later, I sat *at* the table and listened to their stories. And in her last years, when I would visit my mother at the nursing home, I asked as many questions as I could, writing down new information on a memo pad I kept in my purse. When I got home, I would tack the notes to my bulletin board and make a promise to myself that I would one day write her story—that one day I would gather all those childhood memories and scraps of paper and fit them together.

I am fortunate in that I have my mother's scraps as well. She could write in Yiddish, in Polish and in English, and there were times when I typed her stories out for her and corrected her grammar and spelling as I went. But there are many more pieces of paper than I have ever edited or even known about, and although some of them are the same stories written more than once, every now and then I find, as I go through her notebooks and folded, faded scraps of paper, a new memory of hers I have never seen before.

In her own words my mother tells the story of the deportation and her first day in Auschwitz:

January 1943

The beginning of the end...

For three days and nights of dark moaning misery the train moved in fits and starts. Filth piled up among the bodies cast down in seemingly lifeless heaps. You were not sure whether you were alive, and the others dead, or you were dead and the rest alive.

The stench in the car was like the reek of a slaughterhouse. A few of the prisoners banged on the doors and were answered by the rip and tear of machine gun bullets.

Silence again, except for the cries of the wounded. My God, they would not pack cattle like this, unless they were going to the slaughterhouse.

100 people to a car, standing room only. The boxcar loomed ahead, a dark devouring mouth, into which humanity was packed as if refuse.

With enormous eyes, black as night, we stared at each other. The prisoners panted like animals.

And so the survivors poured over the bodies of the dead and dying, the old and the very young. Some crushed and puffed beyond recognition lay entwined there in the blush of dawn. Of the 100 odd ones who entered the car, fewer than half emerged under their own power.

The following hours would be chiseled in my brain as permanently as the legend on a tombstone, and yet it all seemed unreal. I lived apart from my body, observing my own conduct and that of others with disbelieving eyes.

The cheerful little station, heaps of bricks and lumber, the SS officers with their shiny boots and briefcases, their cordial smiles and vibrant whips. The committee of deception.

Cursing, raining blows, the clean-up crew were tossing out the contents of the cars – dehumanized humanity. So many broken breathless dolls to be sent jostling down the platform in carts, to be loaded into dump trucks.

Some, like statues gripped one another and had to be pried apart with crowbars, others barely alive, were thrown aboard with the dead.

I was staring ahead at a black column of smoke that rose from a tall factory, black oily clouds that stung the eyes.

With a thrust of a baton, I joined a line of people waiting with deathlike indifference. In this atmosphere of doom there seemed an intangible quality about each one that said, "this one will live, the others have already come to terms with death."

Up ahead the column was being divided left and right, and I sensed a crisis. Whether or not the whispered warning was true, I did not know, but somehow, I felt sure this man held above them all a power of life, or death.

And yet, I could not imagine even here an end to the faint throbbing which told me I was still alive.

With these few who have been directed to the right, we walked to the destination of the camp, marked by high cement watchtowers, and double rows of electronic (sic) barbed wire fences.

We passed a heavy iron gate and proceeded to a registration center by an orchestra in white suits.

None of this was real, it was not happening to me or was it indeed.

Consider yourself lucky to have a number, I heard a voice as I felt a needle piercing the skin on my arm.

No name anymore, but that's better than taking the heavenly express ... most everyone goes that way; those were the only hints.

My heart and spirit were hiding, not daring to put feelings into words, it did not occur to me to question the absence of emotions.

Next was the barber. There we lost almost all that remained of human identity.

Naked, we waited In line, as the barbers hacked away at heads, armpits, crotches, with dull razors, all those poor bodies deprived of every dignity. Streaming with blood from various cuts, we proceed towards a steam bath. From the steam we pass under an ice-cold shower, and then were given token prisoners clothing, faded stripes, that had been worn and passed around many times before.

And again the voice.

This is a death camp, here you will die slowly of illness, hard work, punishment and hunger, if lice and dysentery don't get you first.

Expect the worst, leave every hope behind, live without hope, forget the names of your fellow prisoners, here there are no sisters or daughters. To stay alive attract no attention, forget escape, no one escapes, forget revolt – this is the beginning of the end.

The first day of Auschwitz was over. Night was nearly as bright as day, for the few clouds were blood-red from the fires fed by human fuel.

Her words haunt me. To imagine my mother, at sixteen, going through this is wrenching, and yet she has not even described what was perhaps the most defining moment of her life. She has not mentioned her parents or her siblings. She has not alluded to the fact that her father, my grandfather, jumped from the railcar, leaving his daughters to travel to hell. She has not talked about the fate of her mother, her brother Velvel, and her baby sister Yehudit.

In her taped testimony for *Shoah*, my mother tells the story as if she is talking about a family acquaintance and not her own father. She starts off by saying her father must have been about thirty-nine or forty years old at the end of January 1943. She sits up straight in her chair to emphasize that he was tall, and he must have carried himself proudly. Then suddenly they are in the railcar, my grandfather and my mother and Fradel, her older sister. Where is my grandmother? Where are Velvel and Yehudit? She refers to them only in passing, which may mean that they must have been in another car and perhaps they were separated during the chaos of boarding the trains. I found out more after searching through her writing.

They had arrived at the trains in horse-drawn sleds in the deep snow of January in Poland. They had been told to pack suitcases. They had made sure there were changes of underwear and heavy stockings for the trip. The girls were instructed to dress in layers, dress over a dress, sweater over sweater, and to be sure to wear their woolen stockings and ski boots. The suitcases filled with tins of cookies to tide them over until they arrived at their destination were brought by Wally from the bakery my grandfather had once owned. Along with so many others, their suitcases were piled up on the train station platform, each with a name and a hometown printed on them, as if there were a delivery service in place to return them to their rightful owners once the journey had been completed. The deception was carefully thought out and ruthlessly enacted. The owners, of course, never saw their suitcases again.

In my mother's papers I found a scrap that details the end of the Pruzana ghetto. I had never heard her talk about this, and I was unaware that this excerpt existed. It details her last moments with her mother, Velvel, and Yehudit, and suggests that she was considering running away and not going with her mother and the younger children to the station.

She writes:

And so, after three years in the Ghetto, swollen from hunger, forgotten by the world, came the day of the final solution: Deportation.

And so we begin our journey without a backward glance at the abandoned streets, the dead empty houses, the gardens. On everyone's back was a pack, in everyone's eyes was suffering drowned in tears. Slowly, heavily, the procession made its way to the gate of the Ghetto.

I was sliding out my hand from my mother's. She turned her head towards me and let my hand drop, her eyes full of understanding and quiet approval. Words were not necessary. She knew what I had in mind. (I must explain here that an able-bodied young woman might have a chance of escape, a chance to run away. A mother with two small children was helpless. My mother was about to make a choice that would change the course of her life.)

And so I stood on the payment(sic), unable to make a move. One by one they passed in front of me, teachers, friends, others, all those I had been afraid of, all those I once could have laughed at, all those I had lived with over the years. They went by, fallen, dragging their packs, dragging their lives, deserting their homes, and the years of their childhood.

The street suddenly became empty. Everything could be found there, suitcases, briefcases, plates, faded portraits, all those things that people had thought of taking with them, and which in the end they left behind. They had lost all value. I heard the dogs barking and the German soldiers rushing the last ones to hurry, knocking them down and stepping on them. I saw bullets flying on the air, bodies falling to the ground and streams of warm blood coloring the snow. I glanced towards the Ghetto. I heard singing and laughter. I saw dancing and clapping. I saw looting and burning as one house after another was set on fire.

I started running in the direction towards my mother. I caught up with her, took my baby sister from her arms, put my other arm around my little brother's thin shoulders and together we went.

I saw my mother's red eyes and felt her trembling body relax near me. My desperate will to stay alive left me. At last, I was at peace with myself.

It is hard for me to reconcile this girl with the woman I grew up with. My mother was not a risk taker or a planner. To imagine that she might have considered running away is incomprehensible given what I know of her. That she decided to be with her family is much more characteristic of her. Yet, I am surprised and heartened to know that at some point she showed such a spark of defiance.

My mother is correct when she describes the number of people in the car. There were about one hundred people packed together, with only room to stand up. She tells us in her *Shoah* testimony that on the second day in the train car, men in the car began urging action. My grandfather was told by others that he should do something, even if it meant risking his life or all their lives, something must be done. I can only guess that others believed he was capable of some sort of physical action having been a leader of the community for so long.

He drew his daughters close to him and gave them some coins, telling them to hide them somewhere on their persons. According to my mother, his last words to them were that if any one of them survived that person should return to Pruzana. There, they would meet after this nightmare had concluded. In her taped testimony, my mother emphasizes that her father would never have done anything like this, that this was not characteristic of him, that leaving his children and his wife was not an action she would ever have dreamed him capable of taking.

And yet, he did. He made his way to the small window in the cattle car, and he and another man jumped from one side of the train, while two others jumped from the other side. My mother believed shots were then fired, but she could never be sure. From my research I know many of the trains had soldiers riding on the roofs of the cars, but I have no proof this was the case on this train.

How could he have left them there *alone*? What could he have been thinking? I will never know the answers to these questions. As much as I want to believe he was doing what he thought was right I cannot imagine a father leaving his children at such a moment. My grandfather was never seen again. In her testimony, my mother reports that after the war she encountered the two men who had jumped from the other side of the railcar. They knew nothing of her father's fate. The entire time she was in concentration camp, in Auschwitz and then in Ravensbrueck, my mother believed she would meet her father again. In her darkest days, she still held out hope that he had survived and was waiting for her to return, and when the war was over, it became her mission, on her journey home to Pruzana in the autumn of 1945 to either find him or find some news of him.

Her Lucky Day

I always wondered where my grandmother and the two younger children were when the events in the cattle car occurred. When my grandfather had jumped from the train, why had he consulted his daughters? Where was his wife? The mystery was solved recently when I did a careful reading of an interview my mother gave in 1984. In it, she tells of going to the trains with her family but there only being room for her mother and the youngest children to board. When my grandfather was separated from his wife and the younger children, he took the opportunity to go into hiding with my mother and her sister, and his older brother and two cousins. Because this was completely unplanned, they had insufficient provisions, and the cold weather made survival in the forest bunker where they hid impossible. After two days they went back to the station and surrendered themselves to the Nazis. They left on the last transport from Pruzana, two days after my grandmother and the younger children had been deported

I now understand why my mother asked about the whereabouts of her mother, brother and sister when she arrived in Auschwitz Birkenau. They had been told when reporting to the trains that their destination was a labor camp. My mother expected her family would be there waiting for her. As the train cars were emptied and people were being sorted, I believe my grandmother and the two younger children, Velvel and Yehudit, were sent to the left, to their immediate deaths, two days before my mother arrived there. Women with small children were not valued in the camps. There are stories of inmates who were working on the arrival platforms, whispering in Yiddish that younger women should hand their small children to older women. The warning was not always understood, but it became clearer as the sorting began. Younger women without children stood a chance of being selected to live. Older women, women of forty-five and older, were automatically sent to the left, and to their deaths. Children, except for twins, were of little use in the camps, and if the switch could be made without detection by the guards, handing over a child might save a young mother's life. My grandmother, who was in her thirties may or may not have been given that information. I only know she did not survive the selection, that she probably walked to the back of the Birkenau camp with her two children, and they most likely died on January 30 or 31st of 1943. No records exist of those who were killed upon arrival.

When my mother and her sister finally reached a barracks late that first night, they asked if anyone had seen their mother. The more seasoned inmates, women who had been there for a while, pointed to the smoke belching from the chimneys, and told them that their mother was there, that she was part of the blood-red cloud above them. Did the girls believe this right away? Or did it take time for them to understand they were completely alone, that their father was gone and their mother certainly dead.

In talking with my mother, I have learned more details about that first day. She remembered that after being stripped of their clothes, she and her sister were put in a long line of naked women. They had never seen any woman completely naked before and they certainly had never stood naked in front of men. The humiliation and shock they felt was followed by the horror of being shaved and then tattooed. Mom said she could not even recognize her own sister without her beautiful hair, that everyone now seemed to look exactly alike. Being handed a pile of clothes that did not fit was the next humiliation; tall people received clothes best fitted for short people and vice versa. The wooden clogs they were given were rough and unsized; there was no left or right foot. The woolen stockings and long underwear they had worn when leaving home had been taken away, probably being sent to Germany with the rest of the belongings plundered from so many carefully packed suitcases. All my grandmother's exhortations regarding how to dress for the cold journey were meaningless now. And the cold must have been excruciating with nothing to protect their bodies from the winter wind other than their thin striped uniforms. February in Poland is brutal; snow certainly covered the ground and the barracks to which they were sent were heated only by a small stove that could in no way keep pace with the elements.

All that they knew was taken from them—their hometown, their belongings, their family, their names, even their hair. What was left were two sisters, numbered consecutively by the tattoos marking their small arms. Fradel was first, and then Dora who was number **33960**.

Many years after my mother's entry into that hellish place, I visited Auschwitz Birkenau on a teacher seminar. The night before I was leaving for Poland my mother and father took the family out to dinner. My mother could not hide her fear that I was going to Poland, that I was going to Birkenau. She had never returned, had not once set foot in Poland since coming to America, and she could not fathom why I had the need to go. Her parting words to me were "You'll find Barracks # 9. You'll know it because it is near the fence. Go there and stand there. Then maybe you will begin to understand." She had never mentioned Barracks# 9 by number before. She had never said anything about the fence except that at one time, in her despair, she had contemplated committing suicide by throwing herself on the electrified barbed wire. But now, she had given me orders to try to understand what she had been through, as if I might absorb that knowledge by walking in the places she had once walked and standing where she had stood.

What my mother did not know was that most of the barracks in Birkenau had since been destroyed intentionally or had disintegrated from harsh weather and lack of repair. They had been built by slave labor, quickly and poorly, most during the winter when the ground was so frozen that proper foundations could not be poured. If I could block out from my field of vision the barracks that did remain and the ruins of the exploded gas chambers, I might be able to forget **that** this was the largest Jewish cemetery in the world.

Yet somehow some buildings survived, and I searched for Barracks # 9. Our guide told me the buildings had been renumbered more than once and that Barracks # 9 near the fence could now be one of the fallen buildings in the women's camp, or one of the ones that still stood. I went into one of the remaining barracks and took a long look around.

At the entrance of the block was a private room given to the *eleste*, the prisoner given special privilege for keeping the others in line. It was as big as a closet but given the circumstances, any private place must have seemed palatial. In return for the title, the *eleste* carried out duties such as keeping an accurate count of the inmates, ensuring no one received preferential treatment, and maintaining order in the barracks. If prisoners were lucky, the *eleste* was one of their own, someone from a similar background, a Jewish woman who cared about the girls she oversaw. If they were unlucky, she was a hardened criminal or a political prisoner who had secured her elevated status by displaying her ability to be cruel.

Walking past the tiny room I entered the main area of the barrack. There were cement bunks on the lowest level, more cement or wooden bunks on a second and even a third tier. I remembered my mother telling me how important it was never to be on the bottom bunk, because the entire population of the camp suffered from dysentery and the lower tiers were in danger of being covered by the waste of those sleeping above them. I remembered her stories about sleeping three or four or five to a bunk, having to turn over when one person in the bunk turned, hoping to conserve what little body heat there was. In the summer, conversely, the buildings were stifling, and the wet, swampy ground of Birkenau bred malaria in the muck. Certainly, the lack of proper sanitary facilities added to the misery of the camp. An open latrine ran the length of the *lager Strasse*, or main thoroughfare. Prisoners were punished or killed by being thrown into the latrine and left to drown in the waste accumulated there. As I stood there that summer, remembering my mother's words, I felt a chill pass through me at the thought of such horrors.

These stories of hunger and deprivation are what substituted for fairy tales in my childhood. There was never enough to eat, there was never clean water to drink. My mother was dirty, ragged, with sores all over her body from not being able to wash. In the winter she was freezing as she stood in the *appels* (the roll calls) that lasted for hours, waiting for the count to be complete and accurate so the prisoners could go to their labor or return to the barracks. In the summer, they stood for hours in the blazing sun, in the winter in the harsh winds and blowing snow, holding each other up lest someone stagger and fall, which would automatically make them fodder for the ovens. What kept her alive was that she had her sister, and the hope she might see her father again.

The facts about the deportation from Pruzana and the fate of those inside the cattle cars are stunning. I was able to find them on a subsequent visit. A caring guide helped me to discover the exact number of people on the trains that deported my family. The old saw about the Nazi fixation on *ordnung* (order) was true. Everything other than the names of those who were killed immediately was in the records. Those lives were evidently not worth noting.

The precision of the details shocked me. The trains carrying my mother, her sister, and her father left Pruzana on January 30, 1943, and arrived in Auschwitz Birkenau on Feb. 2, 1943. Inside the cars were 1265 Polish Jews. There were 35 children under the age of four. There were 60 children aged from four to ten. After the selection, 254 men and 105 women were checked into the camp and numbered; the men received numbers 99211-99504. The women received numbers 33928-34032. The other 866 people were gassed upon arrival.

The Nazis knew exactly how many people came off each train, even though the scenes of the trains arriving and unloading are often depicted in photographs and films as chaotic. They also knew exactly how many people were sent to their deaths. The condemned had to walk from the arrival area to the back of the camp after the selection. Did they understand what the "left" and the "right" designations meant? That being sent in a particular direction meant you had been selected to live or die? For those condemned to die, as they walked the path to the gas, did they know they were living their last moments? In the grove of trees where they were ordered to sit, were they aware that "the showers" were a deception? That there was an entrance but no exit? They were told to undress, to pile their clothes neatly with their shoestrings tied together so nothing would be lost, so they could retrieve their clothes after the shower. Those women who had small children were urged to keep their children with them as they entered the gas chambers, to keep them close, to carry the small ones in their arms. I think of my naked grandmother with Velvel and Yehudit. I wonder if she had a sense of where she was headed as she walked. Was the acrid smoke a clue to what awaited her? I walk that same path each time I visit Birkenau, specifically retracing what must have been my grandmother's last steps. I look at the beauty of the birch trees and the blue sky. I listen to the birdsong and wonder what my grandmother knew or did not know.

When I came home from that first trip, I wanted to share everything I had experienced with my mother. I explained that I didn't think I had found Barracks #9, but that I had been inside one of the women's barracks and seen what it looked like. And after each subsequent trip, I always found another fact or story to offer her. When I learned the details of her transport, I wanted her to know. Sitting by her side I realized, as I looked at the paper I was holding, my mother had never known the date of her arrival, which I now knew had been February 2, 1943; she had never known how many days or nights they were in the cattle cars. All time had stopped there. My parents had been married on February 2, 1946,

37

just three years later and a miracle's distance away. When I showed the dates to my mother she said, "I guess February 2 is my lucky day." It was the day she had been chosen to remain among the living, and the day that she and my father had begun their new life together.

Fradel's Death

In my teenage years I no longer wanted to hear about the War. I wanted to be "normal." I wanted my parents to stop talking about the past. We were, at that time, a very visible family in our community. My parents owned a popular shoe store on the main shopping street of our neighborhood, and everyone recognized our last name of Freilich. Hearing other people refer to my parents as refugees made me bristle. Remarks about my mother's tattoo flustered me. I wanted to defend her and at the same time, I wanted to run from the room and disavow any knowledge of either of them. My parents spoke with a noticeable accent, their English peppered with consonants that were not part of standard pronunciation. Because they both worked in the store and waited on people who were our neighbors, everyone was aware of their *otherness*. I remember having this same accent when I was first learning to speak English. I actively chose to get rid of it, practicing the accent of my teachers on the walk home from school each day. I was ashamed of anything that marked me as *other*, and like many children of immigrants, I had a keen sense of detecting where the differences between my family and other families were and working to erase them.

When kids at school asked where my parents were from, I would say France, because it sounded more exotic than Poland. I wanted distance from the survivors' legacy I considered a burden, and I was sometimes even ashamed of. This was the era of ignorant statements like "the Jews went like sheep to the slaughter," and questions like "why didn't they fight back?" Even though I knew the details that could refute those remarks, I remained silent. Unlike those who did feel compassion for my parents and who admired their work ethic and success, I wanted to move myself as far away from a refugee stain that I felt colored everything about our family. Feeling pride in your roots was not a thing in the 1960s. It was still considered better to bury what you didn't like about yourself. When I look back at my teenaged self, I see the shame I felt at not being the all-American girl next door, what I thought everyone was supposed to be.

My parents' shoe store flourished and the summer I turned eleven we were able to move from the apartment over the store to a single-family home about two miles away. For the first time in my life, I had my own bedroom. I no longer had to sleep in the living room, and I could close the door and separate myself from the rest of the family. One wall of my bedroom shared a common wall with the kitchen. I could hear what was going on in there, but I could also pretend that I didn't. I remember my mother telling me how lucky I was to have this beautiful room all to myself. When I asked if she had shared a room with her sister, she told me they had always slept in the same bed. Until her sister was killed, they even shared a bunk in the concentration camp.

The story of Fradel's death is so painful that even now I can barely tell it. It must have taken place around the end of the first year they were in Birkenau, sometime in late winter of 1943 or early spring of 1944. In her *Shoah* testimony my mother says the girls from her barracks were assigned to breaking rocks and carrying them from one spot to another. The work seemed purposeless, designed to tax the strength of the girls more than accomplish anything useful. It was outside work, lifting heavy sledgehammers and rocks, and the year they had spent in the camp had weakened them considerably. On that fateful day, Fradel, my mother's older sister, was assigned with some other girls to bring the lunch soup. Working outside meant you were given an extra portion of food midday. From the way my mother describes it, the soup was brought in large cans, almost like trash cans, on a dolly of some kind. The rest of the workers were at the bottom of the quarry, the soup cans at the top.

My mother describes the day as cold and rainy. The food carriers were ordered to bring the soup down to where the girls were working, and the wooden clogs they wore could grip neither the icy stone nor soil. The slope down was slick and as they tried to maneuver the heavy cans, the girls lost their footing, and the cans turned over on them, scalding them as they fell. At the bottom of the slope, the SS guard, a boy of about eighteen, stood and waited. He hollered at the girls for spilling the food. "Now, they (meaning the other workers) will have nothing to eat until tonight."

He raised his rifle butt high and slammed it down on each girl's head until he had killed them all. As he did so, he repeated, "So beautiful and so young." One of the witnesses to this atrocity, incensed by what she saw and emboldened by the brutality yelled, "Why did you do that? You didn't have to do that!" He responded, "Well, if not me, someone else. All of you will die. None of you will get out of here alive."

At seventeen years old, my mother watched as her sister was bludgeoned to death. And the horror was not yet over. At the end of the day, she then had to help carry her sister's body back to the barracks, because the number of people coming back to the camp from work detail, living or dead, had to equal the number of people that had left that morning. The prisoners on outside details always carried body boards for this reason. On that day, so many prisoners were killed that the guards were punished for their excessive brutality; and on that day, my mother's sister, her one link to her family, was gone.

In that first year, when her sister was alive, the two girls could comfort each other and remind each other about family, about home, about their father. They could cheer each other up, to buoy each other's spirits if possible. But now, my mother was alone. She knew for certain **that** her mother and the two younger children were dead, and she had seen the murder of Fradel with her own eyes. The only hope she had left was that her father might have survived the jump from the train. My mother was despondent and wanted to die.

I found this in her scraps of paper:

Just as our hunger is not that feeling of a free man missing a meal who knows that he can satisfy his hunger anytime he wants to, or he is skipping a meal for a purpose or time limit, so is our being cold cannot be compared with being cold of a free man, who knows that he can get warm when he comes in to his home, or puts on warmer clothing. We say "hungry, we say "tired," "fear," "pain." We say "winter", and they are different things. They are free words, created and used by free men who live in comfort and can help themselves to any above situations or avoid them to his convenience.

If the concentration camp had lasted longer, a new harsh language would have been born, and only this language could express what it means to toil the whole day with the temperature below freezing, wearing only a shirt and trousers, and in one's body nothing but weakness, hunger and knowledge of the end drawing nearer. When we saw the first flakes of snow, we thought that if at that time last year they had told us that we would see another winter in concentration camp we would have gone and touched the electric wire fence, and that even now we would go, if we were logical, were it not for that senseless pride of hope, which is our weapon to fight and survive. I am not even alive enough to know how to kill myself.

With Sadness in my Heart

The following was composed by my mother in her head in May 1944 and remembered well enough to be written down after liberation, first in Yiddish and eventually in English. She added a paragraph or two at the end in later years.

One day resembles another. The dusk ushers us into the Shoe Detail and darkness of night sends us back to Birkenau, Auschwitz. The barracks in Birkenau, Auschwitz are the same, dank and bleeding. They are damp, dirty; the beds called the "Koop" are hard, gray boards. I hear the same lamenting, weeping, and begging, but now the voices are getting weaker; they are being forgotten. Bodies are getting thin; energy is ebbing.

The rows of my campmates are thinning out against the stark electric barbed wire fences in the gates of hell. There is very little hope left. No one even dreams of freedom anymore. The only dream left to us is the dream of the Promised Land, lost now and forgotten. Lost forever is the only hope and prayer left to us, the dream of being one with You, Lord, in the Promised Land.

If my time will come, let it come quietly, without bitterness on my numb lips in accusation towards a God that I cannot see. Nevertheless, I feel Him near in my heart, hopes, and dreams. I feel His touch as He tells me to hold on. As He speaks to my bleeding heart and tells me so softly, I am the one who will survive to honor the haunting memories in all their eyes. That I am the one child chosen by the Lord's eternal will to bear witness to all I have seen for the future betterment of all humanity.

We will go where thousands went before me. Our fate is decided for all of us here. No one cries anymore. There are no more tears left to weep within dry sockets. Among us, there are girls who have a bit of courage, who talk about their families, freedom, and the future; even of making hopes, dreams, and plans, which they know are sheer fantasy. All alone, they dream of make- believe futures that will never be. Oh Father, unto Thine eyes, tell me where is sanity? Where is the hope. the prayers for all the bleeding hearts in humankind? Their hearts are heavy, and fright permeates their skeletal bodies. It is hard to dream with longing on an empty stomach when death is all about and looks you straight in the eye.

Over there in heaven high above, far from the brutal sordid world and the crackling flames, the gasps and the gagging in the throats, the dirty world is soaked through with blood. Why God, why?

Four large buildings accommodating twenty thousand people at one time with no trouble, only several men directing traffic to keep operations running smoothly, and the thousands flow like water from an open tap. All this happens just beyond the trees of the dusty wood.

Ordinary trucks bring people, return then to bring some more. Why is it that nobody cries out? Nobody spits in their faces; nobody jumps at their throats? If our number is called, we obediently go with them to die and we do nothing. We starve, we are drenched by rain, we are torn from our families.

What is the mystery? This strange power of one man over another, this insane passivity that cannot be overcome? Our only strength is our great numbers; the gas chambers cannot accommodate all of us at one time.

I think about these things when people speak to me of morality of law, of tradition. I, who have lived on intimate terms with the crematoria, the itch and the tuberculosis, having understood the meaning of wind, rain and sun, of bread and turnip soup, of work to survive, of slavery and power, having so to say, broken daily bread with the beast. I look at these people with indulgence and sympathy, because to grasp the pattern of those daily events is beyond anybody's imagination.

Despite that madness we live for a world that will be different, for a better world to come, when all this is over. It is that very hope that makes people go without a murmur to the gas chambers, keeps them from risking a revolt, puts them into numb inactivity. It is that hope that compels you to hold on to one more day of life, because the day may be the day of liberation. Hope for a different, better world, for life, a life of peace and rest.

Never in the history of mankind has hope been stronger than man, but never has it done so much harm, as it has done in this war in this concentration camp.

We were never taught how to give up hope, and this is why today we perish in gas chambers. Still, we continue to long for a world in which there is love between men and peace.

I don't know if I will be able to throw off the concentration camp mentality, the effects of helplessly watching others being beaten and murdered. I suspect I will be marked for life.

I don't know if I will survive but I like to think that one day we shall have the courage to tell the world the whole truth and call it by its proper name.

I tried to follow the slim threads of reality, through the events of the past year. I could not believe that this was the end. Each time I ran into a black space where nothing followed logically, that place where there was no hope, no peace, and no escape from the chores.

Powers far beyond my control seemed to have taken possession of my life and my future.

It was cold, winter came early that year, it was gray outside and damp.

I had no more fight left, no more anger, no more spirit of survival.

I had cried my eyes and my heart out, and I was exhausted by the sheer onslaught of so much sorrow.

My eyes had no more tears; my body had no more strength. I was drained of the last shred of hope.

Everything I held dear,00 everyone I loved was gone and slowly I felt myself slipping away.

I was too tired to think anymore, too tired to move. The world faded away, day melted into night, melted into day again. And it was all the same.

I did not care anymore. I wanted to die, I was so hungry, so unbelievably alone that I wondered if I was going to lose my mind.

I knew how people went mad, and they gave up fighting. They went mad because it comes to be a far better place than dying from the slow pain of hunger and loneliness. You get tired of the constant battle with no victories. You lose your grip on the world, and slowly you drift into your own world, that stretches endlessly into the future, no hope, no relief, no change. I lost all desire to think. I just sank away into peaceful floating, where there were no harsh voices, there was no pain. There was no terror, very peaceful. Nothing hurt me anymore. It was all very far away. I lived my life in daydreams. I made up stories and people and entwined my life around them from a distance.

I felt nothing, not anger, not fury, not rage, not love, not hate – nothing. And nothing is worse than anything. Nothing is the worst.

I first read these words as a teenager. My mother had recopied them from her own notebook and asked me to transcribe them for her. I began typing, not yet aware of what the words were conveying, not yet alert to the despair and hopelessness they held. I had thought I understood what she had been through. I had heard the stories so many times before but typing them onto paper gave them new meaning. I could see her whole heart on every page, feel her wish for death which she so clearly articulated. There were times, as I typed, that I wept. At other times, the enormity of the horror I was transcribing was so great that I would attack the work as if it had been written by someone I didn't know. It was the only way to keep myself from being overwhelmed by her pain.

When I finished typing, I came to my mother with the pages and handed them over. She never asked me if I had read them, but rather there was a silence about what she had shared with me that marked a new understanding between us. I now understood a part of her that had been there all along but that I had not been able to see, either because I had been too young or, and perhaps more likely, too unwilling or unable to absorb the truth of her story.

I was immediately aware that the parameters of my relationship with my mother had changed. She had handed me the truth of her life on those handwritten pieces of paper, revealing, ultimately, her courage. I was now the custodian of her stories, and that new responsibility and the insight that came with it made it impossible for me to ignore the impact of the Holocaust on her and on me.

The Infirmary and Mengele

Sometime after Fradel's death when she was at her lowest both physically and emotionally, my mother contracted an illness that was most likely malaria. How does one get malaria, a tropical disease, in Poland? The conditions in Birkenau were so awful and so unsanitary that stagnant pools of filth and filthy water lay throughout the latrines and in the canals dug alongside the *lager Strasse*, the main thoroughfare of the camp. Flies bred there all spring and summer, and the prisoners suffered not only from their own inability to clean themselves, but from the insects that incessantly plagued them. The ground was always muddy; walking meant pulling yourself out of the muck with each step. The barracks were stiflingly hot with little ventilation to cool the air, which added to the possibilities for infection and disease.

Mom wrote about this event that took place in late 1943:

I am rudely awakened by the civilian overseer's voice. "Get up you cow, get up you pig, you Polish swine. You slept enough. Go to work, it's high time." The shower of whip lashes and rubber hoses falls on our heads and bodies. I hear the laments, the wailing and groaning we alone hear. Our innocent blood is again being spilled. Hell opened its doors wide, over and over. The door to this Hell is never closed. I got up quickly with the last ounce of my strength. The wet clothing that I wore yesterday clings to my weak and worn body. My feet are swollen and bruised; the blood dried on my feet. My face is deformed, someone knocked a tooth out of my mouth. My dear God, my only God, you are sitting up in Heaven, up on your luxurious throne. You passed out the laws for all your children, the laws of love, freedom, liberation, salvation, for whom?

Outside the night is dark. The rain pours with raging might. Where is your moon and stars, the shiny stars that always light up your sky, the heaven and your whole wide world?

Are you ashamed to look at your world. The world you created in Auschwitz. The dirty world which is soaked through with our Jewish blood? Eight months have gone by for me in this eternal Hell. In pain, grief and misery. The rows of campmates are daily dwindling, thinner and thinner. But the corpses are all around us. We step on the corpses. We sleep with them. They are so much better off now.

Oh God, when will you make an end to this torment? when will the sun shine on us? You have hidden the sun, the moon, the stars and you sent us darkness. The bleak night of no hope, only strain and tension. Take mercy upon us, release us from this Hell or send us quick death. Don't you see all of this? Don't you hear anything? Doesn't the smoke from the chimneys sting your eyes when the bodies of my sisters are consumed by fire? The weeping, the laments of your children is not heard at all. Perhaps you really don't exist but are a figment of imagination. You, the one who has the power to hold the whole world in the palm of your hand, take one good look please, at the Hell on earth you created. Forgive me, dear God. I'm losing my mind and senses. I do know You exist, and You are not a figment of my imagination. You are the Almighty and Your compassion and love for Your children will not vanish. Take pity, have mercy and send me Your Angel of Death. Please send him quickly and suddenly and then perhaps I too will acquire a peaceful face with a faint smile on my lips.

(Composed by Mom and remembered until she was able to put the words down on paper.)

So sick that she wanted to die, and so hopeless without Fradel to boost her spirit, Mom decided to go to the infirmary. The deception that there was a camp hospital is another one of those examples of Nazi-speak, a euphemism that allows the uninformed reader to imagine things could not have been as bad as we have been led to believe. No medical care was ever administered, in fact much of what went on there was as far from accepted medical care as one could get and was in fact cruel experimentation designed to test specious medical hypotheses on victims who had no say over what was happening to them. Going to the hospital voluntarily was tantamount to committing suicide. The infirmary was usually a waystation on the road to the gas chambers, and going there meant you were giving up, you no longer cared if you lived or died, as few ever returned to their barracks from there. But Mom didn't care anymore whether she lived or died, and so she trudged to the infirmary.

Every conversation I have had over the years with Auschwitz survivors will eventually involve the mention of an encounter with the infamous Dr. Mengele. Most survivors will tell you that he was on the platform making the selections when they arrived in the camp, pointing to the left or right, determining life or death. If this had been true, he would have been there day and night for months.

But I am never one to argue with people's stories, so I will only tell the one my mother told me.

My mother sat down on the steps outside the infirmary waiting for someone to let her in. or to throw her onto the truck to the gas chamber. A man drove up on a motorcycle. He was wearing a very clean uniform, and although everything else in the camp was covered in mud, his boots glistened. He dismounted and grabbed my mother by the collar. He asked what she was doing there, and when she answered that she was sick, he opened the door to the infirmary and threw her inside. She landed on the floor, and there she stayed for she knew not how many days. No one tended to her, no one asked her who she was or what the problem was. Mengele was called the Angel of Death, but for my mother he had served the opposite purpose. He saved her life.

In another one of her writings, I found this fragment:

After twelve months of pain and misery I find myself in the hospital. Swollen from hunger and burning with fever, I lay piled among bodies, cast down in seemingly lifeless heaps. I am not sure weather (sic) I am alive, and the others dead, or I am dead and the rest alive.

I lived apart from my body, observing my own conduct and that of others with disbelieve.

I could not imagine even here an end to the faint throbbing, which told me I was still alive.

Suddenly it is quiet again, just faint moaning and crying from adjoining bunks.

I move closer to the wall and rest my burning face on the cement.

In this atmosphere of doom there seemed to be an intangible quality about people that have come to terms with death.

When she recovered enough to realize that she was still alive, she left the infirmary on her own and went back to her barracks. Her fellow inmates could not believe their eyes. They had been certain that she was dead.

I heard this story many times during my childhood and was always struck by how easily a life could be lost or saved in the camps. Was my mother simply in the right place at the right time to benefit from Mengele's decision not to kill her? The concept of luck is very real in all the stories that my parents and their survivor friends told me over the years, and in those I heard in my many interviews with survivors throughout my travels. There seems to be nothing else that can explain some of the life-altering events that have been told to me. Stories of miraculous escapes, of reprieves from death, guns that jammed, nooses that broke, train doors that opened in the middle of nowhere, injuries that should have been fatal but from which a recovery somehow occurred with no medical intervention. What else could explain these things but luck?

When I heard stories like this it only reinforced my belief in the heroic nature of both of my parents. In the movies, people died from malaria or were saved by a fortunate dose of medicine in the nick of time. But in my life, people survived in ways that could not be explained except for a stroke of luck. My parents would insist they were saved so they could live to testify—to tell the world what had happened. I believe that is true. My father never missed a chance to share his stories, and my mother left me the treasure of her writing. Both wanted us to remember, not through the pages of a history book, but through the eyes of a lived experience.

In the Camp

The following piece was written and excerpted several different times, and this is the most complete iteration. From what I can tell, specifically from the reference to Disneyland, it was written and amended finally in English. It is the piece with the most detail about the camp and the miracle of the *shoe command* that seems to have saved not only my mother's life but the life of the woman who went on to marry my Uncle Sam and become my aunt, Basha.

My mother wrote:

The night is dark, and the rain pours with raging might. Through the windows of the barracks I see the thick gray smoke of human bodies leaving the chimneys of the four huge crematoriums. Throughout the night the transports of Jews keep arriving. The heavy trucks move slowly, passing the concentration camp, moving behind it to the crematoriums. The newcomers aboard the trucks are baffled. They do not know where they are being taken. But to us older inmates whose doom is temporarily stayed, the mystery is a bitter knowledge. We know that these newcomers will be the material that will feed the fires anew. We know that they will be burned to cinders in the four huge furnaces, often pushed alive into the yawning openings. Their last traces will be the oppressive thick smoke belched out of the chimneys, the smoke that keeps me awake tonight.

I could not sleep. I kept listening to the cries of the children and their mothers, I wished I could stop my aching ears from listening. If only this were a nightmare instead of the horrible reality that I know it to be. As the sounds come to me, my heart beats faster and I clench my cold fists. The hours of the night pass slowly but the ovens of Auschwitz work very quickly. The heavy gray smoke keeps gushing out and blowing in my direction. The acrid taste of human flesh is in my throat and burns my eyes. But even the knowledge of such horrors cannot keep me awake all night for I am too weak to resist sleep. My eyelids are heavy, and my eyes begin to close.

Suddenly it is the silence which arouses me. The work of the ovens must be done for all is quiet again. I drift off for the night. The night is my heaven, the time when I can pretend that none of this is happening, the only thing that keeps me from going insane. I rock back and forth feeling warm and safe, praying for the silence and the night to last forever. If only tomorrow never comes, how light my head feels as I drift from one thought to another.

There is in our barracks a stir among the girls, a sudden rumor flies from mouth to mouth, a rumor that a new work detail is being formed, the whisper of something to do with the dead's shoes. Pulses quicken. Who will be the lucky ones for this detail? Whose sanity will be prolonged by the oblivion that work provides? No one knows what the work will be or where the workers will be taken. Does it make a difference? Can it be any worse than this? Perhaps they say it will be better. We are in Block # 9. The girl who is in charge of the block is named Ester, a Slovakian Jewish fragile girl, who takes all her icy orders from the S.S. She is not a bad person; she pretends to strike one and if she does hit you, it is not brutal. She pretends to yell, but the yelling is not loud and frightening.

Two hundred girls, who are just innocent children, are chosen. I am among the two hundred chosen. Basia, my dear friend, is with me. The whole night nobody sleeps. I hear whispers, all kinds of thoughts twist and tangle in each individual's heart, soul, and mind. Perhaps, this is a new Nazi trick to take us into the fires of the crematorium, those poisonous odors that I choke upon day by endless day. Nobody has an explanation. Suddenly the voice of the civilian overseer wakes us up. Solemnly, we get dressed for certain death. We dress, each girl helping another; each girl pats the pale cheeks of her companion, hoping to stimulate a blush of color, to banish the look of death which covers us all.

In seconds, we stand in rows of five, waiting alone and forgotten. My mind begins again to wander into illusions. It must not and I snap back into reality. However, I look around and see where the hand of death touched young girls who would have been in their bloom of life if not for the horror that has befallen them. They were sheltered innocent girls once, full of smiles and blushing throats whose tender glances eyed the world with wonder and anticipation. What are they now? They are like slender marble statues, cold and dead. The blood in my veins begins to pound and floods me with an overpowering desire. Nobody is praying a prayer for the still young life all around me. As I pray to YOU oh Lord so far away in heaven. I pray for the dying and the memories of the dead ones You have called Your chosen ones. I stare at them. Suddenly, I do not want to become a lifeless statue. I want to live. I want to live. I want to live. Oh Lord, can You hear me. I want to get out. Beyond a doubt, I want to get out. Will anybody ever hear my tears, my crying, "Let this soul out!" I want to see the end of torture and brutality. How can one escape this calculated, determined trap?

Suddenly, a German S.S. woman in S.S. military uniform appears. She is about 50 years old. She does not look brutal. She even has a smile upon her red lips. She looks at the rows of girls. She counts us in a haunting way. She recounts and then looks, as she keeps writing in her little black notebook. Walking half dead and half alive at her side is a girl in a striped Auschwitz prison dress. Her name is Marisa, a Polish Jewish girl, who is thin and small. Marisa's nose is heavily scarred, but her face is beautiful. Her eyes are black, and they shine as two starry diamonds in the midnight sky. Her eyes nod in silence; she knows something, and her looks relax us. After the counting has been done several times Marisa gives a signal to proceed toward the gate. I look back into the lunatic asylum of Satan and Dante's Divine Comedy.

At each forgotten cold gray barrack stands a column of weeping young girls. They too are about to go to work. They do not even recall the name of the word "school." For they are now all alone, being brutalized in every hellish, demonic, satanic way, by the ones who stand for the now forgotten Third Reich, who's (sic) icy demeanor I shall cast off to hell today as I have in my yesterdays. The chaos among these young girls is unbelievable as each girl scrambles to get into line for the special work group. Whoever the overseer lays her hands on is struck with a heavy truncheon and when fallen, they are still beaten until their crushed skulls are shards of broken bones scattered red and bloody in the freshly fallen snow. Then their once pitiable youthful bodies are dumped into the sewers of Auschwitz. Innocent blood is spilled again and again, a faceless face, never to be remembered. For they are now in the putrid sewers drifting silently with the worms and grossly oversize rats in one red muddy bloody inferno. In frenzy, the girls are running in all directions without a place to run to. They run from Hell straight into the fire.

We walk in the direction of the gate. The Auschwitz orchestra, usually about fifty to seventy Jewish musicians plucked from among the nationals transported into Auschwitz, continue to play on and on as if this is some forgotten Disneyland. Oh, they are forced to play their melodies inside the gates of hell for the sunrise in Lucifer's eyes, as we march on to a lonely forgotten song. Only the German Nazi, a humorless, gross, merciless, and macabre being, could plan this bizarre musical accompaniment.

We are counted and scrutinized again. At the gates of hell, the S.S. guards eternally stand with their police dogs. These demonic heartless guards and their dogs always accompany all to our details of horrid work. The German Sheppard (sic) Guard Dogs are primed and ready, on their masters' command, to tear into any one of these innocent victims. Laughing Nazis target the dogs, to rip apart flesh, limb by limb, of one innocent girl after another. At a signal from the German S.S. overseer, the gates of hell are opened. We are out, on the other side of life. I look around and see the gate close. On the other side of the fence, two hundred girls, the German S.S. woman, Marisa and I. Suddenly, there are no guards, and no hungry barking dogs. We look at each other silently; the same question mirrored in everyone's eyes. We ask each other" is this true?" It cannot be possible. Is it a trick? We walk slowly, each girl submerged in her lonely, icy forgotten heart and thoughts. We are walking in the direction of the city of Auschwitz.

A deep sigh of relief escapes 200 dry throats. We walk slowly, each submerged in thought. No, we are not walking in the direction of the crematorium! The German woman guard even speaks to us. She encourages the girls to sing in the never-ending pouring rain. As we sing, for the first time in months, something within us, within our hearts, begins to ease. Am I hearing for the first time in my life the music of the angelic spheres? Oh, as I wish my life goodbye in the Lord's eternal eyes, we take this singing for a symbol of hope in our forgotten future days. We sing thereafter on the way to our horrid work each day. The public civilian highway we walk with bare feet, is bustling and busy. People are going to work, riding bicycles, some in vehicles, all going to their places of work in factories and fields of green. They look at us; they keep looking, thinking, oh, what a joyful merry group of girls. They too begin to hum and sing. I see now that music is the universal language and eternal key to open all our hearts to the wellspring of the eternal Lord. For the first time in months something within our hearts eases; we take this singing as a symbol of hope.

We pass small village hamlets. The houses are low, the roofs covered with thatched straw. Light gray smoke drifting from the chimneys, is rising to a blue sky. Here and there are women who come out of their houses. They look at us and wave handkerchiefs. Oh, dear, sweet, God, are their (sic) still people on earth who live in a house, sleep in a bed, and eat at a table. Is this possible on this same earth, under this blue heaven, as I watch innocent children being born while other innocent children are being burned alive in the fiery ovens?

Finally, we come to the city of Auschwitz. We go in the direction of the shady grey, large barracks. Around these barracks is a huge yard. In this lifeless once green field, now is a memorial graveyard of tons and tons of shoes piled miles high. Millions of shoes. Little children's shoes, big shoes, black shoes, white shoes, all colors, high shoes and low shoes. I keep looking and staring and thinking, and suddenly the picture before me is not of shoes. The picture is of people. It is a picture of a family. It is a picture of a city. It is a picture of a country. Oh, these shoes walk no more. These are millions of my people, my burned brothers, and sisters. Oh dear God, show me now, at this moment, Your big, brightest miracle. Breathe life back into each pair of shoes. Please wake up the children; kill the enemy of the children. Take pity on us and take us under Your protection. End this hideous nightmare. Nevertheless, this is no nightmare. It is not a nightmare, but a stark reality.

Marisa's voice cuts into my thoughts. "Girls, Girls," she says, "we are going to work here. The work will not be hard. We are going to work under a roof, need I say more? You know what it means to work under a roof that will keep us dry from the pouring icy rains. The rain will not soak us today. The sun will not scorch and bake us. The cold wind will not chill you through your thin tatters. Here the dogs will not be able to feast on pieces of your flesh torn from your bodies. We must behave girls. Do well, do as we are told, and most of all do your work. Then Auschwitz will become a haven to us." Two large tears slip from in-between Marisa's eyelids as she finishes speaking. Marisa looks at the rows of quietly weeping girls and speaks again. "Perhaps we will live through this, to tell the whole deaf world of this ghastly camp."

Slowly we walk into the shoe barracks. We are separated into groups of 20; we are given tools, hammers, knives, clippers, and nails. We are seated on low benches. The girls are permitted to walk out of the barrack to bring shoes for each group, and to take out with them the finished product of our work. Our job is to tear the shoes apart and sort out the soft skin from the hard skin. The shoe soles are separated from the shoe. In the morning of each workday, we receive our portions for the day; it must be finished by nightfall. At the end of our workday, we gather the tools; each group must account for the tools it uses. The tools are counted; nothing is permitted to be missing. This is the beginning, the creation of the Shoe Detail. A gleam of hope brightens up our sad lonely forgotten hearts today.

And so starts my second year of imprisonment. We helped and humored each other in the group of twenty girls that worked together at each table. We played a game of remembrance to preserve our sanity and to remember our loved ones. Each day another told about her family and from the stacks of shoes that we worked with we tried to put together a family. We picked shoes for every member and every age and put them together.

To me the most striking detail in this piece is not the formation of the shoe command but the encounter with the townspeople who step outside their thatched straw homes or who are on their way to work as the girls of the shoe command march by them. At the end of the war, it was common to hear civilians say they knew nothing of what was going on in the camps, that they had no idea of the brutality, the selections, the gas chambers, the crematoria. Anyone who has been to Auschwitz or other camps knows these are lies. The death camp, Birkenau, is about three miles from the older fort and camp of Auschwitz. Both lie within walking distance of the town of Oswiecim (Auschwitz is the German renaming of the town and camp). From my mother's *Shoah* testimony and in this piece of writing, her mention of passing by people on the way to work is quite clear. It is 1944. These girls are walking skeletons. They are foul and covered with lesions from lice and the inability to clean themselves. Their clothes are rags, they are barefoot or in broken wooden clogs. Can the passersby really say they did not know what they were looking at because the girls had been told to look happy and sing? Did they imagine this was a cheerful band of young women enjoying their walk to work? Did they not smell the smoke of the burning bodies or find the ashes from the crematoria blown by the wind onto the laundry they hung on the lines outside their tidy homes? And yet they sang along when the girls were told to sing.

How many of the townspeople were employed in some enterprise directly or indirectly related to the camp? Having visited more than just Auschwitz Birkenau in my travels with teachers I was struck by the proximity of the camps to the towns in Germany and Poland. Sachsenhausen sits inside of Oranienburg, Germany. Ravensbrueck across the lake from Furstenburg, Germany. Majdanek is on the main road leading into and out of Lublin, Poland. Belzec was so interesting to the rural Polish locals that they planned Sunday picnics on the hills above the camp, watching the arrival of trains and the lines of the condemned filing into the gas chambers. The only camp I visited that was somewhat hidden was Treblinka, but even that was no secret; the locals harvested whatever valuables they could by digging up the soil the Nazis had plowed under when they had finished killing the 400,000 Jews of Warsaw. The scavengers proudly posed for pictures on the mounds of the excavations as they hunted for gold teeth or other treasures that might have somehow eluded the strip searches as the condemned were marched to their deaths.

My anger is directed first and foremost at the Germans, both those who participated actively and those who stood by and did nothing. My mother used a saying in Yiddish that translates into "making yourself not know," a description of purposely avoiding what is in front of you. But I also harbor anger at the complicit Poles who now rebrand themselves as victims of the Nazis as they rewrite history to hide the truth. How many of them gloried in the destruction of the Jewish people? How many of them benefitted directly by taking the jobs, the homes and possessions of those who were displaced or killed? How many of them actively abetted the Nazi destruction? And how many of them had the opportunity to help but did not? I am aware of the penalties for helping. I am aware of the upheaval that caused neighbors to forget the long history of Jewish presence in Poland, the chaos of war that destroyed people's moral compasses and allowed them to be participants, passive or active, in the murder of their neighbors and friends. For every baker like Wally, how many others were there who not only did not lift a finger but who did the wrong thing, the immoral thing by giving people up to the enemy? Don't tell me about the righteous who did save people? The righteousness of those who did save people is overshadowed by the fact that six million people were slaughtered by a combination of evil and inaction. The numbers tell the story. We may want to glory in the goodness of those who helped, but most turned a blind eye, which should be a lesson to us about human behavior. They made themselves not know.

Dora, 5th from right in front row at memorial meeting
for Pruzana victims of the Holocaust. Event held in
Feldafing DP camp, Germany.

Camp Sisters, the *Lager Schweister*

Writers who specialize in analyses of concentration camp life are unanimous in their recognition of a phenomenon known as the *lager schweister* or camp sister. This was a woman who was an intimate, possibly a relative or a friend but not necessarily, whose companionship kept another woman alive, with whom she could share a bunk, her bread, and her dreams of one day being liberated from the hell they endured. Having a camp sister meant **that** there was someone waiting for you each day, someone propping you up during the *appel*, someone pinching your cheeks or pricking her finger to smear blood across your pale cheeks to mask your weakness.

After Fradel's murder, Mom wanted to die. She thought often about going to the electrified fence, but she could never summon up the courage. Instead, she spent a great deal of time crying and hoping **that** death would find her and take the work of dying out of her own hands. But ultimately, what kept her going was the offer of friendship **that came** from those left in her barracks, among them her "angel," Shoshka.

This woman, who was from a nearby town, saw a desperate young girl, and took it upon herself to keep my mother alive. She was not someone who knew my mother's family. She was from a much poorer background, uneducated and several years older. Yet, somehow, she felt it was her responsibility to help my mother to live. Shoshka was a big woman with a countenance that was almost masculine. She was used to hard work and had scrambled for survival even before the war; and while the conditions in the camp were horrible, Shoshka was someone who had the skills to find a way to overcome them. It was not that she took advantage of others, but rather she understood how to fend for herself, how to make it through. It was this tenacity and strength that was what she had to teach my mother and along with her, a girl called Nina, whom my mother had known in her days in the ghetto.

Shoshka wrestled my mother out of her bunk during her deepest moments of despair, pinched her cheeks in the *appel*, and held her up, both mentally and physically when she was starting to collapse. And she did the same for Nina. Shoshka's spirit was indomitable, and she somehow maintained her strength even though both her husband and child had been killed. Perhaps, her age and experience meant she valued life more than the two young girls she helped to protect and survive. What was clear in the stories told to me was that it was crucial to have someone who cared about you, to whom it mattered that you were still there day after grueling day.

My mother's devotion to Shoshka and Nina continued after the war. I can remember the Aeropostale letters arriving from Palestine, where both had gone, arriving on a regular basis, sometimes containing pictures of children and family gatherings. When my mother and I visited cousins in Israel in 1964, Mom wanted most of all to see Shoshka and Nina. Over the years, each of them made several trips back and forth, and each time they rejoiced at being in each other's company once more. My own trips to Israel always included a visit with both women, and it was especially with Nina's family that the bond remained.,

Many years after this friendship had saved my mother, I was in Milwaukee giving a presentation for community members about my mother's life. In the audience was a man and his wife who came up to speak with me after the presentation. Steve Russek told me that his mother's story was very similar to my own mother's. She had been from Grodno, a city very close to Pruzana, and had been deported to Auschwitz three days before my mother's transport. Her name was also Dora. Perhaps they knew each other? I did not recall my mother speaking of her, and given the size of the camp and the many people that had been brought there, how could we be certain that their paths had crossed? Then he remarked that like me, he had also been born in East New York and wondered where we had lived. When I told him the address, 397 Georgia Avenue, he was stunned. His parents had lived on the 400 block of Georgia Avenue! We felt that our mothers had to have known each other, but we could not establish a real connection because neither mother was still alive.

Steve gave me a book written by his mother detailing her war experiences. At home, I flipped through it and was struck by the fact that his mother was the niece of Herman Yablokov, the famous Yiddish singer and songwriter. I remembered that my mother had mentioned that she knew Yablokov's niece, but I had no proof of that. In doing my research for this book, I read through transcriptions of my mother's interviews. In one of them, given for the Gratz College Oral Archive in 1984, she says:

I was with a girl that was not from my town, and she was from Grodno, Poland and she was in our ghetto. (This is an error. Dora Russek was not in the Pruzana ghetto. My mother met her in Birkenau.) And her name was Dora, too, and we, for a little time, shared our life. We slept on the same bunk together and we shared our food together and she used to tell me, "You'll see. We'll live. I have an uncle in America, and he is a big actor, and we will come to him. He is my uncle, and you will see, we will have it so good." Her uncle was an actor. He played in Papirossin on the Jewish stage. I can't remember his name right now, that was her father's brother, and they stayed in contact. She even knew Brooklyn. She called it "Broklyn" and she said, "You'll see, He will be so good to us because he always sends us money. He sends us for every yomtov (holiday), and we have something to live on. We'll be with him. He lives in Broklyn."

Later on in the interview, Mom remembers:

Yablokow, that is the name of the famous actor that I knew. And he played on the Yiddish stage, in Grodno. In fact, when we came to the United States, he was still alive.

And so here was the connection. Here was my mother establishing that it was in fact Steve's mother that she was remembering! Had I read this interview at any other time, I would not have remembered this detail of the uncle who was a singer in America. And if Steve had not come to my presentation in Milwaukee, or come up to speak with me afterwards, there would have been no connection at all. What's more, my mother does not mention many names in her interviews. She always speaks about Shoshka and Nina and sometimes mentions other women that populated the barracks and the various workplaces, but most campmates are nameless. Miraculously, a conversation with a stranger became another link in my mother's story and in Steve's as well. And the camp sisterhood that helped to sustain my mother had one more member to whom I am grateful.

Steve sent me an email with an audio excerpt from his mother's *Shoah* interview. In it, she talks about a time when she was very ill and had lost all hope. She talks about three girls who persuaded her to live, two girls from Czechoslovakia whom she does not name, and a Dora from Pruzana, my mother. What Steve tells me in his text is that his mother's expression in the videotaped interview is very solemn as she talks about her illness in the camp and her feeling that the end was near. But when she mentions my mother, her face comes to life. Yes, not only did she know this other Dora in the camp, but they remained friends well into their senior years when they would visit together in Florida.

Here was a part of my mother's story that I did not know. I knew my mother had been saved by the kindness of others, but I did not know she was also one of the ones that did the saving. In my search through her papers and in writing that others have done, I looked for mention of her in this new role and found it. A campmate, a woman named Marisa who was the leader of the shoe command writes in her diary in 1944 about Dora, my mother, and her friend Sara, a girl from home:

Sara and Dora are with me in the shoe detail. Dora has a very close girlfriend, Basia (this woman will marry my uncle Sam), who is a very capable girl. She is also a devoted friend. The comradeship between them under Auschwitz circumstances is unusual – endearing, warm and loving. In the group of Litvaks is a girl named Syma... Her appearance reflects a heavy, coarse, common character, rather swinish than human. A pig has plenty to eat, this who I must call a human being has plenty to eat, like a swine, but only for herself. She does not share a thing. Sara and Dora are weak, they are barely holding their own. This stuffed pig of a human being is punished by God, she is sick with malaria, the disease which is spreading through the camp. Sara and Dora on their weak shoulders and young hands pull her back and forth to her work. They do not leave her behind to the fate of certain death, which awaits her by leaving her behind. This creature of abundant packets of food packed into her clothing, plus a sack which she carried slung from her arm. Sara and Dora are hungry, they don't touch a thing of her provisions. Sara in Yiddish is talking to Dora, asks her if they can give some of the bread and whatever food they have to "our boys," who they meet on the way to work. "Because you cannot eat it all Syma," Dora says. Syma nods yes. I see from a distance the way Sara and Dora throw the bread and food to the Jewish innocent boys as the girl and boy inmates pass each other towards their work details, For themselves they keep nothing, all bits and scraps go to the boys. Also Sara asks Dora, "Dora, is it worth saving the life of this girl," and Dora with a faint smile on her lips answers Sara in Yiddish, "Sara, dear, dos is doch a heimisze Pruzana meidel." (She is a girl from our hometown of Pruzana). The two young, sweet girls look at each other and after these words from Dora, Sara helps Dora pull Syma into the shoe barracks. Thus is she rescued from day to day and I see that she survives...

My vision of my mother has always been that she needed the help of others to survive, that she was unable to fend for herself, but it was a great gift to learn she was instrumental in the saving of at least two others. What makes this even more remarkable is my mother was no more than seventeen at the time. I feel a certain sense of pride thinking that she had this goodness in her even in these most dire circumstances— she would put the life of another above her own. I wish I had known this before she died. Of course, she never mentioned any of it to me.

Dora and Bernie in Florida, 1996

Cousin Lola standing behind Fradel, Velvel and Dora, around 1932

Lola

The girl with long braided hair in the photograph, the one standing behind the smaller children with her arms around them, is Lola, a young teen, but I don't know her exact age. What I do know is she is spending time in Pruzana with her cousins, visiting from Lodz, the big industrial capital known for its textile mills. I know this because my mother has told me about her. She is my mother's cousin, or should I say, she *was* my mother's cousin. My mother is the little girl next to the teddy bear. The other two children were her older sister and younger brother. Perhaps their maternal grandmother is still alive, and this visit will allow Lola to see the old woman who lives in the home of her little cousins, my mother's childhood home. Or maybe it is summer vacation, and she has come to spend a few weeks in the country before she returns to school. As was the custom, they have all gone to the photography studio to have their portrait taken. It will be sent to America, to their uncles Abe and Eli who have left for the *"goldene land,"* the golden land of America. Only one person in the photo will survive, and it is my mother. And it is from her that I will come to know what little I do know about Lola.

Lola, whose real name was Leah, was the only child of my maternal grandmother's sister, Bryna. Or so I thought, until I found a census record that indicated there had been another daughter who had died very young. My mother never mentioned another cousin, so this information, like so much of Lola's story, was another unhappy surprise. Lola's father was the manager of the Poznanski textile mill in Lodz. He was from a very distinguished family and the heir to a family fortune, albeit a small one in comparison to that of his wealthy employers. Handicapped from birth with a paralyzed arm and partially paralyzed leg, but with a brilliant head for business, he was wealthy enough to employ a valet who helped him with his daily dressing and who lived with the family in their apartment in the center of Lodz. Lola attended a private girls' academy and was headed for university. Her life was much more cosmopolitan than that of her small-town cousins. The Poznanski family, her father's employer, was well-known in Lodz. Not only was their factory the largest, but they were the second wealthiest Jewish family in Europe after the Rothschilds.

My mother's memories of Lola's visits are filled with joy. Mom and Fradel loved their cousin, and when she came to visit there was great excitement. The rules around bedtime and the restrictions about what the girls could and could not do were abandoned during her stay. Lola's father sent trunks of underwear and socks from the mill for the family. Sometimes Lola's mother Tanta Bryna accompanied Lola to the small town, to spend time with her aged mother and her sister (my grandmother Chava), but as Lola grew older, she would travel on the train alone and would be picked up at the station in a horse-drawn cart. My mother remembers visiting Lola's family in Lodz, traveling on the train to the big city, being taken to the mill office to be measured for new underwear and hosiery. But most often, Lola came to Pruzana.

In 1939, sometime before September and the invasion of Poland, Lola was sent to England, to a prep school to perfect her English in anticipation of her eventual education there. The year coincides with the outbreak of the war, and with my mother's loss of information about Lola's whereabouts. At one point Mom thought Lola might have come back from England to be with her family, although that would have been difficult, if not impossible. When we discussed the fates of our family members, Mom said she believed Lola might have survived by staying in England. But there is no record of her that I can find anywhere, under Lola Groslejt (the way my mother told me it would have been spelled in Polish), Leah Groslejt, Lea Groslajt, or Groslait, or Grossleit, or Grosslight, or any other variation of the spelling of her last name. Even the records of the transports from Lodz to the death camps do not reveal a clue. I have searched in person at the Lodz memorial to the deported Jews, poring through loose-leaf books filled with plastic encased pages of lists of Jewish names beside the dates of their deportations. I have searched online, only to find nothing. Lola's fate remains unknown to this day.

When my mother emigrated to America in 1949, to the home of her maternal uncle Abe (the brother of Tanta Bryna and my grandmother Chavah), she was given the picture of the children that had been sent to the family many years before. She had never seen the photo but did remember going to the photography studio for the sitting. It was not the last time she saw Lola, but it is the only photo of the children all together. For me, the photo is a treasure and a mystery. My mother's siblings, so young and beautiful, would die in Auschwitz. There are so few pictures of them, so little proof that they once existed. And while my mother would survive to tell us about them, about their lives and their deaths, Lola remains a mystery. I can't help but feel if not for the photo, she would not exist at all.

Can I mourn for someone I did not know? I mourn for grandparents whose death occurred years before I was born, grandparents whose names my brother and I carry. In the synagogue list of those my family remembers at Yom Kippur, a day when we traditionally remember our dead, I have listed my grandparents and the brothers and sisters of my parents, those who would have been my aunts and uncles had they lived. I have never included Lola, or even her parents for that matter, because if I were to add everyone on both sides of my family who was killed in the Holocaust, I would need pages and pages in the memorial book. That is not the way it is done. Each family limits its list of those they want to memorialize to the most immediate members. But most families are not like my family. Most of the families who have deeper roots here in America were not destroyed by the Nazis. They may have a distant relative or two that was lost, but it is unlikely they even know their names let alone the details of their deaths. With Lola and with her parents I have something in common with them. I have no information.

Yet, there is something that attracts me to wonder about Lola's fate, something that brings her story to my mind at random times. Who mourns for her? Who remembers her, if not me? Doesn't every life deserve to be remembered? She might have had a brilliant academic career in England. She might have been a wife and a mother. Perhaps all these things occurred, and I do not know it. Whether she was famous or unknown, a shining star or just an ordinary person, she does not deserve to be forgotten and to go unmourned. And so instead of allowing her to be yet another casualty, forever young, and almost faceless save for the picture **that was** sent to her uncles in America, I take up the weight and the honor of remembering her myself. Surely her life should hold some meaning in the world.

Arrivals

I was in awe of my parents and when I measured myself against them, I always came up short. I was not brave or cunning like my father, and I knew I could not endure suffering like my mother. My father would tell me I was too soft to have survived the war, that I didn't have the smarts to outwit the enemy, that I was too trusting. I knew he was right. My upbringing had held no real danger. My problems were not real problems. My only enemies, schoolyard bullies or snobbish girls, were not real threats. I had nothing to complain about in comparison to what my parents had gone through. As my mother would remind me when she wanted to show me how silly my worries were, "Hitler is not at your door." It worked. That remark stung enough to make me realize my concerns were petty by comparison. Mom and Dad had endured so much—they had lost almost everyone in their families. They were homeless and penniless at the end of the war, but they were unbroken, or so I thought. They seemed almost superhuman in their courage. They had survived death camps, forced marches, starvation and disease. They had felt the pain of losing family members and yet they still married and had children, despite the losses, or perhaps because of them. With great optimism they had left Europe and come to America, ready to start a new life, ready to face whatever challenges lay ahead. It wasn't until I began to listen more carefully to their stories and to read my mother's writings that I discovered how difficult the transition to America had been. I knew the war had left its scars on them, but I never realized what it must have been like adjusting to their new world.

The war ended in May of 1945 and Mom and Dad married in early 1946 after a very quick courtship. For three years they waited for permission to travel, first to Palestine and then to the newly formed state of Israel. They revoked their initial papers and decided to come to America when they realized immigration to Israel would land them in another war. America was a dream destination, but an unfamiliar reality. Neither of them spoke English and their contacts here were family with whom they did not have a close relationship. My mother's two uncles, Abe and Eli Tanenbaum, my grandmother's brothers, agreed to sponsor my parents to come to America. I am not sure if Uncle Abe had ever met my mother. He had left Poland for the U.S. in the 1920's, perhaps before Mom was born. His younger brother, Uncle Eli, had

Dora's citizenship certificate, 1955

lived in Pruzana with his mother, my great-grandmother, but he left Poland to escape the Polish army sometime in the early 1930's. My mother did remember Eli from her childhood. The only picture that we have of my grandmother is one that Eli brought to America, a photo with my grandmother, my mother and her older sister, taken before Eli left. Eli could not come directly to the States because of the quota restrictions, so he spent years in Cuba waiting to immigrate to New York. Drafted into the army during WWII, he found Mom in a DP camp in Germany after the war, her name appearing on lists of survivors. He had not seen her since she was a small girl. Now she was all that was left of their once large family.

Changing their intended destination from Israel to America meant my parents were put on another waiting list. By the time all their paperwork had cleared, Mom was seven months pregnant with me. The American consulate in Germany, in charge of those deemed eligible to immigrate, determined Mom would have to fly to New York because of her advanced pregnancy, while Dad would sail several days later.

"I was on a plane for the first time, all alone. In those days it took 24 hours to fly from Europe to America," she told me.

Each time she talked about this I was astonished by her courage. She was alone, headed to a family, only one of whom she had ever met. "I could not speak much English," she said. "Just some sentences I practiced before I was leaving, but I was so scared I couldn't remember how to say them. I was sick the whole flight, throwing up all over my clothes. I did not have anything to clean myself with. I was so ashamed."

She had no way to communicate on the plane, and she had no change of clothes or toiletries on hand to clean herself before meeting her family. In Europe after the war there had been no such thing as maternity clothes. A woman wore what clothing she had or bought larger clothing. With very little money and saving everything for America, Mom continued wearing her few dresses even as she grew bigger, and the dresses grew shorter and tighter. She was quite aware that she looked disheveled and unwell when her new family saw her for the first time.

At customs she was detained. She told me the story many times. I remember it this way:

"Your father was holding the papers. We did not separate them, mine from his. In the confusion of saying goodbye my papers were still with him when I got on the plane. I did not realize this until they asked me for my documents."

As her uncles watched helplessly, Mom was taken to Ellis Island and jailed for the night as an illegal immigrant. The uncles promised her they would return in the morning with a bond to assure their responsibility and support until my father would arrive with her documents.

"They came the next morning, I mean the aunts came, because the uncles had to go to work. Anna and Celia were there. What must they have thought! I was seven months pregnant with a dress that barely covered me the way it would be proper. My coat was covered in vomit. They were really getting a bargain with me, huh!"

I knew her stories about the war, but I never thought much about what it was like to come to America—to arrive to so much confusion, to be taken to Uncle Abe's house in Brooklyn, to meet the American family that she had only heard about in letters. Uncle Abe and his wife Aunt Anna had two children, Melvin who was 14 and Marilyn who was five or six. Uncle Eli, now married to Aunt Celia, had twin daughters Linda and Janet, about three years old. Though Eli and Abe understood Polish, no one else in the family did, but even the aunts and Melvin spoke Yiddish. Curious neighbors dropped by to see the new immigrant. The house was filled with chatter Mom could not understand but which was clearly about her. This new outsider was a bit of a spectacle, an actual Holocaust survivor, a pregnant one at that.

"The next day Abe and Anna went to work, and I was left in the house with Melvin who was home from school with a broken leg. Melvin was a sweet boy. He wanted to know what happened to me and my family. We talked for hours." Mom and Mel developed a special relationship in her first days in America, one that lasted for the rest of her life. "He really listened to me. I did not know then that most Americans did not want to know about the war or what happened to us. I would find that out very soon."

Mel remembers being fascinated by his newly arrived cousin whom he found to be very beautiful. He showed her a map hanging in his bedroom where he had tried to keep track of the war, where their family might be and where the American army and Uncle Eli were landing. Mom was grateful for the companionship he provided, and they spent the days together until Dad arrived a week later. Mel described my father as a "force of nature."

My father was never one who enjoyed taking charity. At twenty-five, he was determined to make it on his own, and within days he had secured a job in a small factory that fabricated orthopedic shoes and braces for patients, particularly children, who had been stricken with polio. The skills he had learned from his father, which were then honed in the labor camps, made him a valuable worker. The fact that polio raged every summer meant there were plenty of customers for the goods he produced. Dad's goal was to move out of Uncle Abe's house as soon as possible into a place of their own. It was a feat he accomplished within weeks.

Two months after they arrived, I was born. Mom went into labor without knowing what was happening to her.

"My mother and I never talked about babies. In those days it wasn't a topic," she told me.

I reminded her she had lost her mother before she was old enough to have that discussion. My mother would nod in agreement when we talked about this. She was only sixteen the last time she had been with her mother, and so there had been no one to explain things to her when her own time came.

"I felt sick. Then my water broke. I was in the new apartment by myself. Your father was at work. I called Melvin. He didn't know what to do, so he called Celia, who told him to tell me to get into a taxi and go to the hospital."

Again, her lack of English became a barrier. Mom and the nurses in the maternity ward could not communicate. She told me they wanted her to stay in bed, and she wanted to get up to use the bathroom. Climbing over the raised sides of the bed, she disappeared and returned to their disapproving faces. "What an animal, they must have thought! Straight from the camps, look how she behaves!" My father was at work and could not leave to be with her. Men didn't often accompany their wives to the hospital to deliver a baby in those days. It didn't matter; Dad would not have done anything to jeopardize his job. My dad arrived when I had already been born, carrying a bouquet of flowers that had wilted in the heat of afternoon.

The nurses gave my mother a baby naming book and told her to pick one. No matter that she could barely speak English. They needed a name for the birth certificate, and she was holding up the process. There were papers to fill out, procedure had to be followed.

Her own mother's name was Chavah; it meant "companionship" in Hebrew, the name for the first woman created to be a helpmate for the first man, translated to Eve in English. It was Jewish tradition to name a child after a departed relative and my mother had more departed relatives than she could count. But of course, she would name the baby for her own mother. In her heavy Polish accent, my mother told the nurse the baby girl would be named Eva.

"That's not a name for an American child. Look in the book under the *E*. You can find something more modern there." Somehow my mother understood the disapproving tone and so she looked.

There were no questions asked or answered. There was no empathy for the new mother with the fractured English, the twenty-two-year-old with the tattooed number on her arm, the one who had seen more death and destruction than any of these nurses could possibly imagine but who still had enough hope left in her to want to bring a child into the world. It was 1949; everyone knew what those tattooed numbers signified, at least everyone who worked in a Jewish hospital in Brooklyn knew.

The nurse opened the book to the appropriate page and handed it to my mother, who was intimidated enough to believe that she could not name her child Eva, not in this new land where she had arrived only two months before. She was on her own again and had to follow orders. Auschwitz and the Nazis had taught her that.

She looked through the list and selected *Elaine*. Had she heard the name somewhere? Was there someone she knew named Elaine? I could never figure it out. It did start with an *E*, but it was a far cry from Eva. My parents never called me Elaine as a child. I was *Chavah* in our house, my grandmother's name, I was *Ellinke* to my parents' Holocaust survivor friends and few relatives, a European-inflected diminutive of this new-fangled American name. I was *Iya* years later to my little brother who couldn't pronounce my name, and I was *Eleanor* when my mother was angry with me for behaving like a silly American. That was always a distinction I

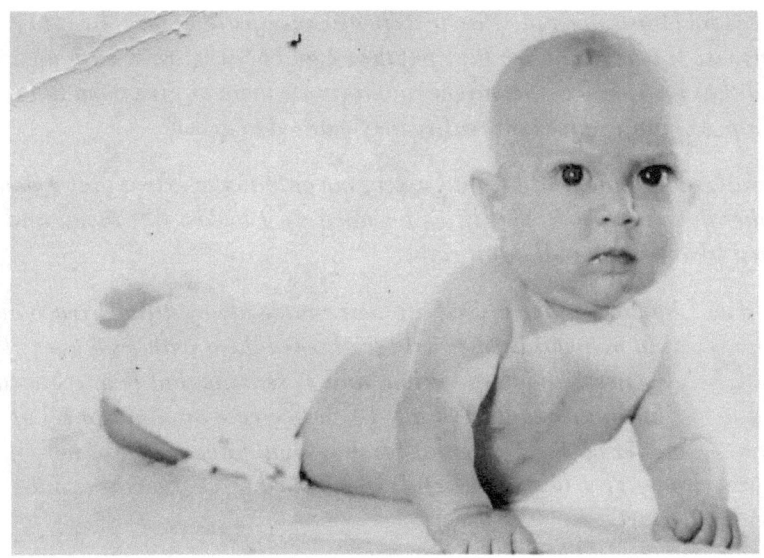

Elaine at 3 months, 1949

knew— Americans behaved in ways that did not please my mother. They were impolite and abrupt. They thought everything could be forgiven with a simple "I'm sorry." They had no initiative and no self-respect. I was Eleanor when I acted like one of them. *Elaine* was the girl I would become when I was old enough to play in the street with other kids from the block in the Brooklyn neighborhood where we lived, when I began to discover the difference between the world inside my house and the world inside theirs.

Everything about the new world was different and confusing for my mother, but what was most difficult was the adjustment to always being the "other. "After about a year in the U.S. Mom wrote:

The constant staring at my tattoo, my concentration camp number on my arm, the silent whispers and stares, and the sideways glances, made me realize how different my life will be, no matter how I tried to cover it up, with long sleeved blouses, pretending not to notice. It was always there, eating away at my little confidence that I felt, thinking that I am the same as other people, except that this problem happened to me. But I began to see that the rest of the world did not share my view. In their eyes I was not like everybody else. An invisible barrier had been erected and I was on the other side.

I was no longer normal. People were always afraid of me. I could sense it. It was as though they felt that I had been touched with a curse and that too close contact might contaminate them or give them a glimpse of an unpleasant reality they wanted to avoid.

I realized that the world would accept me only to the extent that I don't bother them too much, that if I pretended, if I looked like them, and acted like them, it will be all right.

And so I had to remake myself in their image. They did not reach out to understand my world. My world frightened them with its echoes of pain, helplessness, and desperation, and I, sensing that fear, realized that to maintain any contact at all, I had to create an atmosphere of calm, of matter of factness (sic), so they would not be afraid to approach me. If I looked cheerful, if I looked in charge, they could risk the contact.

I withdrew behind this façade of confidence. No one will know, I vowed in despair. In fact, the more despairing I felt, the more I tried to project calm. I think it is impossible ever to shed that habit. If I had allowed what I felt to show, it would have destroyed me. But behind this, how I hated it all. How lonely and isolated I felt. I got sick of being asked "How are you?" that all-purpose meaningless formula that sets up barriers of false interest. There is only one answer, "I am fine, managing well and adjusting beautifully." Any other answer is unacceptable.

They examine you with their eyes and unbelievable remarks they whisper behind your back, and you constantly hear the same refrain, "I don't know how you can go on." I knew I could not, as if anyone wants to struggle and suffer for the pleasure of it.

When others had been talking, I found it hard to express myself. I was searching myself for answers, so I started to write my feelings down, and this became my constant companion, and this I feel made me capable of surviving impossible trials.

I mostly wrote when I was very depressed and lonely, and the times were many, and through the years I accumulated a vast amount of material. I never altered anything. I wrote that day how I felt and why, and that helped me in going on with my life and making a place for myself in society.

Though I knew she longed for her family, I never knew how lonely she really was or how much her otherness burdened her. When she wanted to talk about her war experiences in those first years, people asked her to stop. It was too horrible for them to hear. "That was then, this is now. That was over there, you're here now," they would tell her. When she stopped talking about it, people assumed that she had overcome it and that her life was proceeding normally. Caught up in my own childhood and then adolescent struggles to fit in, I never imagined that my mother was going through much the same thing, with the important difference that she was always going to wear the mark of the refugee on her, if not the tattoo, then the accent that accompanied every word she spoke even after she had mastered English quite well.

Dora in Brooklyn, circa 1950

Many years later she delivered a speech about her experiences:

I will give you a glimpse of the two wars that I have fought. One I survived, the war which the world called the Holocaust, an American term, too grand and remote to touch such a familiar devastation. The other is my private war, of living and surviving in a free society. Through the years I tried to block out the memories. I would cover my ears and close my eyes, but the turmoil always was there. The outside world knew so little about the war, so to them, seeing one alive, a survivor, was enough. But you can be alive, hooked up to a lifesaving machine, and this means living. You can sit in a chair and stare at the world as it passes you by, and you are also alive, but to live and adjust to a free world, to work and raise a family when the ground under your feet is so shaky that you feel it tremble? When your little boy comes running from school crying, saying that his friends don't want to play with him because his parents are refugees, or when you sit at your daughter's graduation, and she is among the first in her high school class and gets four scholarships and you hear somebody sitting behind you saying, "but this is impossible. Her parents are refugees." And so, your little world that you tried so carefully to put together crumbles, and you are again back from where you started. When you look into your children's eyes and see the pain when you answer their questions, when you try to make their world so smooth and painless when your own is so complicated. This is no small task. But standing here before you and being able to speak about it is a victory for me. So, I think that I am winning my other war too.

Then there is pity. People drench you in it, which is not at all what you need. Compassion is what I needed, but compassion demands stronger emotions, love and courage, sacrifice and discipline, and the outside world that is not affected does not want to get involved. I grew to hate society, the happy untormented society that did not want me. Did not try to understand me. They were well, they were happy, and above all they had families. They could make plans, they had a future.. I only had a bare existence. I felt alone and lonely, it was me against the world. I longed to find a place where I could nurse my wounds and not have to put on a bright face, but there is not such a place. You must adjust slowly, making one step at a time, being careful in choosing your path in life. Many people I met on the way offered individual acts of kindness, moments of understanding and help, for those I will always be grateful. But most tried to stay away, not to get involved. Mine was a long internal problem, that could be only resolved with my own determination and carefulness.

The loneliness is sometimes so great that you feel yourself floating away from reality. I know that there are some sorrows that will never be healed and sometimes there is no ground for happy thinking. But with determination and positive thinking, you pick up, and live, and hope and dream again. And this has made me capable of surviving impossible trials.

God works quietly and slow. I began to learn patience, instead of turning frantically in circles, seeking answers to my dilemmas. I learned to wait and trust. In the dark night lying lonely and terrified I prayed for strength, strength to go on. I will not give in. Years of frustration and fear I endured and survived.

Grandfathers

A few weeks after they arrived in America, my parents moved out of Uncle Abe's house and into their own apartment in Brooklyn. Dad commuted every day on the subway into Manhattan to the orthopedic shoe shop near Union Square. Their apartment on Williams Avenue was small, and after I was born in May, they realized they needed a bit more space. Friends who had traveled on the same boat as Dad, the *General Hahn*, were living in a building on Georgia Avenue where an apartment was available. My parents' desire to be among other survivors was strong, and this couple had a baby boy who was exactly a year older than I was. This connection would provide companionship for Mom while Dad was at work.

An elderly man who owned the brownstone building was interested in sharing his first-floor space. The apartment had an eat-in kitchen, a large front-facing living room which he would use as his bedroom, and a small room off the kitchen where we eventually put a television and where Dad would work on custom shoemaking projects he completed at home to make extra money. There was also a large bedroom on the other side of the kitchen and a small bedroom off that. There was one bathroom that we all would share.

When Mom came to inquire about the apartment, she had me in a pram. I think I must have been about six months old, which would make this sometime in November or December of 1949. Mr. Nitzberg was the landlord's name, and though I don't really know his age at the time, he must have been in his late seventies or early eighties, and a widower. Mom had been told by her friends that the old man spoke Yiddish, so she felt comfortable coming to inquire about the apartment on her own. When he saw the baby carriage, Mr. Nitzberg told Mom that he would not rent to a family with children. He needed peace and quiet, not the tumult that babies caused. Mom began to cry. She told him she needed to move and that it would be so nice for her to live in the same building as a few people she already knew in America.

As she spoke, Mr. Nitzberg listened to her Yiddish and asked her where she was from. He recognized her Litvak Yiddish (northern Poland, Lithuania). When she told him Pruzana, he reacted with disbelief. He asked her who had instructed her to say that. She didn't understand. It turned out that Mr. Nitzberg was also from Pruzana but had come to America many years before. He recognized her family name but did not remember her parents and thought that Mom had been prompted to soften him up by lying about where she was from. But he finally understood no one had told her anything about him. He was so taken with her that he agreed to rent the apartment to her, and Mom used my pram to move their few possessions that very day.

And so it was that we lived at 397 Georgia Avenue and that Mr. Nitzberg, that crusty old man, became my "grandfather." Though he had grandchildren of his own, they lived in Philadelphia, and he saw them only on special occasions. He went from someone who did not want the noise and mess of children to someone who could not get enough of playing with me and taking me with him on his

Dora and Elaine at her 1st birthday, 1950

82

neighborhood jaunts. He took me to the park, sat me on his lap while he ate, and allowed me to put my hands into his food. My mother begged him not to spoil me, but it was to no avail. I was his Ellinke, and I could do no wrong.

The arrangement was so successful that Mr. Nitzberg began to eat all his meals with us and became a part of the family, which meant my mother had a built-in babysitter and Mr. Nitzberg had a reason to enjoy life again. Since my parents spoke Yiddish to me, so did Mr. Nitzberg, and my budding Yiddish delighted his old buddies in the park. What baby spoke Yiddish? When my brother Harold was on the way, Mr. Nitzberg was delighted. He was the one who paid for the bris (the ritual circumcision and party to celebrate a boy's birth). Sadly, soon after Harold's birth, Mr. Nitzberg suffered a stroke and died in the apartment. It was a painful time for all of us. For Mom, a tiny bit of home that she had found with this stranger, turned adopted family member, was also now gone.

The building belonged to the Nitzberg family, and we now forwarded our rent to the son who lived in Philadelphia. Knowing how well my mother had cared for their father, they were only too happy to let us stay in the apartment at the same rent and to redecorate it to suit our needs. My parents converted Mr. Nitzberg's bedroom into a living room, and now had full use of the apartment, but there was a void in our lives that I, even at four years old, felt and remember to this day.

This was not my only experience with a substitute grandfather. Years later when we had been living in Philadelphia for two years, my parents' best friends, Jack and Tillie Hershenberg, also survivors, had the opportunity to bring Jack's father to the U.S. from communist Poland. Joseph Hershenberg was in his seventies at the time. When his son and daughter-in-law had emigrated to America, he had not chosen to come with them. Now, he was alone and needed their help.

We all called him "Zayde," Yiddish for grandfather. Few in my parents' group of friends had a parent who survived the war. Most of the children I grew up with had no grandparents at all. As honorary family he became my zayde as well. He never learned to speak English; communicating with him had to be done in Yiddish. He sat in a large, upholstered chair near the door by a picture window that provided the light he needed to read the Yiddish paper, *The Forward.* I am not sure he ever knew my first name. He always called me "maidele," little girl. Coming into the house, one had to greet Zayde first, usually with a kiss while asking the question, "Was machst du?" (How are you?). I remember his scratchy beard, and his very strong grip as he held my hand each time I visited.

Since these were my parents' best friends, we visited often, and Zayde was always in his chair. On Saturday nights he loved watching the Lawrence Welk show, and when there was a pretty girl on television, he made us move out of the way so that he could see past us as we perched on the floor in front of the TV set. That always made us laugh. He may have been old, but he wasn't *that* old.

Zayde's dominion was Passover. He expected all of us there for the seders (the traditional meals on the first two nights of the eight-day holiday), and he had a very strict view of the way the seder should be performed. Everything was done in Hebrew and there was no shortcut to the food that came at a break in the service. We sat obediently, waiting for it to be over so we could eat and leave the table. There were few parts of this event that interested us as children. The youngest child had to ask the Four Questions, an explanation of the seder meal and the meaning of all the traditions. After that came the part, we waited for—the stealing of the afikomen by the children and the holding of it for ransom so that the seder might conclude. This was problematic for Zayde, but we didn't understand why.

Zayde hid the afikomen (a piece of matzah wrapped in a napkin) under a pillow on his chair. We plotted to get it away from him, but he was vigilant, perhaps somehow tying his possession of it to his sense of dignity and seniority in the group. My brother Harold, who was about six that particular year, crawled under the table, and while Zayde was standing during one of the prayers, slipped the afikomen out from under the pillow and scooted back under the table. Zayde was so absorbed in the Haggadah (the book of the retelling of the Passover story), he never knew what happened. But the rest of us did. We couldn't wait for the moment when we might get as much as a dollar each for the afikomen. Jack and my father were more than willing to pay us, but Zayde was furious. He had been fooled. I had not been around many older people, and I was very scared of Zayde's reaction. Somehow, Jack was able to calm him down and we children were rewarded. Though the story became one we told every year at the seder, we realized **that** it was at Zayde's expense. He had been outwitted and was indignant.

Zayde lived a long life. He was at my wedding in 1971 where he had the honor of saying the blessing over the bread to start the meal after the ceremony. Though his hand was shaking as he cut the large loaf, he still had the same aura of authority that had scared me a bit when I was nine. But on that day, what I felt most was appreciation for having him in my life.

Not having grandparents made me aware of how lucky my own son was to have my husband's parents as well as mine. He was even blessed with a great-grandmother, my husband's Nanny, who lived long enough that my Josh knew her quite well. They say you don't know what you've got till it's gone. And perhaps you also don't know what you have missed until you experience it. My two substitute grandfathers gave me a sense of the love and the tradition grandparents bring to a family, something I would not have known without them.

My Little Brother

My father bundled me up in my red winter coat and matching leggings, not the kind of leggings women wear today, but the old-fashioned kind, wool pants held up by suspenders that a girl wore under her coat. He settled the matching fur-trimmed hat snugly over my ears. It was December, and the wind was strong. What a treat to have my father all to myself! My mother was away, something that had never happened before, and I was enjoying my dad's undivided attention. He was not much of a cook, but that didn't matter. At least he didn't make a fuss about what I ate or whether I had gone to the bathroom, the way my mother did.

I had been told we were going someplace special, and my dad had dressed me in a party dress. He was clearly excited about our adventure together and his enthusiasm excited me as well. Wherever it was we were going, I wanted to be there, if it meant being with him. We didn't have a car in those days, not many people did in 1952, so we took the elevated train, and I felt very grown-up sharing a seat with my father. We walked from the train to a big building that took up the whole city block. I had never been there before either, but I was with my father, so I was not afraid.

My dad explained we were going to see my mother and that there was a surprise in this building, one I would be very happy about. I imagined it was a toy, a big doll perhaps, or maybe a kitten or puppy, and I approached the building with great happiness and anticipation. I was three and a half years old.

We took the elevator to the correct floor. There were other people in a large room, some sitting, some standing near a window and pointing and smiling. My father approached a woman in a white uniform and told her our last name. He pointed to me, and the woman nodded. She went through a swinging double door that had oval glass windows. My father grabbed hold of my hand and told me to look up at the window.

What I saw was not the toy or cuddly pet I was hoping for. It had a red face that was as red as its hair. The nurse held it up for us to take a better look. It was swaddled in a blue blanket. It was screaming, contorting its face, and it seemed to me it might explode from the force of its cries. My father pointed at him and said, "That's your baby brother!" I felt the heat rise in my body and a sense of what I now know as dread crept over me.

"Will he stay at the hospital always?" I asked hoping that the answer would be yes.

My father laughed. "No, we will take him home tomorrow," he replied.

Why would they want him to come home, I wondered. He looked to me like he was going to be very troublesome. The entire time I stood there watching him, he had never once stopped crying. It was a harbinger of things to come. What had I done to bring this problem into my perfect life?

I was right. Life changed drastically. Now there was Harold, and everything that had once revolved around me suddenly revolved around *him*. At three and a half, I was now expected to act like a big girl because there was a baby in the house. Harold's birth was the cause for a big party, and at the bris, a great many people came to our house, most of them asking me how I liked my new little brother. I didn't.

As he grew older, Harold went from a constantly crying red-faced baby into a devoted little brother, so devoted that I couldn't get him away from me. Whatever I did, he had to do too. The problem was I didn't find him nearly as interesting as he found me. Harold was a big fan of cowboys, wore a holster and guns all the time, and was always ready to defend me. If someone hurt my feelings or made me cry, he would say, "Show me who did it." The little pipsqueak was only too eager to do battle for his big sister. My parents admired his spunk and devotion, and my mother would remind me constantly that Harold had a more generous heart than I did. She was right. Would I have defended him? I doubt it. But still her words stung.

Many years later I was driving my mother to visit my ailing father in the hospital when she said:

"I am so happy I am going to eat lunch with Harold today."

A bit taken aback, I replied, "What about me? Aren't you eating lunch with me too?"

"Yes, of course," she muttered.

Staring straight ahead and gripping the steering wheel to steady myself, I responded, "Well, the truth finally comes out. I know you always loved Harold more than me. I'm over it now, but I admit it did hurt me when I was younger."

My mother was flustered for a moment. "Oh no, I loved you more, but Harold needed it more than you. A boy needs his mother's love. But you were my first baby, and I loved you more." My mother's face was serious as I cast a sideways glance at her. I realized she might be telling me her truth and so I decided to back away from an argument I could never win.

"It's okay, Mom. I felt Dad's love more than yours. Now that he has been so lost to us in his dementia, I can't expect him to show it. But I remember what it felt like to have his love."

"Mamaleh, don't make such a big deal of it. We both loved you and we loved your brother. Did you ever want for anything? Didn't we take care of you?"

The same old song: we gave you everything. Why can't you give us credit for that? Doesn't that prove our love?

"Mom, it's not what you bought for me. It's deeper than that. But you're right, let's not go into this. It won't end well. Here's the important thing, Harold and I are good with each other. You don't have to worry about that. No jealousy, no resentment. And like you always say, when you and Dad are gone, we will only have each other. He's my little brother, forever."

We tabled the discussion. We all had lunch together after visiting with my father who was no longer able to recognize us.

My brother and I love to reminisce about our family, but he doesn't always remember things. I excuse him, thinking it must be because he was three years younger, but sometimes I tell him it's because he was outside playing ball. This always makes him laugh. In my recollections he was always outside playing ball, no matter what hour of the day or night. Maybe it's the difference between girls and boys, girls being more interested in what's going on with the family. When we start wandering down memory lane together, we always end up laughing or feeling sentimental. Sometimes he will tell me that the only reason he remembers a particular incident is because I had already told him that story. Other times he will be amazed at the details **that** I can recall from events that he barely remembers.

"That's how my head works. The past is so vivid to me."

"I'm glad, because I would never have known that" he'll say.

Writing has allowed me to reflect upon our relationship more than I had done in the past. My brother, no longer a pain and a responsibility, is a person I admire and love. Talking with him brings me great pleasure. As we talk about our parents and our lives, we realize how precious we are to each other, and I see how he has changed from that unwanted interruption of so many years ago. Or maybe the change was all mine.

Penny Loafers

Growing up in a ladies' shoe store had its perks. At first, I was more interested in the large cartons that held shipments of twenty-four boxes of shoes than in the shoes themselves. My brother and I would build intricate forts in the basement by connecting one box to another. If we were lucky, the teenage boys who worked in the store would put us inside the cartons and rock them back and forth to give us a scary ride. Once they even tumbled me down the basement steps inside the carton. But that was a bit too scary and was very painful, since I bounced down wooden steps and crash landed on a cement floor. Had my father known he would have fired those boys.

"This is not a playground," he would yell if I was getting on his nerves. "These boys are not here to play with you. They are here to wait on customers and put the stock back on the shelves. Get moving, all of you. Elaine, go upstairs or go outside."

I could also play with the handbags that Dad sold to match the shoes, making pretend I was a grown-up going out shopping. If my father wasn't looking, I could play with the shoe polish tins, stacking and unstacking them in the display. There was always the box that held the ornamental buckles and bows that could be added to plain shoes. Those were fun to put in my hair or clip to my clothes when I played dress-up. When the front window was being redone for the coming season, I could rearrange the artificial flowers or ribbons that adorned the sides and floor of the showcase, fashioning costumes for my dolls or designing dioramas of dream houses in cast off shoe boxes.

Our store was not far from my elementary school. Sometimes teachers from my school came to shop during the lunch break or after school. I would hide then, thrilled and embarrassed at the same time, secretly peeking at what they were trying on and hoping that they weren't noticing me as I spied on them. If I saw them wearing the shoes they had bought in my dad's store I felt a special sense of pride.

As I grew older the shoes began to interest me. I was first to see the new styles for each season as the cartons arrived. I could try on the shoes and imagine myself wearing them to all sorts of wonderful places. All I wanted was a pair of cordovan penny loafers. I was tired of my black and white saddle shoes or the red buckle straps that were my everyday shoes. I saw the teenage girls who came into my father's store wearing penny loafers with bobby socks. If only I could have a pair of those! But my father insisted that my feet were too narrow and that seven-year-old girls were too young for slip on shoes. Even though I had big feet for my age and could just about fit into a ladies' size four, he insisted that the shoes would fall off. He was the shoe man after all. I could beg and plead all I liked, but nothing was changing his mind.

Whenever I was in the store, just downstairs from our apartment, I would spin the large revolving display and look longingly at the flats. I would never dare to ask for a pair of ballerinas or a suede or jeweled number. I knew they were way beyond my possibilities. Even the high heels that were prominent in the store window and throughout the wall displays were of little interest to me. I had plenty of years to grow into those. But those loafers were the thing! I couldn't resist them. I would steal into one of the back storerooms and take a box off the shelf, trying the loafers on while sitting on the floor, hoping no one would come back there and find me. I would never stand up in them for fear of marking the sole, but I could admire them while lying on my back and imagine myself out in the world wearing the epitome of teenage style. There were penny loafers in every color of tan or brown imaginable. There were even white ones for summer, but the ones I wanted were the cordovan ones. With every new shipment I looked to make sure there would be one pair in my size.

When winter turned into spring, I started pleading again for penny loafers, and to my astonishment, my father gave in and brought out a pair to try on. I stood up and looked at my feet in the special mirror that allows you to see your shoes and nothing else. If I hadn't known they were my feet, I would have sworn that they were the feet of a very with-it teenager. I spun and twirled and walked only on the carpet.

"Please, Daddy! See how good they fit? I am old enough now to have them, aren't I?"

"You will start out fine, and then they will fall off your feet. Wait another season or two. Maybe in the fall…"

"Daddy, please! I have been waiting for *years*! I am almost eight. I can't wear those buckle strap shoes. I look like a baby." I was tall for my age and could easily pass for a girl of ten. The shoes I wore looked childish. They may have been the right choice for my age, but not for my physique. My father must have seen my point. He let me take the shoes upstairs to the apartment where I practiced walking in them. I spent the entire afternoon with the loafers on my feet. Even dancing to American Bandstand seemed more fun because of the loafers. I was sure they would be fine, that I could manage them. I felt extraordinarily glamorous and mature, and if I had just stayed in the apartment everything *would* have been fine. But I was determined to wear them to school. I wanted everyone to see them.

We lived about five blocks from Spruance School, and the journey involved traversing a very large schoolyard in order to get to the door closest to my classroom. But on that day, it didn't matter how far the walk was, because I was floating on air, at least I was for the first block or two. Before I had even walked two blocks, the loafers had begun to slip, just as my father had predicted, and I had to slow down to keep them on my feet. The only way to keep them from flipping off entirely was to scrunch up my toes in a vain attempt to grip them from the inside. It didn't work. I stopped several times to adjust my slipping socks. The other children were passing me on their way to school and soon I was the only person left on the last block before the schoolyard. I heard the bell ring indicating that school was starting and I was frightened. I had never been late for school before. Even the crossing guard, Betty, remarked at how slowly I was walking when I reached the corner of Magee Avenue and Horrocks Street. The only solution was to run.

I ran into the schoolyard and immediately lost my balance. The shoes and I fell, tumbling down the incline that led from the outside fence to the appropriate door, the gravel in the yard and the hard cement tearing into my bare legs. When I put my hands down to stop my fall, I abraded them as well. Finally, I lay alone and crying in the yard, afraid to come in late and afraid of what would happen to me if I didn't.

A teacher on the second floor happened to look out of her classroom window and saw a second grader lying on the cement. She sent a big sixth grade boy out to help me, and he brought me to the nurse who cleaned my wounds and wiped my tears. I walked in my socks to my classroom, holding the loafers in my hand. My teacher, Miss Wilson, looked up from the lesson, acknowledged my presence with a nod, and motioned to me to go to my desk. The other children just stared.

I did not go out for recess that day. I explained to Miss Wilson that I had no energy or desire to play, nor could I have done so in the offending shoes. Being outside in my socks was not a possibility, so she let me stay in and water the plants. She never asked why I was late or about the shoes that were now on the cloakroom floor. I imagine it was clear to her what had happened.

Those were the days when we came home from school for lunch. I knew I had a long walk ahead of me and that at the end of it I would have to deal with my father. Now, along with trying to keep the shoes on my feet, I also had multiple bandages on my arms and legs. Moving my limbs was slow agony.

By the time I made it home, lunch period was almost over. When I stumbled through the front door, my father was standing behind the front counter, working on a pair of shoes that needed an innersole cut to fit his customer. He looked up and saw me and the look he gave me was withering. He commanded me to sit down and take the shoes off. Still wielding his special leather knife, he picked up the shoes and took them into the back of the store where he kept a big carton for trash. I followed him, moving as quickly as I could to see what he was doing. I could hear him muttering under his breath about letting a child make her own decisions. As he mumbled, he cut each shoe into ribbons with his knife and tossed the pieces into the trash. I knew enough not to protest.

He never asked me what had happened, but given my condition and his expertise, he obviously knew. Instead, he went upstairs to our apartment, brought down my saddle shoes and a clean pair of socks and sent me hobbling back to school. The pair of penny loafers he gave me when I turned twelve stayed, as he predicted, comfortably on my feet.

The Hitler Clause

I might laugh at it now, but it was frightening then. My mother would be arrested for child abandonment or child abuse if she did this now, but then she thought what she was doing was not a problem. My brother does not remember the incident— he was too young. It happened when I was four and he was about six months old. We were living in the apartment on Georgia Avenue, and Mr. Nitzberg had died some months before. I know it was late spring or summer, because the windows were open and I could hear street noises, cars and people. I can remember what I was wearing— shorts and a short-sleeved shirt, and Harold was in a diaper with those plastic pants on top, and a white T-shirt. The apartment was warm, and we were playing on the linoleum floor, hiding under the kitchen table, unbothered by the heat.

My mother was cooking dinner when she discovered she was missing an ingredient, or perhaps she needed milk for Harold's bottle, I don't remember that detail. (I hate to think that she had run out of cigarettes and that this was the reason for the errand.) Whatever it was, she decided she had to go to the grocery store immediately and putting Harold in the carriage was too much trouble for such a quick trip. She had an easier solution.

She picked Harold up and put him down on the floor in the small television room, between the kitchen and the living room that had separated our part of the apartment from Mr. Nitzberg's when he was still alive. Then she called me into the room.

"Mamaleh, you take care of Chaimke (my brother's Yiddish name) until I get back from the store. I am putting him down on the floor. You sit in the doorway of this room and make sure he doesn't crawl into the kitchen and get hurt. Don't move. I will be right back."

She was, I quickly realized, leaving me *entirely* in charge of my brother. It was now my job to entertain him and keep him from going into the kitchen. I was four.

My brother was a fast crawler by this time and the television room was small. He made a speedy circuit of the room, then concentrated his energy and attention on being next to me. I stationed myself in the doorway. He crawled quickly over to me and began yanking on my braids, which provided an attractive toy for him. For such a little guy, he was strong, and the whole game that came at my expense delighted him. He would pull and laugh, and I would try to get my hair out of his fist. I remember thinking I didn't want him to cry, but he was also hurting me. I couldn't really push him away, which meant I couldn't really defend myself either.

I don't know how long Mom was gone, perhaps no more than fifteen minutes, but to me it seemed like forever. Tears were running down my face when she walked through the door, but my brother was enjoying himself enormously as he sat next to me, yanking on my hair and laughing.

"Why are you crying?" my mother said.

"He's been pulling my hair since you left for the store. I was afraid to move and I didn't know how to make him stop."

Mom was surprised I had let this go on for as long as I had. I was afraid he would be upset if I stopped him, afraid that she would be angry if she came home and found him crying. I was four.

I have often thought about this event and tried to understand her behavior. I believe we were the most important part of her life, but I also believe she did not always understand or want the responsibilities of parenting. Why didn't she put him in the crib? He might have cried, but she would not have had to worry he might get out, and she wouldn't have had to put me in charge of something so important. Why leave him on the floor and entrust his safety to me?

I know that during that same summer she left Harold napping in his carriage under a tree. When the sun shifted, she never bothered to move him, and as he slept his face was so badly sunburned that he had sun poisoning that left him with freckles for the rest of his life.

I know we did not eat proper meals, that vegetables were a rarity in her menus, and that we were allowed to drink coffee at an early age, albeit very milky coffee. I know when we moved to Philadelphia, when I was almost seven and Harold was three, she left us in the apartment alone for long periods of time. I remember Mom and Dad would go out for a walk and leave us alone in front of the TV. There was never any thought something might happen. There was never any instruction about what to do in case of emergency. Somehow, she trusted that everything would be all right. How she was able to do that, given what she had been through, was impossible to understand. Didn't she know that the world, as my father counselled, was a dangerous place?

Discussing this with her when I was the parent of a teen, she acted as if I was too judgmental.

"Nothing happened. You were both fine when I came back. Why are you making a big deal out of it now?"

"What would you think of me if I left Josh (our son) alone at that age? Or even older? Eight or ten? Would you think that was okay?" She loved her grandson with all her heart and if anything ever happened to him, she would be inconsolable.

"No, of course not. But the world was a different place then. We didn't worry so much about possibilities like we do now," she said.

"What are you talking about? The dangers were the same. Harold could have choked. He could have banged into something. I was a small child. Anything could have happened, and I was scared to death."

"You always did have an *alte kop* (an old head). Any other child would just have played with the baby until I got back. You must make a big deal out of this. Making me into a bad mother. I was not a bad mother."

"But you put me in a very bad position. You can't make a child that age into a babysitter!" Both of us were raising our voices at this point in the conversation, which meant she knew that what she had done was wrong.

"That's now in America. In Europe children were always watching their younger brothers and sisters. That's how the mother could get something done in the house. One child watched the other. The children raised each other. Now everyone has a babysitter for everything. We didn't know from babysitters. We were the babysitters."

"Mom, as I recall, you had a maid that worked in your house and lived with you full time. I don't think you were left alone. Maybe you saw that in other families, but not in your house."

"Always so smart! Always with an answer for everything. What are you trying to prove? That I was a bad mother. I was not. Everything was for you and Harold. But you find one little mistake and you talk about it until it is big. Didn't I love you enough? Didn't we give you a good life? But you need to make me into something I am not."

She insisted everything had turned out well, that there had been no incident, and she wondered why I even remembered this non-event. I tried to explain the level of fear I experienced, but it was impossible to convince her my fear had been legitimate. This was one of those times when she invoked the Hitler clause: unless Hitler was at your door, you really had nothing to cry about.

"Mamaleh you never wanted for anything, and you never had anything from what to fear. You want to know a hard life? You want to know fear? It's not taking care of a little baby. Tell me, was Hitler at your door? Now, that is something to be afraid of!"

All parents make mistakes. None of us is perfect. We look back on what we have done and silently thank God that nothing serious came of it. But for my mother, no blame could ever be assigned. The fact that she loved us, she believed, overrode any lack of judgement on her part. In her worldview, nothing she ever did could harm us when the ultimate harm was not ours to ever fear.

Freilich's Shoes

If there is a place that defines me, that taught me most of life's lessons and that provided every luxury I was lucky enough to have in my childhood, it is my parents' shoe store on Castor Avenue. My parents bought a store that was in financial trouble in 1956 when I was almost seven, turned it into a success and sustained it for more than thirty years. Our Northeast Philadelphia neighborhood was filled with young Jewish families. The prospects of financial success and being one's own boss caused us to uproot from Brooklyn and from my father's secure income. My father wanted to try his hand at retail, and shoes were not only the family business in Poland, but they were also what had saved his life in the camps. This next step of his American dream was calling.

The base that my parents had established in Brooklyn, their circle of survivor friends and the few family members that had come to America before the war, were what had sustained my parents in those first few years after their immigration. Leaving upset everyone.

My parents chose this store and this neighborhood over another possible store in South Philadelphia. The South Philly neighborhood was not what my mother wanted. My father had argued that the South Philly store was doing better business. And he wanted to be close to his brother Sam whose own store was just a few blocks away. Seven years ago, when they left Europe, my Uncle Sam and Aunt Basha went to my aunt's family in Philadelphia, while my parents went to my mother's family in Brooklyn. The time apart had weighed on my father. The brothers had been raised to value family over everything else. This is what had sustained them during the worst times.

"Bernie, I need a quieter place, not the *tummel* of South Philly. That's what we are trying to get away from, the crowd, the changing neighborhood. We have that here in Brooklyn. This would put us right back."

"But I want to be close to Sam. I have one brother. Now we have the chance to be together. We've been apart for seven years. And the South Philly store is doing better business."

My parents were sitting at the kitchen table in our Brooklyn apartment when this conversation took place. On two successive weekends they had traveled to Philadelphia to look at possible stores to buy. The stores they looked at were very different and so were the neighborhoods. It was a tough decision to leave their friends in Brooklyn and take the risks that would come with being self-employed. I listened in to the adult conversation, hoping they would choose the store in the neighborhood with all the trees. Even though the apartment above the store was small, the area was prettier and the school I would attend was newer. I dared not interrupt their conversation to voice an opinion. This was grown-up talk.

"I don't want to live in that neighborhood. I want to be among my own. The store in South Philly may be better for business, but this one is better for our family. The neighborhood is newer. There's a synagogue nearby, the neighborhood is Jewish. Here we can make a home. We can visit Sam on Sundays. I can't live in that other place." My mother was close to tears. She knew my father wanted to be close to his brother. That had been his original motive for exploring a move. Now she was asking him to choose her and my brother and me over what was left of his birth family.

"Don't worry. We'll make the business better. If there is one thing I can do, I can work for my family. You will never want for anything; I promise you that. If this neighborhood is better for you and the *kinder,* then we will make a success there."

They bought the store in Northeast Philadelphia, and we moved in January of 1956. For the first weeks after the move my father worked in the basement of the store throwing out old stock that he knew would never sell. Dad bought wood and built shelves in the stockrooms and the basement, investing in the store even though there was not enough money to buy a refrigerator for the apartment where we lived. When he wasn't waiting on customers, he was in the basement or in one of the back stock rooms reinforcing the shelves or reorganizing the stock and shelving new merchandise that was arriving almost daily. Mom had been a housewife but now worked in the store part-time while taking care of my little brother who was too young for school. Everything revolved around the store. From morning till night my dad was occupied with improvements. And it worked. The store, which had been a middling business at best, thrived.

After the first months of sharing a bed with my little brother, I slept in the living room of the one-bedroom apartment above the store on a sofa bed whose pillow buttons I could feel through the sheets my mother used to make up my bed. At night the streetlights made patterns on the ceiling. I could hear the trash trucks rumble down the alleyway in the early morning, and the squeal of the electric bus brakes on the #59 were part of my new bedtime lullaby. Each night my parents would put me to sleep in their bed, and then carry me or, as I grew older, walk me to my sofa bed when they were done watching television or talking in the living room. My brother slept in a single bed in my parents' bedroom. In the books I read and the shows I watched on television, the girls always had a room with fluffy curtains and a pretty bedspread. They could close the door and be alone in their rooms. I had no such privacy, but I dreamed of having all those things someday.

The first few months in Philadelphia were unhappy ones. We moved in January, and it was terribly cold. The ceiling in our new apartment above the store caved in during a snowstorm, and the landlord and my father argued over whose responsibility it was to repair it. While we waited for a resolution, we shivered in the freezing cold apartment.

My dad needed to establish credit to buy inventory to sell in the store, but no one knew him in Philadelphia, so every purchase had to be a cash transaction. And while he knew how to make a shoe from scratch, he did not necessarily understand the retail shoe business or how to predict the styles that would be popular. In the beginning there were probably more misses than hits as he attempted to buy new wares to sell.

My father found the new responsibilities that came with being his own boss to be more burdensome than liberating. He wanted a store that catered to a fashionable young crowd, like the people that he saw on the avenue. The previous owner had been content to sell odd lots and cancellations, orders that had not been picked up by the original purchasers, things that could be bought at discount and sold at low prices. But this was no way to build the business my dad had dreamed of, so there had to be what we would now term a "rebranding" of the store. It took a while for people to realize that not only had the store changed hands, but the merchandise had changed as well.

I was enrolled in the local elementary school, struggling daily to keep people from making fun of my Brooklyn accent. It was not just that people wanted to hear me say "chocolate," the word that seemed to distinguish a New York accent from a Philadelphia drawl. There seemed to be a different way of speaking in Philadelphia that was unfamiliar and daunting. Walking home from school in the afternoons, I imitated my teacher's pronunciation of every word I could remember her saying that day.

My brother was three and too young for school; my mother had to develop some strategies for keeping him occupied while she helped my father in the store. I think my parents' English was a bit of a barrier as well. They both had graduated from night school classes and obtained literacy certificates along with their citizenship papers, but their interactions in English had been limited. Now they had to face the public every day. They had to understand and be understood, and I imagine that it was not easy.

My mother was lonely and depressed. When I see pictures of her taken during that first year, she is gaunt and rarely smiles, as if she is worried about what they had gotten themselves into. We had moved from a lovely, spacious apartment in a neighborhood where they knew their way around and had many friends, to living above the store in a one bedroom on a busy, commercial street where we knew no one except my uncle's family that was miles away across Philadelphia. There was nowhere for us to play, inside the apartment or out. I slept in the same bed with my brother for the first few months, in the same room as my parents. We could not even afford a living room sofa bed for me in those first months.

In Brooklyn, my father had worked overtime only if he wanted to, but now he had to keep the store open in the evenings and on Saturdays to compete with other shoe stores in the neighborhood. Every penny they made was reinvested into the store for stock to sell. Buying shoes in the wholesale district downtown and trying to carry them home on public transportation, tied in bundles with string was almost impossible, but Dad did it every week for the first few months after our move. He eventually learned how to drive and bought a car, but this was yet another expense we could not really afford. I was too young to understand exactly what was going on, but the atmosphere was charged with despair. My brother kept asking when we were going home.

My father hired a salesman to help him in the store, a very experienced man who gave him some tips on how to run things. He advised my parents not to speak Yiddish to each other in front of the customers, noting that people felt uncomfortable around foreign languages. As people in the neighborhood realized that my dad had the ability to alter the shoes in ways that made them more comfortable, specifically dealing with bunions and hammer toes and the like, business increased. Buying more fashionable stock brought the younger crowd that my father hoped would become his clientele. Eventually, with a little more money coming in and with the spring season upon us, things began to seem brighter. My mother made friends with the woman in the apartment next door, giving her someone to talk to other than my dad.

As business increased there was more of an opportunity to meet new friends and that is precisely how my parents' dearest friendships were formed. Word spread in the Philadelphia Holocaust survivor community that a *landsman* (a fellow countryman) had bought a store on the Avenue, and soon the Philadelphia survivor community, largely headquartered in the Northeast, became regular customers. Of that larger group, ten survivor families became a surrogate family for us. They named themselves the Family Group.

My parents' store would be the backbone of our family for the next thirty years, and it was the source of everything good and bad in our lives. The boys my dad hired to work in the store after school helped my brother and me build forts out of cardboard boxes, taught me to dance, picked us up from school or Hebrew school in my dad's car, and roughhoused with my brother when there were no customers to attend to. At one time, at the height of the business' success, there were four teenage boys, my father and mother, and their most trusted employee, Toby, a fellow survivor and family friend, all working in the store. The young boys attracted the young girls, which made the store a mecca for teenage girls' after school get togethers.

My father found he had a talent for matching colors and dying shoes and he built that into a business hallmark. He also had a steady hand and a good eye, and began to decorate the shoes with rhinestones, pearls and other beads. He learned how to applique lace and feathers onto the shoes and soon, people came from all over the city to have their shoes dyed and decorated. My mother and

Toby were the steadying influences, waiting on the older customers, especially the women who had problem feet and whose shoes my dad could alter with the special orthopedic tools he still had from his past work. Often, my mother and Toby mitigated my dad's temper when he lost it with difficult customers.

The busy store needed a lot of stock to remain profitable. In 1960, after we moved from the apartment to our family home about two miles away, my dad rented our old apartment for a short time, but later he converted it into a huge stockroom. That meant that there were now three floors of inventory, and that everyone who worked in the store had to know where each style was located. It also meant a lot of running up and down the steps, carrying shoe boxes to customers and putting away what hadn't been sold. On busy days, the traffic on the stairs was mayhem.

As the store flourished, both my brother and I were recruited into working there. I admit I opted out most of the time and that my brother put in many more hours than I ever did. I hated working in the store because girls my age would come in as customers and I disliked waiting on them, putting shoes on their feet, or making small talk with them. I was embarrassed to be there, even though I knew everything I had was because the store was flourishing.

My parents could never attend anything at school that took place in the daytime, because they could not leave the store. I saw other mothers come to school plays and awards ceremonies, but my own parents were never there. They had to work late on Wednesday, Thursday and Friday evenings, so we had to learn to entertain ourselves when we lived in the apartment, and to take care of ourselves when we moved to our house. In the first few years, we took no vacations because money was tight. Later, both parents could not be away from the store at the same time, so my mother, brother and I would vacation at a rented bungalow, or my father would take us to the Jersey shore for a few days in the summer. I realize now we were living the quintessential immigrant success story, but at the time I resented that we couldn't do what other families did.

My dad would open the store in the evening after the Jewish holidays were over, much to our dismay. He was always sure that there would be customers around, people out for a stroll who might come in to buy shoes. Sometimes he was right. In the winter, if it snowed and driving was bad, my father and mother would walk from our home to the store. Harold and I would be home waiting for them, and there were times when we were afraid something might have happened because it took them so long to come home. As I look back on it now, I can see my father's drive to succeed was all consuming. Everything my parents had lost in the war was an impetus to work harder.

When we still lived above the store, we had to keep the noise level down. My father insisted that any sound we made disturbed the customers. We learned to tiptoe around in the apartment, particularly in the living room which was directly above the front of the store where the customers' chairs were situated. We could never have friends over because of the noise level. When I watched American Bandstand after school I could only dance on my tiptoes, lest the ceiling sound as if it might be falling on the customers' heads. The phone in our apartment was an extension of the store phone, so we could not tie it up during business hours. If we answered the phone we learned to say, "Freilich's," and if the call was indeed a business one, we had to run downstairs to find an adult to answer.

The store had its joys, too. I loved trying on the shoes as they were delivered; I liked helping to log the shoes into my dad's stock book and to find a place for them in the stockrooms. I liked helping my dad on Sundays when he did his paperwork, addressing and stamping envelopes for the checks he used to pay his bills. And not many kids I know had their birthday parties in a shoe store.

My dad urged Harold and me to wait on customers and to ring up sales at the cash register before we reached our teens, and we became adept at figuring out how to give accurate change. My dad made us learn how to add and calculate percentages in our heads, and we were able to tell customers the cost of a multiple sale without using an adding machine before walking to the register to ring up the sale. But most important of all, my brother and I learned how to deal with the public, how to talk to customers, how to be polite even when the person you were dealing with might not be polite in return. That of all things was the most necessary life lesson the store taught us.

The back of the store had two small stockrooms on the same level as the store front. Both were lined with shelves filled with shoes, but in one of them, a small TV set and a stool provided a place for my dad to eat lunch and dinner. When we lived above the store, my mother would cook and bring the food down for him. When we moved and the apartment was rented to someone else, my mother would either bring something from home or buy food on the Avenue. After it was decided that the apartment was needed for stock, my mother reclaimed a part of the kitchen and cooked up there, although the kitchen did not escape being used as a stockroom as well. Mom's famous meatloaf was the house specialty. She was not a particularly good cook, but my father was not a particularly discerning eater either. One time she served him some chicken parts that my dad refused to eat because there were three drumsticks on the plate. He thought my mother had cooked a three-legged chicken, which would not have been kosher. He did not realize that chicken parts were available to purchase. His refusal to eat the chicken is the source of one of our favorite family stories.

I used to laugh when I had to run upstairs for a customer, and I passed what was once the apartment's bathroom, only to find shoes in the bathtub. I would have a quick moment remembering having my hair washed in that tub and hollering that my mother was getting shampoo in my eyes. Once we had moved to our own house, every available space in the apartment was taken up with stacks of shoeboxes.

The TV was always on in the back room of the store and depending upon the time of day and time of year, the programming changed. Mom and Toby were big soap opera fans and couldn't miss an episode of *General Hospital*. Sometimes Dad would have to come get them from the back because there were customers who were not being waited on promptly. If it was baseball season, Dad would be watching a Phillies game, and if the Olympics were being held, Dad would be glued to the set, his heart set on German and Russian defeat. I have a very clear image of my father sitting on his stool, eating as he watched television. One of us would be standing in the tiny hallway, looking to spot a customer entering the store. It was impossible to get my father to finish eating; he would always jump up to make sure everything was going according to the way he wanted it. He was ever vigilant about the work.

When my son Josh was small, my parents would help me with his care. On days when public schools were open and Jim and I had to work, but Jewish day school was closed, Josh would accompany my parents to the store for the day. He would sit in a corner and play with his action figures or his blocks. Sometimes he would draw and "sell" his drawings to the customers as they were trying on shoes. And he had the chance to be with my dad and watch him work with his tools. One of Josh's most prized possessions was the set of dice my father carved from small pieces of wood on a day when Josh realized he had forgotten his dice and needed them to play a game he had devised. My dad loved Josh so much that there wasn't anything he would not have done for him.

Of particular interest to Josh was the walk up the Avenue with my mother on her trip to the bank. On the way, they would stop into several stores so my mother could show her beloved grandson off to her friends. Then they would walk to the hot dog stand, a treat that Josh loved and that his Bubbie indulged. Josh and my mother had a conspiracy about the number of hot dogs that were consumed on any given day, and I was not supposed to know that he had eaten more than one. I loved that they were in cahoots— that the special relationship between grandparent and grandchild was one that they both could enjoy. It was particularly precious because it was something Harold and I never had. Somehow, when Josh had an event at school, my father would find the time to go. He would leave my mother in the store and go to Josh's school for a play or for Grandparents' Day and I was overjoyed that Josh would experience the feeling of having someone in the audience, a feeling I had also never known.

One of my favorite stories about Josh's adventures at the store took place when the mother of Eddie Fisher, the famous Philadelphia singer, came into the store to buy shoes. She was a regular customer at that time, and my mother introduced Josh to her and made a point of mentioning Eddie Fisher. Josh was of the generation that had no idea who Eddie Fisher was and did not seem very impressed. Eddie's mother solved the problem. She said, "I am Princess Leia's Bubbie." Josh was overwhelmed. He couldn't wait to tell me that he had met Princess Leia's Bubbie!

The heyday of the store was the late 1960's and early 1970's. My dad liked to remind me that the busiest day ever in the store was the day of my wedding, Saturday, October 2, 1971. I was afraid that my father would be late to the wedding, since the store was overflowing with customers well into the late afternoon. Somehow, he tore himself away and came running home to grab his tuxedo, take a quick shower and rush to the synagogue for pictures.

As my parents grew older and more tired, the unrelenting hours of the store began to give way to a more relaxed schedule. Dad would close on Mondays during the summer so he and Mom could have an extra day at the swim club. He would no longer stay open late on Thursdays, and he would not open after the end of Rosh Hashanah or Yom Kippur as he had all those years in my childhood. He still would not close during the summer, but Toby and Harold and I could persuade him to go on vacation, leaving us to handle things. Running the steps and the long hours of work were getting to be too much for both of my parents, and eventually, after Dad had to have surgery, they decided that it was time to sell the store and retire. It was not an easy decision, but it certainly saved their lives.

For years afterward, I would see people carrying the pink plastic drawstring bags that advertised "Freilich's Shoes" and I would be flooded with memories. To this day, people who ask my maiden name will ask if I am related to the people from the shoe store. I am always proud to say yes and to hear their tales of the shoes my father dyed to match their special outfits. That the store was an integral part of the neighborhood and of many lives is its own reward. My parents' hard work paid off in so many ways.

In the Night

During the war, my parents had been taken from their homes, separated from their loved ones, and endured personal suffering and familial losses that left them permanently scarred. They were plagued with the kind of emotions that most people did not understand or even acknowledge in the 1950's. Today we would label it Post Traumatic Stress Disorder (PTSD), but in those days their trauma was not recognized or even mentioned, except perhaps when Americans who did not understand or care whispered about them behind my parents' backs. Their experiences had affected them differently: my father was feisty and faced the world with bravado; my mother was just the opposite, timid and certain that the worst would happen. She had good reason to believe that. She was the one who would scream in the night. While she was the one who was rendered inconsolable by her nightmares, my father was determined to make her safe, to make things better for her if only by the force of his will.

One night when I was about eight, and I was sleeping in the living room of the apartment, I thought I heard a male voice calling from the stairs that led down to the store and the street.

"Is anybody home?"

I told myself I was dreaming, but then, as I kept hearing the same phrase being repeated and getting louder, I got out of bed and inched my way to the door. I opened the door but kept a grip on the door handle just in case I had to close it quickly. In the dark stairwell I could see a uniformed policeman standing about halfway up the steps. It was dark, but the light from the streetlamp coming through the transom window of the downstairs door backlit him enough that I could tell he was wearing a uniform and a policeman's hat. I was sure I was dreaming, and I started to go back to bed.

This time the voice said, "Little girl, go get your daddy."

I remember thinking that this man could not really be there—that this was a dream. He was now on the landing that turned the corner into our apartment, having come up from where he initially stood.

"I think I am dreaming. You are not real," I said out loud and scurried back to my bed, amazed at how human and alive he had seemed.

"Little girl, go get your daddy. Tell him the police are here. Go now, get your daddy."

I got out of bed again, stared at the policeman closely, and now convinced that this was happening, rushed to the bedroom. My parents and my brother were asleep, unaware of any disturbance. I reluctantly tried to wake my father. Sleep was sacred in our home, and I had been taught that I was to disturb my parents only in an emergency. I judged this might qualify as that, and although I feared my father's anger, I persisted.

"There's a policeman on the steps." I touched my father on his shoulder, and I repeated it again. "Wake up! There's a policeman on the steps."

"Go back to bed," my father growled. "I have told you not to wake me up with nonsense."

I had never woken him up with nonsense.

I repeated, "Daddy, there is a policeman on the steps! I mean it. I am not making this up."

"Go back to bed and stop bothering me in the middle of the night. You're too big to be making up stories like this."

"Daddy, please. There's a policeman ..."

My mother, awake now said, "Bernie, take her back to bed so we can all get some sleep. Go before the little one wakes up."

My father rose from bed sure that I was having a bad dream and propelled me with his hands on my shoulders back to the sofa bed in the living room. The policeman, in full uniform including a gun belt, had now stepped into the apartment and was standing there waiting for my father as we turned the corner into the living room. My father reared back but kept his hands on my shoulders. I could feel his grip tighten.

"Sir, your back door was unlocked. I can't lock it from the outside. You'll have to come downstairs with me and secure it. You're lucky I was the only one that came in."

In those days, the police would check the back doors of the stores to make sure everything was safe for the night. My father had put out the trash at the end of the workday and had forgotten to lock the back door. Now he hurried to put pants on over his boxer shorts and followed the policeman down the steps. By this time, my mother was out of bed, having heard another man's voice. Only my little brother slept through the entire event. When my father came back upstairs to the apartment, my mother was sitting on my bed, holding me in her arms.

"Someone could have come upstairs and killed us all," she cried. "I knew this was the right neighborhood for us. In South Philly we would all be tied up or God knows what.

"And my big girl! She didn't scream or cry," my father said. "She just came to get me, and she wouldn't stop until I got out of bed. And the little one just slept right through it. I'm glad. He would be very scared, not like Elaine."

I can only imagine that my parents must have had a more complex reaction than mine, a feeling as reassuring as it was disturbing. I had been taught that the police were our friends and so maybe there was something reassuring about knowing the policeman had been there to help. But for my parents, finding the police in uniform in your house must have brought back some terrible memories from a time not that long past. In their stories, the police, especially police who arrive at night, were not there to help you; they were there to do you grave harm.

The Incident

Saturday is always the busiest day in our shoe store, particularly in the fall and spring when the new styles have just come in. My father and mother and four salespeople work on Saturdays, waiting on customers, running up and down the steps to bring out shoes and then quickly re-shelving what doesn't get sold, taking turns at the cash register and spelling each other for lunch when time permits. From noon until about five, all sixteen chairs in the showroom are taken, with a constant stream of customers and a continuous back and forth between the stock rooms and the front of the store. My father has made it clear that my brother and I are not to come into the store when it is this busy. I am outside on this brilliantly sunny spring day, working my hula hoop skills, near the edge of the sidewalk close to the parking meters, but always within earshot of the store. The door is open, the air conditioner has not been turned on yet. It is early afternoon and Castor Avenue buzzes with foot traffic.

A woman enters the store carrying the pink plastic bag with the logo of the store on it, "Freilich's Better Shoes." When a customer arrives with a bag it is always a bad sign; it indicates that something is being brought back, that there is a problem. It is always best for my mother to handle this kind of interaction since she has a sweeter way than my father with customers, but this time my father steps to the counter. I can see the back of the woman with the bag, and I have a clear view of my father's face. I stop my hula hoop and inch closer to the door.

The woman has come to return a pair of shoes—shoes that she pulls out of the bag and thrusts into my father's hands. Her voice is shrill, so shrill that customers turn their heads away from their prospective purchases on their own feet and focus instead on the interaction at the counter.

The shoes she has given to my father are completely worn out, even torn in places, yet she insists that she should get her money back for them. My father turns the shoes over in his hands, looking at the holes in the soles and the frayed linings that are clear indications of a great deal of wear. I can see the expression on his face change from one of accommodation to one of refusal.

"These shoes have been worn through and through. You can't expect me to give you your money back."

"That is *exactly* what I expect. They are defective. Look how they fell apart."

"You have made good use of these shoes. They were bought last year. I can tell by the style. We don't carry this style any longer. They've been worn and torn. There is not enough left to repair at this point." My father knows his stock well enough to know when these shoes had been purchased.

"I want you to make good on them. I want my money back!" Her voice is louder now, and she turns to look at the seated customers for support. Most of them turn their heads away. A few still stare.

"Lady, shoes wear out. That's the nature of it. When they do, you buy new ones." My father's voice is louder now, and his face is stern. I know this look. I have seen it many times in my own dealings with him. He will not change his mind. The two glare at each other.

He tells the woman that he will not refund her money. When she insists, my father raises his already quite loud voice and repeats with anger that he will not give her a refund. There is a moment of strained silence, and then she turns and rushes from the store, slamming the door that had been open to the street. My mother moves quickly to reopen it, watching the woman stomp away from the doorway. Mom has a worried look on her face. She doesn't like this kind of confrontation. It upsets her. It is not good for business. She and my father have argued about this before. Her position is always to give the money back, my father's is never to give the money back.

The open door allows me to see and hear what is going on. The silence in the store is broken as customers begin to engage with the salespeople again. My father walks to the back room and disappears from my sight. I move away from the door, not wanting my father to warn me that I am blocking the entrance with my hula hoop. He usually does this with a smile, but I don't think he will be smiling this time.

About ten minutes later, a stocky man, near my father's age, wearing a rough looking khaki jacket over work clothes bursts into the store. This is a ladies' shoe store, and the male customer is rare—usually a husband sent to pick up something his wife has purchased. This man is screaming, insisting he wants to see the owner. His gruff manner and strident voice must be shocking to the customers and the salespeople who exchange frightened looks. Everyone freezes, and then I see my father come out of the back room. He is wiping his mouth, having had a bite of his very delayed lunch.

"I want you to give the money back!" The man shouts at my father as if it is clear what he is referring to. The man is looming over the customers who are seated closest to the door. They turn to look at my father. Some of them had been in the store when the man's wife had demanded a refund, but there has been some turnover, and a few are startled and don't know what is going on.

My father stands near the back of the showroom and looks the man over.

"You've upset my wife. You embarrassed her! You're trying to cheat us!" the man yells.

My father moves a step closer to the man. I see my mother grab my father's hand. I can't hear what she is saying, but I can figure out that she is urging my father to give the money to this man and get him out of the store. Whatever it takes, avoid any more confrontation. The customers are horrified, cringing at the intruder's shouts.

"The shoes are worn out. I am not refunding the money." My father shakes off my mother's hold on him and moves even closer to the man.

The man, not retreating, rushes toward my father and screams, "You dirty Jew! Hitler should have killed you all!"

In one swift move, my father picks up the metal measuring stick that had been lying on the floor and hits the man with it. Blood spurts from the man's forehead and he turns and runs from the store, followed by all the customers who throw off the shoes they have been trying on, and struggle to put on their own shoes as they run to the door and out into the street. The customers gather in a group on the sidewalk. My father stands in the store, his face red, his chest visibly rising and falling. He still has the measuring stick in his hand, but he drops it and looks around as if somewhat bewildered. My mother is crying, her hands over her mouth. She stares wide-eyed at my father with worry and fear. Slowly, the customers come back into the store and sit down, collecting themselves and their possessions, whispering to each other. I wonder if they have come back into the store to show support for him or just to retrieve their belongings. My father turns and heads to the back room. He sits down on the little stool where he takes another bite of his lunch.

I drop my hula hoop on the street and break the rules. I run past my mother, past the customers and salespeople to the back room. My father's face is filled with pride, like he has just won a contest. He grabs my hand and asks if I saw what happened, if I heard what the man said. When I nod, he says, "This is what I have been trying to tell you. This is why you can never trust anyone. This is why you can never let your guard down. Even in America!"

"But Daddy, you could have given his money back. It was not that much, was it?"

"It's not the money, my girl. I had to stand for what I believe. She was wrong to bring the shoes back, and he was wrong to come into my place and threaten me. To use Hitler's name, in my place of business! In front of my wife! In front of the customers! I can't let these people think I am afraid. Not the customers and not that bastard. Not after what I went through."

I don't know how to answer him. I wrap my arms around him and hold on, burying my face in his shoulder. He tells me to check on my mother, and so I leave the back room and find her in the front of the store. She is pale and nervous. I put my arms around her now, and she hugs me back, running her hands over my hair and holding my face close to her body. She whispers in Yiddish to comfort me, "Go, Mamaleh, go back outside and play. Be a child for as long as you can."

We never do this in front of the customers; we never speak Yiddish, but this is not an ordinary time. Some of the customers are consoling my mother, telling her how shocked they are by what has happened. No one says anything about my father, at least not while I am in the store. Then my mother pats me on the back and shoos me out onto the street.

I am not interested in my hula hoop any more today. I go upstairs to our apartment and think about what has happened. I am careful not to make any noise, not to disturb my father or the customers with loud music from the television or treading too heavily on the floor by dancing with the doorknob as my partner. I make myself small, wanting to disappear. Even at eight I know what my parents endured during the war, the murder of their families, the destruction of their homes, the starvation and brutality of the ghettoes and the camps. I had thought they were safe here in America, that we were safe. That someone has come into our store and threatened us is something I cannot make sense of. I am torn between being proud of my father's strength and fearful that his lessons are clearly more important than I ever imagined.

The story of what happened in our store is all over the neighborhood in no time. Some deem my father a hero for defending himself against the man's words, others think he is crazy and that the war has twisted him in some way. I worry there is truth in both notions. I am proud of my father, proud that he defended us, but worried that he will have to do it again and again. The guy who owns the hardware store across the street starts calling my father Rocky Marciano, a prizefighter of the era, joking about his willingness to battle, but I don't want people to think my father is violent. I don't want them to talk about him that way. For a long time, I worry that the man will come back and try to hurt my father, but he never does.

Rescued

The only way to deal with Brooklyn's steamy summers for families like mine who couldn't afford air conditioners was to take public transportation to Prospect Park or Jones Beach. There, we could cool off and escape the torrid air rising from the cement sidewalks and the asphalt streets. Getting there was complicated. None of my parents' friends had a car or even a license, for that matter. So, we shlepped everything we would need for the day on the elevated train, the subway or the bus. And *everything* included chairs, blankets, towels, and lots of food. One thing my parents rarely did in the first years of being in America was buy food from the concession stands or the guy with the huge ice box of frozen treats strapped over his shoulder. Only occasionally were we allowed an ice cream from him. On that one item my parents would relent, but everything else we brought from home—not just snacks but whole meals, and drinks too. While other people ate hot dogs and sandwiches, we ate soup and cholent (beef stew) even on the hottest days. I have strong memories of being fed tomatoes that had a sprinkling of Jones Beach sand on them as the wind blew into my face.

"Daddy, it has sand on it!" I spit out the food he had just pushed into my mouth

"We're at the beach. Everything has sand on it. Make pretend it's salt. Take another bite."

In the summer of 1952, months before my brother was born, we spent many afternoons in Prospect Park. My parents would meet their survivor friends at a specific spot each Sunday. The kids were allowed to play a bit apart from where the parents sat. The survivors told war stories and compared notes about their new lives in America. The older kids, those of about five or six, could wander farther away from the chairs and blankets their families had spread on the grass under the trees. I was the youngest of that group of first-borns or the oldest of the younger ones. I held the distinction of being the first one born in America.

I was three on one early summer day I remember so vividly. I should not have been able to wander off to the fishpond, but there were many children around and my parents probably felt there was safety in numbers. They must have believed I would not do anything foolish. What the older children were doing, pushing sticks around in the pond, using longer sticks to propel shorter ones, pretending the sticks in the water were boats, looked like a lot of fun to me, and I wanted to do it too.

I found a long stick and stood next to some of the bigger children. They were not the children of my parents' friends. There was a lot of laughing and shrieking as the "boats" were pushed out into the deeper part of the pond. If you were tall enough, you could reach out and extend your stick to bring back your boat, but if you were small, like me, your boat would soon be a bit too far away for you to reach it. Unless you leaned out over the water, your boat would drift out of reach. I can still remember feeling a bit dizzy and out of control as I stretched my arms out and finally lost my balance.

I fell into the water and went under quickly. I remember seeing small fish and grass and a little bit of light. But I couldn't swim, and I had no idea what to do. The water was not more than a few feet deep, but for me it might as well have been the Marianas trench. I was under and did not know how to get up. I closed my eyes tightly and then felt myself being yanked out of the water by my hair. A man who had been sitting on a bench near the pond had seen me fall in and had pulled me out. I remember him saying, "Little girl, open your eyes!" But I could not. I was afraid to. And I have been unable to open my eyes underwater ever since.

One of the older children had run to get my parents, and as I lay there, I remember my father arriving, hearing his heavy breathing and his shouting. He was panicked and he was angry. He picked me up and started back to where my mother had been sitting with her friends, though by this time they were running toward us across the open field. My mother was screaming. I opened my eyes when I heard her.

I don't remember exactly what happened after that. My father and mother often expressed their fear through anger, a strange kind of punishment that was mostly unarticulated relief. It was likely the emotion a parent feels snatching a child back as he tries to run out into the street, relieved he is not hurt, but angry enough to smack him on the bottom for risking his life—grateful for the near miss and upset at what might have been. I guess that is what they felt. My father lectured me for being silly enough to risk my life. I was three.

Throughout my entire life, my parents smothered me with their overprotective behavior. Given their past and the losses they had both suffered, I cannot imagine how they allowed a three-year-old to wander off in a park with a large pond. Perhaps they were relying on the older children to be the guardians of the younger ones. How could my parents become so absorbed with their friends that I could wander away and nearly drown? This was such a complete departure from their usual vigilance, a behavior I would struggle against my entire life, and one that prohibited me from doing so many of the things my contemporaries were allowed to enjoy. Why it happened this way, I'll never know. To ensure my future safety however, my father taught me to swim that summer, and I was never again afraid of the water. My mother continued to be petrified by it. Which brings me to the second part of this story.

The summer I was fourteen, my parents took a hotel room in Ocean Gate, a sleepy little resort town across Barnegat Bay from Tom's River, New Jersey. Most of the inhabitants lived there year-round, but my parents' survivor friends had discovered this place and started renting some of the available apartments and smaller houses for the summer months. My parents worked all week in the store, but every few weeks my mother would take some days off. My dad would drive us to Ocean Gate on a Sunday, and then he would drive back to the city alone, leaving my brother and me or sometimes just me with my mother at the hotel. We might stay for an entire week, or maybe until Tuesday evening when my dad would pick us up and return us to the city.

I loved being there. I loved swimming in the calm water of the bay and living in the hotel, even though it was the most run-down, shabby place one could imagine. The beds always had sand in them, the shared bathrooms were always filled with yesterday's wet bathing suits and towels, the mosquitoes that tormented us all night were as big as hornets, and our entire family slept in the same room. My brother and I had to share a bed when he was there. None of that mattered. I loved having my mother available to me. She would take us out to breakfast, sit with the other mothers on the beach, give us money for hot dogs at lunchtime, and then take us out to dinner. After dinner, the women would play cards while we kids listened to records and danced or told dirty jokes, laughing into the night. We became suntanned from the long days in the water, exhausted by nighttime from all day in the sun and water, and slept with the windows open to catch the breeze off the bay at night. There were days when the mosquito truck would drive down the street spraying poison all over us, but no one had any idea what those chemicals might eventually do, so we walked through the mist without a care.

My mother and the other ladies would loll in the water using inner tubes from tires as their flotation devices. None of them could swim, but they enjoyed bobbing along in the soft waves, yakking the entire time in Yiddish, watching their kids cannonball off the pier or swim around them. On one afternoon, my mother caught her foot in the inner tube in such a way that she was suddenly capsized, and her head went into the water. I was swimming nearby when I heard the other women exclaiming:

"Look at Dora! Look how she is making tricks!"

"Dora, you put your head in the water. You'll ruin your hair!"

"I never knew she could swim, did you?"

I knew right away something was wrong. My mother's hair was sacred territory. She had it done every Saturday morning, and she spent the rest of the week combing and recombing it, using ever more hairspray to bring it back to the full amplitude of its original height. She would never get it wet willingly. Plus, she did *not* know how to swim.

I made my way over to the ladies' ring of inner tubes as they marveled at my mother's aquatics. My mother's feet were sticking up in the air, out of the center of the inner tube. Her head was completely under water, and I could see she was struggling. I pulled her head up and pushed the inner tube off and away from her. She sputtered and coughed as she grabbed hold of me with all the strength she could muster. I swam back to the shore, dragging her along with me and then walked her onto the beach. It was only at this point the ladies realized my mother had not been showing off.

As I settled her into her beach chair, I realized my mother was panicking. She gripped me and would not let go. To calm her down, I told her that as soon as I heard the words, "Look at Dora swimming," I knew something was wrong and I had rushed over to save her, knowing she would never do anything to get her hair wet.

She began to laugh, both in gratitude and at herself. It was precisely because I knew her so well that I was able to swim over to her in time. The rescue became the most retold story of the week. Everyone knew about it, the mothers who were there, the fathers who came on the weekend, and of course the kids with whom I spent my days.

I have never thought of these two drowning stories in juxtaposition until I started writing about my mother and me. Both stories are about being rescued, but I was rescued by a stranger and then chastised by my parents for endangering myself. My mother was rescued by her own daughter, and the panic she felt, although it looked to be for herself, must have tapped into some previous trauma far more dire than the one she had experienced on the beach.

Mom always struck me as somewhat helpless. My father perpetuated that perception of her by marveling she had survived Auschwitz at all. He would always say she needed someone to rescue her, whether that was Shoshka in Birkenau, or him, or even me, she was lucky because someone always came to her rescue. Perpetuating this story of course, erases the strength my mother had summoned to keep living, but what we both did not know was that in Auschwitz, my mother had *been* the rescuer in at least two different situations. She never once said anything about those circumstances. It was only through reading what others have said and written about her I learned about her selflessness. Now that I know the truth, I wonder why she kept those stories to herself. I know it is my job through these writings to bring those stories to light.

I Navigate the World

Parents teach their children how to navigate the world, but this held true in our family only up to a point. There were certain aspects of American culture my parents either could not understand or refused to understand. In those instances, I had to look around me for other cues or models. I often had to learn my lessons the hard way.

One year, I needed to bring money to school for a musical instrument. I had been begging my parents for a piano, but that was a major purchase, and I think my parents were reluctant to invest before they had a sense of my dedication to practicing. The opportunity arose to buy a set of resonator bells housed in a small black suitcase. They resembled a small xylophone or marimba and were played by striking the bells with wooden mallets. Children who were in the bell orchestra sat on the stage during assemblies and accompanied the classes as they sang. To me, being a bell player was the height of acceptance and popularity. I would be a part of the orchestra, no longer sitting in the seats, but up on the stage. I also loved music, and the idea I would be a real musician was extremely enticing.

The bells cost eight dollars. In 1957, that was a lot of money, especially for a school purchase. In those days, going on a school trip cost about fifty cents, and candy bars were a nickel, so eight dollars was a considerable amount. My parents had purchased the store only a year before and though business was improving, we were still on a tight budget. We never lacked for anything, but the bells were a true extravagance. I didn't understand this or want to listen to reason. I worked on my parents for a week, alternately begging and explaining how important this was to me, how it would be good practice for the piano, reinforcing my ability to read music. Finally, they succumbed to my arguments. On the day the money had to be brought in, my father gave me a five-dollar bill and three ones.

We stood in the kitchen as he rolled the money into a small bundle and closed my left hand around it. He warned me not to lose it.

"Daddy, I need an envelope to put the money in." My dad had ordered envelopes printed with the name and address of the store. I thought one of those would be perfect to bring to school.

"What for? That's a waste of a good envelope. I need those when I pay bills."

"Everybody brings money to school in an envelope. Please, it's just one envelope," I begged.

"This country is so wasteful. What will they do with my envelope at school? Throw it in the trash the minute they take the money out. You can bring the money to school without an envelope!"

No matter what I said or how much I pleaded, he refused. There was nothing I could do, and I had a sense of dread as I went off to school. We lived about five blocks away, a walk I normally enjoyed. I would daydream and sing on the way, sometimes skipping for whole blocks at a time. That morning, I trudged to school overcome with nerves about the money in my hand.

I was holding the bills so tightly my hand began sweating and the money became what felt like a lump of wet seaweed. When I finally reached my classroom, I was afraid to put the money in my desk. I wasn't worried someone would take it, but that I would forget where I put it. As the morning wore on, I kept waiting for the teacher to ask who had brought in their money for the bells, but it didn't seem to be the first thing on her agenda, although it certainly was at the top of my list. All morning long I held the money tightly, barely managing to accomplish any of the classwork. I could not concentrate on anything else.

By the time Miss Wilson called for those who had brought in their money, I couldn't unclench my fist. We were to walk up to her desk to give her the money while she took down our names. I watched as the other potential bell players filed up to her desk. When it was my turn, I had to open my paralyzed left hand with my right hand and peel the bills apart. The teacher looked at me with surprise and perhaps a bit of scorn.

"Elaine, when we bring money to school, it should be in an envelope, with your name on the front of it."

I don't know if the other children could hear her. In my mind she was speaking into a megaphone and the entire universe was listening. I could feel my cheeks burning. I was humiliated, and it was all my father's fault. I went back to my desk and tried to disappear until lunchtime when I could walk home. It was a beautiful day and when I arrived for lunch, the door to the store was propped open to bring in the breeze. My father was behind the counter fixing a pair of shoes.

I had worked myself up on the way home and was ready to shout at my father about how things had to be done in America, how this was another instance of being shamed as the child of refugees. I didn't care if he thought I could just bring the money in to school in my hand. That was *not* the way things worked. By the time I reached the store I was crying. I tried to explain to my father what had happened, but he was totally unsympathetic. He was *not* going to waste his envelopes.

"Did you give the teacher the money? Then everything is all right." He dismissed me and went back to work.

I determined I had to take matters into my own hands. Several days later, when my father was occupied with something else, I stole some envelopes from his supply box. I hid them in my underwear drawer, where they would wait until I needed another envelope for school. I am sure my mother found them at some point, since I was too young to be putting away the clean laundry by myself, but she never said anything about it.

I replenished my supply every year. At some point my father offered to give me used envelopes from mail that had been sent to the store. Perhaps my mother told him about the envelopes in my drawer. But I didn't want his used envelopes. Dad had a way of opening them by cutting off one end rather than breaking the seal. He suggested I could reuse them by folding down that open end. This was worse than no envelope, in my opinion.

My brother was three years behind me in school at that time, and those stashed envelopes came in handy when he had to bring money to school. I told him never to ask my father for an envelope, that I had it under control, and I continued to practice this kind of subterfuge as long as it was necessary.

But what of the bells? Being in the orchestra was fun, but not as satisfying as I had hoped. Eventually my parents did purchase a piano. I took lessons for about five years, but the sad truth was I had no talent and practicing bored me. Perhaps they had been smart to hesitate before investing in the piano. Either way, the piano they bought was chosen not for its musical quality but to match the living room furniture, so it was not a complete loss.

The envelope event was not the only time I felt I had to do an end run around my parents. I was the girl in school who wore her hair in a very old-fashioned style. My mother kept my hair long, in two thick braids, the same way she had worn hers as a child. Sometimes I could sport a long ponytail, but neither of those styles was something I could handle alone. The mode of the late 1950's was a pixie haircut. I longed to be rid of my hair—it was too heavy and thick for me to manage myself. Each morning my mother had to untangle it and pull the strands into tight braids. I can still feel her hands tugging at my hair, and my scalp tightening as she pulled. I stood in the kitchen for what seemed like hours until she was satisfied with the way it looked. Washing my hair was a grueling process. It was so thick it rarely dried before I would fall asleep, and if my mother braided it, it was even less likely to dry. This was way before the era of handheld blow dryers, and I didn't know anyone who had any kind of hair dryer until I was in my teens. Walking to school on icy mornings with wet hair made me even more determined the time had come for a new hairdo. I wanted to be free of it all, the pulling and the crying every morning, the tangles, and most of all what I thought of as a style from my mother's childhood—not one I wanted. I went on a campaign to persuade my parents to let me get a haircut.

For weeks I talked about nothing else, but both my parents ignored my pleas. I became furious and then grew desperate. My mother went to the beauty parlor every Saturday morning to have her hair done, and I often stopped in there, as it was on the next block, to watch the stylists at work. I knew the woman who did my mother's hair each week, and she knew me. A few weeks after my tenth birthday, I devised my plan. After school on a Thursday, I went to the beauty shop on my own. I told the stylist I was there to get my hair cut and that my mother would pay on Saturday. She was a bit reluctant to do it, but I was calm and insistent. As she combed out my braids, she asked if I wanted to keep the hair after she cut it. I guessed that I should say yes. She told me my mother could make a wig or a long ponytail hairpiece out of it. I agreed and the process began.

True to my request, after making sure I understood what was going to happen, she cut my hair into a pixie. And it was perfect. My head felt so light! I let her spin the chair around and she held up a small mirror to show me what the back of my hair looked like. I could barely recognize myself. I was shocked, but happy. She wrapped my long ponytail in some newspaper and handed it to me. I had never thought of my hair as being separate from my head. It was a strange and giddy feeling.

I walked to my parents' store, proud, defiant, and scared. I knew if I came into the store they would not be able to say anything to me if there were customers present. My plan was to enter the front door of the store and stay just long enough for them to see me before running upstairs to our apartment. It might be hours before the store closed, and my father would not be able to talk to me about what I had done until he had had time to cool off. My mother would probably be upstairs making dinner, and I thought I could deal with her, if it came to that.

Both Mom and Dad were in the front of the store waiting on customers. I came in and my father looked up and stared. A sound escaped my mother's lips, but she did not cry out. My father lifted his hand and wagged his finger at me. It was clear they were both upset, but they were also conscious of not making a scene in front of the customers. I disappeared into the stairwell and ran up the steps. For several hours I waited for one of them to come upstairs. My mother was first. She began to cry as soon as she saw me, asking me why I had done it. I told her I had asked but they had both ignored me. I did not want to be the girl with the long braids. I wanted to look like everyone else. I realize now what I had done was to destroy a little bit of what she had treasured from her own childhood before the war. She had tried to make me look like her and her sister, and I had taken that from her.

My father's anger was different. He did not like that I had been defiant and deceitful. He told me I looked terrible and that it would take a very long time for my hair to grow back. I told him I didn't want it to grow back. And there we were, at an impasse as usual, with him unable to understand why I had done what I had done. I still like to believe he secretly admired my nerve, because obviously that was something he thought was important—perhaps even more important than the long braids my mother mourned.

The ponytail wrapped in newspaper was put into a drawer. Years later, when we were selling the store, one of my father's employees found my hair in the drawer of an old bureau that had been relegated to the basement. The hair had begun to disintegrate, and the newspaper was so old and dry it crumbled when he tried to lift it out of the drawer. I hadn't seen my hair or thought about it since I was ten years old. At the time, it had been of the utmost importance. Now, it was just some more stuff to dispose of as we emptied the basement of our belongings.

In my forties, I was interviewed by a psychologist for a study about survivors and their families. Reading over the transcript of the interview I am struck by how much these little incidents impacted me, and how early in my life I decided to act as a decision-maker. At one point in the interview, I referred to myself as the "superintendent" of the family. I never thought of my parents as stupid or uncaring. I just felt they did not understand certain intricacies of the American way of doing things and telling them about something was often harder than just taking care of it myself. Some people might refer to this attitude as asking forgiveness rather than permission, but I would not characterize it that way. It was a sense I developed that certain battles could not be won, the only thing to do was to act, to make the decision and stop the agony of deliberation. It was the way my father would have handled a problem, and I was like him in more ways than I realized then.

Learning my Lesson

When we lived above the shoe store, my elementary school was about a five block walk from home. On the two weekdays when I went to Hebrew school at our synagogue after the end of the regular school day, I had to carry my schoolbooks, and my Hebrew school books back and forth. That meant two different book bags and an additional three or four blocks added to my route. Sometimes, if the store was not busy, Dad would send one of the boys who worked there after school to drive me home. But most days I walked home. Hebrew school ended at six in the evening. I was tired and walking home with my two bookbags, and on Wednesdays when I also carried my musical instrument case, all that weight really slowed me down.

I enjoyed it when the boys would pick me up from school in my father's car. I liked the fact the boys drove fast and how they would extend the ride by driving us past the high school so they could show off my dad's car to any girl who might happen to be walking by. They played the radio loud, and I could sit in the front seat and pretend I was old enough to be riding with them on a date. But mostly I enjoyed not having to walk while carrying all that heavy baggage.

On one particularly warm evening in 1958 when I was nine, my dad did not send anyone for me. I was trudging home, and my music case was digging into my hand as I juggled my schoolbooks and my Hebrew books. I remember stopping on every other block to switch hands, hoping that I'd see Dad's bright blue Chevy Impala drive up the street to save me. The more I walked, the closer to home I was, the less likely it seemed the car would appear, and the angrier I became. By the time I reached the store, it was already closed, and my parents were waiting for me, standing beside the car so that we could go out for dinner. The sight of them enraged me. I started mouthing off.

"Why didn't you come for me? Or send one of the boys who works in the store? It's hot and I had all these things to carry. My hands are sweaty and red and hurting!" I held out my hands as evidence to support my tirade. I worked myself up even more by recounting my sad tale. I thrust my jaw out and squared my shoulders, dropping my books in a pile around my feet.

"The store was filled with customers until just a few minutes ago. These boys are not your drivers, *madame*! They are hired to help me in the store." But I was so angry I didn't really care what Dad was saying made sense. I was too busy feeling sorry for myself.

"Put your books in the car and get in. We are leaving for the restaurant. We were just waiting for you to get here. Everyone is hungry."

We often went out to eat on nights when the store closed at six. My mother worked full-time then and did not have time to prepare dinner, so the easiest solution was to take us to Horn and Hardart's cafeteria. My parents could be sure that even Harold, the fussy eater, would find something to please him there, and Mom could relax, not having to cook or clean up after dinner. Not only that, but the restaurant was also air-conditioned, and our kitchen was not. On hot nights, it was much more pleasant to eat out.

I was too angry. I didn't want to go. I thought I would punish my parents by refusing to eat. If I did, then my father would have to promise me he would never let me walk home from Hebrew school again. He would have to promise he would always send one of the boys with the car.

"I can't eat. I'm too hot and tired."

I waited for my parents to insist I get in the car. I waited for the apology. It didn't come. My father gave Mom a look that said, "Follow my lead," and headed for the driver's seat. She looked at me, shook her head in a way that told me I was in trouble, and obeyed my dad's signal. I stared at them in disbelief. Were they going to leave me standing there on the street and drive away? When I refused to get in the car a second time, my little brother got out, saying he wouldn't go to the restaurant without me. I had an ally.

Harold was only six years old, but he was angry enough to start accusing my father by saying, "You make me lose my sister!" With his lisp, it came out "shister," but the message was clear. He was not going if I was not going. I had not planned on his support, although he was always willing to fight my battles and be on my side when he was small. In fact, I hadn't planned on this stand-off at all. I thought my parents would give in right away. Now for sure, I thought my parents would apologize to me and insist I get in the car. I saw my mother signaling my father to say something, but he would not. This was a lost cause. My father was an extremely stubborn person and once he took a stand there was no moving him. To expect him to apologize to me, a child, was out of the question. In his world, parents were always right, even when they were wrong, and a mouthy child deserved to be punished. He did not hit me. He closed the car door, and they drove off, leaving me and my brother standing on the sidewalk. Neither of us was old enough to have a key to get into our house.

We stood there in front of the store, not knowing what to do. I kept waiting for the car to circle around the block, for them to come back, for my father to open the car door and let us in. It did not happen. It only took a few moments before Harold started to cry.

"I'm hungry and thirsty. Mommy and Daddy won't come back for us." He was trembling. I felt so guilty. He had been defending me and now I had put him in this terrible situation. Looking at him made me want to cry too.

I tried to hold out, relying on my mother to persuade my father to come back for us, but it was clear they were not returning and that I had to do something. I decided we would walk to the restaurant, and I would apologize for my temper. It was the only thing left to do.

I wasn't sure which restaurant my parents had chosen. There were two Horn and Hardart restaurants that we frequented. One was too far away for us to walk to and involved crossing a very large multi-lane boulevard. The other was the cafeteria. It was closer, but my parents were driving, so they could easily have gone to either one. After stashing my books in the doorway, I took a guess, and we started off. It was a long walk, about ten blocks or so, and the evening was very warm. Harold continued to cry the entire way, and I had to reassure him every block or so that Mom and Dad would be there when we arrived, even though I was not sure that was the case. Walking with Harold was slower than walking by myself, and by the time we got to the restaurant we were both exhausted and dripping with sweat. I still remember the feeling of our sticky palms glued together as we walked hand in hand.

Our parents were seated at a table eating dinner as if nothing had happened, and I was elated to see them and so relieved I had chosen the right place, and they had not finished their meals before we arrived. I could not imagine what I would have done if they were not there. Harold was too tired to walk back home again, and I have no idea how I would have gotten in touch with my parents to let them know we had walked to the wrong restaurant. I also can't imagine how angry my father would have been if he had to drive back to the restaurant to get us. As we walked, I had planned I might have to ask a policeman to take us home. That would have *really* upset my parents. Being brought home by the police would not have pleased them at all.

My mother was surprised and so relieved to see us that she did not hide her concern. She hugged Harold and gave me a look that told me I had done the right thing by coming to find them. I wonder if they had argued in the car, if my mother had not begged my father to turn around and come back for us. My father just kept eating as if this was a perfectly normal occurrence, as if Harold and I always walked ten blocks by ourselves to meet them for dinner.

Harold, between sobs, promised we would never be bad again, we would always from then on, be good. It was not his fault this had happened, and I knew it. He ate everything on his plate for the first time in history, much to the shock of the rest of us. I was so thirsty I only remember asking for more glasses of water. My mother was washing Harold's face with a table napkin and still calming him down, when my father began to lecture me on my behavior.

"If you ever..."

My mother stopped him with the Polish word "Pshestein," which she used to mean it was now "enough." She could see whatever lesson was to be learned from this episode had already been learned and any further lectures were not needed. I was grateful for the silence. Harold, fed and recovering, nestled in my mother's arms. I'm not sure I ever apologized to him.

She was right. I did learn something from that evening. My father, as loving as he was, and he was loving, was stubborn. And this was a fault he could not abide in anyone else. He would call someone a "mule" if they didn't agree with him immediately. He would grow very angry with Harold when he exhibited any kind of stubbornness, a trait Harold was known for as a child. As for me, I had to be very careful with my dad when I disagreed with him. Every argument was personal, there could never be an "agree to disagree." It was best to swallow one's pride, or to let go of one's point and walk away. There was, I came to learn, no way to win.

This was confusing for me. My father valued those who showed strength and often claimed I was not strong enough. He told me many times I would not have survived the war because I was too weak. And I believed him. Yet, when I defied him, he could not accept it was my own strength that allowed me to do so.

Parenting

"You're going to have as much ice cream as you want after the operation! And you'll see. It doesn't even hurt." Whenever they say it doesn't hurt, that's when you should run in the opposite direction.

"And then, you won't have all the sore throats anymore and you'll be able to breathe through your nose. It's like a miracle." This is the sales talk I am getting from my mother before the removal of my tonsils. I didn't care that I would be able to breathe through my nose. I didn't realize people did that anyway. But not having sore throats sounded like a good deal. It was a bit surprising though, because any kids I talked to at school told me having your tonsils out would give you a sore throat, at least for a little while. My mother didn't mention that part.

My brother Harold and I both had infected tonsils and enlarged adenoids. We caught frequent colds and were always congested. It was determined we should have our tonsils and adenoids out to cure these problems. This was a very common operation in the 1950's. Our surgeries were scheduled; mine was first and being the older sister, all of eight, I went bravely. I remember very little about that part, just that an orderly carried me to the operating room. No gurney, just a big man carrying me down the hall, and that a boy in the hospital kept calling for more ice cream as I was being taken to the operating room.

I could not imagine how the boy could have swallowed ice cream given the way my throat ached after the surgery, but the nurses were amazed at his capacity and remarked upon it among themselves, supposedly out of earshot of the children on the ward. I do remember I was wrapped up like a mummy so I could not move my hands during the surgery. I remember the anesthesia mask being placed over my mouth and being told to count backwards. I thought I should mention to them my little brother did not know how to count, so they would have to try something else with him. I never had a chance to tell them. I thought I saw my aunt at the top of the stairs, and I was trying to climb up to see her, and then nothing...

Harold's tonsils were next. He was only five so my mom decided she would stay with him in the hospital. Dad would drive them early in the morning. The surgery would happen that day, and if things went well, Dad could pick them up the same evening. To spare my father the worry of getting me off to school on time, and to enable him to transport Mom and Harold to the hospital early enough to allow him to return to open the store, I was to sleep at the home of their best friends Tillie and Jack the night before. I would walk home for lunch with my father at the store. By then, the surgery would have taken place, and Dad might know if he could pick Mom and Harold up that evening.

I had never slept in anyone else's house without my parents being there as well. Having no grandparents, I had never had the kind of sleepovers other kids might have been used to, so I was both excited and a bit scared. I packed my pajamas in a brown paper bag and made sure I had my school bag with me when we went to Tillie's. Her son Benny, who attended the same elementary school as I did, would walk me to school the next morning. I was to sleep in the same bed as Helene, Tillie's daughter, who was four years younger than I was. This may have sounded like fun to Helene who saw me as a big sister, but it did not particularly sound like it to me. I had not been consulted on any of the arrangements, but I knew better than to argue. There was nowhere else for me to sleep.

I spent many hours at Tillie's as a child. We visited them at least once a week and often ate with her family as well. But I had never been an overnight guest there and I was not used to the rhythms of the house. There was a strict protocol about going to bed, and since there was only one bathroom, rules had to be followed to make sure everyone got in and got out in an orderly way. I couldn't have known this before that evening. At home, I slept in the living room. On weekends I stayed up later than I should have because my parents watched television in the evening, and they often let me watch with them. On school nights, they put me to bed in their room and then carried me to my bed when they had finished watching their shows.

Tillie insisted that I go to bed the same time as Helene, so I crawled into her single bed and wedged myself against the wall. She talked and giggled for a while, excited that I was there with her and then she fell asleep. I did not close my eyes all night. I wasn't scared as much as I was uncomfortable. The sounds of the house were not the sounds I was used to. Every time someone went up or down the stairs, I could hear the creak of the steps. The door to Helene's room was wide open because she was afraid of the dark, and the hallway light made it bright as day. I could hear Tillie and her husband Jack talking in the kitchen downstairs and then in their bedroom across the hall. I could hear people outside through the open window, kids playing ball in the driveway that ran behind the rowhouses, people walking their dogs one last time before locking up for the night. Headlights from cars in the driveway created interesting patterns through Helene's window shade and onto her ceiling. Each little sound and light caught me by surprise. Though my bed at home was near a window that looked out on a busy commercial street with all night light and traffic noise, these interruptions were different.

By the time morning came, I was exhausted, but eager to get up and get on with the day. I dressed and came down for breakfast and this is when my troubles really began. There was a long negotiation with Tillie about what to eat for breakfast. I sensed a bit of judgment on her part about my mother's nurturing abilities, as I did not eat hot cereal or a soft-boiled egg or want very much for breakfast at all. After I agreed to a piece of bread and butter and ate it, Tillie sent me upstairs to the bathroom.

"Go have a BM before you leave for school."

"I don't have to go."

"Of course, you have to go. You just ate and you don't want to feel like you have to go at school. Better go up now while the bathroom is empty."

"I don't have to go."

"Don't even think about leaving without emptying your bowels."

I didn't know what my "bowels" were, but I figured it had something to with the bathroom. My parents did not have these rules. I was not sure what to do. Though I protested, I went into the bathroom and closed the door. I explored the medicine cabinet, reading the backs of the bottles and smelling the perfumes. After what I thought was a sufficient interval, I flushed the toilet and came out. Tillie was waiting for me.

"I told you that you would have to go. I can't believe your mother lets you leave the house without emptying your bowels." I never corrected her.

Before Benny and I could leave for school, I asked Tillie to do my hair. I had not yet gotten my pixie and still wore my hair in long braids secured with small rubber band barrettes.

My hair was my mother's responsibility, but on this morning, it was Tillie's. I had thought being able to comb children's hair was part of a mother's portfolio of skills. Helene had very short curly hair, so perhaps Tillie had never had any experience with long hair. From what went on, it was clear she did not know how to braid, and I could not help her very much.

Between the two of us, we managed to get the barrettes at the bottom of some very loosely woven plaits. I was not happy, but I couldn't criticize her. She was my mother's best friend, and I loved her dearly. She was a great cook, a talented seamstress, and an amateur doctor who never failed to come up with a remedy for every ailment. But she was not a hairdresser.

Soon enough it was time to leave for school, and I was walking with Benny, an older man of eleven. That was a big deal, and I wanted to savor the moment. I was secretly in love with him, something he did not know. He dumped me as soon as we reached the schoolyard, assuming I knew my way from there. He went off to the three-story part of the school reserved for the upper grades while I went to my second-grade classroom on the first floor of the long, low section of the school building. I stashed my brown paper bag filled with yesterday's clothes and my pajamas in the cloakroom and went to my desk.

All morning long, I could feel my hair coming loose, my braids slipping out of the barrettes, long strands starting to fall into my face. I tried holding it all back with one hand as I used the other to write, but it was a lost cause. At one point my teacher, Miss Wilson, walked past my desk and bent down to speak to me.

"Elaine, is everything all right at home?" I looked up at her, not understanding. "Your hair is not its usual tidy self. Is Mom ill?" I felt such humiliation, as if I had somehow fallen in her estimation.

"My mother is with my brother in the hospital. He's having his tonsils out today."

I did not want to explain any further. I just sank into a state of shame, hoping the messy situation would not get any worse, but of course it did. By recess at 10:15, my hair was completely loose. I stayed near the building, not wanting the wind in the schoolyard to exacerbate the situation. The barrettes that were supposed to hold my braids were no help. Neither one was the right kind to hold all my hair or to keep it off my face. As I held them in my hand, I wished I could run out of the schoolyard and back to my father's store that moment, ashamed to have to go back into the class.

I watched the schoolroom clock waiting for lunchtime when I would walk home to the store. I was sure my dad would be able to help. He knew how to braid because he had done it with leather for trim on shoes and handbags when he was younger. But he had not worked with hair, which tended to slip easily out of one's hands. Again, the results were not what I had hoped for. He had managed to pull my hair back and off my face, but even before the lunch break was over, things were loosening up again.

"Dad, can I have some money for bobby pins?"

Dad saw his handiwork had not solved the problem and gave me two quarters. I ran to Manis' drug store on the corner of Castor and Unruh and purchased one of those cardboards that held about fifty bobby pins. I began placing them strategically around my head. With each loose strand, another pin. I took the bobby pin card to school and spent the afternoon session monitoring my hair, paying only a bit of attention to what was going on in class. By the time the school day was over, I had about ten bobby pins left on the card. I looked like I was wearing a helmet of tiny metal pins.

When Dad picked Mom and Harold up in the evening, I had never been so glad to see them. My mother was amazed at how many pins I had placed in my hair, and the next morning, even though we thought we had found them the night before, there were bobby pins all over my pillow. Nevertheless, I slept well, safe in my own space, knowing my mom was there to make things right in the morning. It was the first time I had missed my mother, and the first time I understood people ran their homes in different ways and had different rules for their children.

My mother and I laughed about this episode many times. She never realized Tillie had such strict rules about bathrooms and food, and she certainly did not know Tillie was unfamiliar with braiding hair. But most importantly she never thought I would not like being separated from my family, even if it was only one night. This was something she certainly understood. She made light of my fears. Nothing was going to happen to ever separate us, she assured me.

Just a few months later, my parents and Tillie and Jack decided to attend a cabaret in New York. The show would finish very late, and the two couples made arrangements to stay overnight with friends in the city, rather than try to drive home. Harold and I were to sleep at Tillie's, with Benny and Helene as our companions, but with no adult supervision. The parents assured us they would be home by noon the next day, and there was nothing to worry about. As I write this now, I am amazed at their nonchalance. Two children, one eleven and one eight, in charge of two younger children, both of whom were not yet five. We were not given emergency phone numbers, we were not told what to do in case of a problem, we were just told to stay in the house and wait for the parents to return.

Helene started crying as soon as the parents left, and no matter what we tried she could not be comforted. She wanted her mommy. Her crying upset Harold, who also began to cry, afraid our parents were lost forever. When Benny and I finally got them calm enough to get into bed, I too started worrying that the parents might never come back, that Benny and I would have to raise Harold and Helene on our own. I was more than upset, I was angry that my parents would leave me in this situation.

I have no idea what we were supposed to eat, but I remember breakfast was a disaster. I had been told never to touch the stove, but Benny was allowed to make toast. Fussy Harold just stood in the kitchen with a defiant look on his face. By the time the parents came home, sometime after noon, I was seething. Harold had not stopped whining all morning that he was hungry, although he wouldn't eat anything we offered, and Benny was angry at him and at me by association. All four of us were hungry, tired, and nervous.

I told my parents how scared I had been. They would not accept my fears. They did not understand, and perhaps I did not either at that stage of my life, that I had absorbed all their stories of loss I had heard for years. I knew from what they had said sometimes parents did *not* come home. I knew children might have to grow up very quickly and assume responsibilities that were far beyond their years. Why didn't my parents see I had internalized their experiences and made them my own? Rather than make me strong, their stories had made me fear things I should not have feared at a young age, and those things had festered inside me, scaring me, weakening me. I was too knowledgeable for my years and had too many worries to be carefree. My parents wanted me to have a happy and light childhood like the one they had been denied. But they also raised me to be a person with the foresight to be able to save myself from dangerous situations, as they had done. At eight, I could not hold both of those paradigms in my mind at the same time. I still can't.

Years later, I asked my mother how they could have left us alone, that it was tantamount to child abuse. If someone did that nowadays they would be arrested, or would have their children taken away from them, I told her. She could not answer except to say that times were different and there was less to fear in 1958. *Really?* After what she had been through in her life? Had she already paid her dues, suffering enough, believing nothing bad could ever happen to her or her loved ones again? Maybe that was her thinking? I can't explain this at all. I can only recall looking back on events like these and wondering. Had losing her mother and father made my mother think children could grow up without parents? I would have thought just the opposite. Or perhaps, being too dependent on your parents made you weak, so the sooner you learned to fend for yourself, the better? That sounds like my father's philosophy. Somehow this strange combination is what was planted in my head.

This doubt about them, particularly about my mother, surfaced again, many years later. In 1984, when our son Joshua was eight, I arranged with my parents to have him stay with them while Jim and I took a vacation. We planned to travel with another couple to one of the Caribbean islands and we were looking forward to the trip. Josh loved spending time with his Bubbie and Zayde, and the feeling was mutual. They adored him and he could do no wrong in their eyes. They would have a great time together, they would enjoy indulging him and he would get the full force of their loving attention.

The night before we were to leave my mother called to tell me if we wanted to go on the vacation, we would have to take Josh with us. She could not take responsibility for him.

"What if something happens to you? What if the plane crashes and Daddy and I have to raise Josh on our own? We are too old to accept this kind of responsibility."

"Wait a second! Let me understand what you are saying. You would rather have Josh die in a plane crash with us than have him live with you? Is that what you are telling me?" I was stunned, shouting into the phone. "Does Daddy agree with you? Does he know you are saying this?"

"No, he is in the other room and can't hear me. I am too scared of what might happen. You must take Josh with you."

"Mom, this is a vacation we have already paid for. We are traveling with another couple. Everything is arranged. Josh does not have a plane ticket. We are flying tomorrow. There is no way I can arrange this now. Please reconsider. Nothing bad is going to happen. Let me talk to Dad, please."

"Elaine, I am telling you we cannot take on this responsibility. Either take Josh with you or don't go. That's all."

And she hung up.

We never took the trip, and I never forgave my mother for that phone call. It was not the loss of the trip or the money. It was the fact she would rather have had Josh die than keep him safe with her. For someone who had endured so much loss, I would have expected her to safeguard his life at any cost. But she could not see it that way. She would rather have lost all three of us. There is no way to explain this except to say the damage of the Holocaust was deep and enduring. It crippled her ability to love the way a grandparent should, with no limits.

Street Road and Elbow Lane

In the evening of the last day of school in June, my parents would close the store, pack the car, and take us to the "country," an area known as Neshaminy, or what we sometimes called "the bungalows." Not a real trek, it was less than an hour's drive from Northeast Philadelphia. If we hurried, we could be there before dark. Our version of the country was some farmland off Street Road and Old York Road, past the small suburb of Warrington in Bucks County, but to me it seemed like another world. For all of July and August we lived in part of a rambling, rundown old house that had been subdivided and added onto over many years. Four families shared this space along with the owner, Mr. Diamond, a jolly old man who loved kids and seemed to enjoy a simple life. My family rented the front or the back of the house, depending on where you stood. There was a long, screened porch that ran the width of the building, a kitchen, two bedrooms and a bathroom. It was more spacious than our apartment above the store. I slept in a bedroom I shared with my little brother on a real bed, not on a sofa bed in the living room. But the biggest difference was that my mother was with us all the time. While my father would come out on the weekends, and sometimes on a Tuesday when the store closed early, my mother was always there.

The other parts of the large house were also rented to survivor families, as were the properties across the fence and down the road. It was among these people my parents felt the most comfortable. These were the families with whom I grew up. I don't know who found this spot, but my parents and their friends had discovered a place where they could bring their city children for a respite from the summer's heat. No one had air conditioners in those days except movie theaters that proudly advertised, "Come in. It's cool inside."

Mr. Diamond's plot of land bordered a tomato field that provided produce to the Campbell's soup company. Alongside this space were other smaller lots, some with summer homes, others inhabited by poor families whose circumstances were very different from ours, the summer people. Their children were dressed in rags, and their cupboards and refrigerators were often empty. They looked upon us city people with envy and disdain, but I was too young to understand economic differences then. I only knew the way they lived was different from the way I did. I realize now if my parents had seen the state of their houses, I would have been forbidden to play with them. As it was, we ran in and out of their houses with the same freedom we felt in the homes of my parents' friends. The poor children never came into our bungalows. There was an invisible border they could see, and we could not.

Every morning was busy with friends and the creation of new adventures. Our favorite pastime was playing Robin Hood and Maid Marian. We climbed trees, skirmished with imaginary enemies, and executed daring escapes. Being Maid Marian was the greatest honor a mere girl could achieve in this male-dominated game, and I relished the part. I didn't have much to do besides assume an abject air when captured by the enemy and then wait for rescue. At times I might have been able to affect my own rescue, but that would have spoiled Robin's opportunity to show off the manly skills he was honing. So, I languished, prisoner beneath a tree, delighting when Robin vanquished the evil Sir John. When called to lunch, we assumed our real identities, ran to our respective bungalows, ate quickly, and waited to hear the call of the first person summoning us back to the woods. The mothers returned to playing cards, gossiping, or telling stories about the War, until the long shadows told them it was time to fix dinner.

Only the littlest ones stayed with their mothers. The older girls, who were eleven and twelve, too sophisticated for Robin and Marian games, ran a day camp for the younger ones, charging the mothers a penny a day to look after the toddlers and babies, those still in diapers up to the age of four. None of the women drove, but in truth, there was nowhere to go. We were marooned in our idyllic spot, playing outside or in our bungalows on rainy days, running through downpours to share a game or a book if the bad weather persisted all day.

Mr. Diamond would show the same old movies every Friday and Saturday evening. We had seen the films so many times we could recite the dialogue along with the actors, but somehow that made it even more fun. We knew when to cringe, when to laugh, and when to shout at the actors to look out because someone was behind them. We would hold talent shows before it was dark enough to show the film, using an old microphone and an amplifier that Mr. Diamond kept in a shed in one corner of the property. On Saturdays and Sundays, when the fathers would come from the city, we might go swimming at Warrington Club, a private pool that allowed day guests, or go roller skating at a nearby rink. If I swam during the day, the nights were filled with the smell of Noxzema as my dad gently smoothed the cream over my red-hot shoulders and back, trying to ease the pain of my inevitable sunburn. If it rained and we went roller skating instead, we would skate alone or hold hands, helping those who hadn't quite mastered the sport. If I close my eyes, I can still sense the motion of gliding around the ellipse of the rink to the records played over the loudspeaker. These were the most glorious and carefree summers of my life; from the time I was eight until I was eleven.

The family that lived next door to us at the bungalow, the Zygmuntowiczs, had four boys. The oldest, Erland, was my contemporary, and with him I was taught to dance by two older girls, Debbie and Marlene. Erland and I were Robin Hood and Maid Marian in the woods, and to this day, almost seventy years later, when we see each other, we address one another by those names. His mother fashioned a quiver for his arrows, and he created a bow out of a branch and string. I don't remember if the arrows were ever shot, but I do remember the adventures we dreamed up and acted out.

Erland's mother, Itka, had known my mother in Auschwitz Birkenau. I don't know if it was a coincidence that we were their neighbors during the summer, or if our parents planned it, but the opportunity to be together and share reminiscences was precious for the two women. Itka was very different from my mother. Her spirit was indomitable, and she looked on her experiences in the camp as contributing to her strength and independence. My mother was just the opposite—what had happened to her had damaged her, had deprived her of her family, had made her helpless and dependent on others. Though they shared a special fondness for each other, and could certainly understand each other, Itka and my mother saw the world through different eyes. I envied Erland his mother's spirit and her encouragement of his adventures. My own mother was always fearful, always cautioning us against trying something new, always worried that something bad would happen, always sure it would.

Still, having my mother available all day every day was a special treat. The shoe store had eaten up her time and her energy, and I did not get to be with her very often. I wanted to love her more than I did. I can say that I loved my father, but my mother was harder to love. I felt a bit of a rivalry with her for my father's attention, and I always knew that she favored my brother. Her way of paying any attention to me was to braid my hair, to make sure that I was cleanly dressed and then be done with me. She would hold my brother and cuddle him, but I do not remember she ever did that with me. Even in the summer, when she had the time, I don't remember ever being the focus of her full attention. I was happy she was there, but what I anticipated most was the weekend when my dad would arrive. Then I would bask in every second until he had to leave again on Sunday evening or very early Monday morning to open the store.

The bungalows abutted two farms, and there were horses on both properties. These were workhorses that pulled wagons transporting the tomatoes to be packed and shipped. One day the older children were playing horseshoes with the metal castoffs from the farm. My brother, who was about five, and who should have been with kids his own age, was sitting near the far stake. I kept telling him to move, but for some reason he wouldn't. This was not atypical behavior for my brother; he was known for being stubborn. The game continued despite Harold's refusal to move. All at once, someone yelled,

"Elaine, there's something red coming out of your brother's head!

I laughed it off. "Of course there is. He has red hair."

"He's bleeding. Elaine, he's bleeding!

A horseshoe had hit him in the head. I remember grabbing his arm and running back to our bungalow with him. The blood was spurting all over both of us—the faster we ran the more blood there was. When we reached our door, I screamed for my mother, and she came flying out of the kitchen onto the porch, almost fainting when she saw the two of us, covered in blood. It was clear that Harold was badly injured and needed stitches, but we had no car to take him to the hospital. One of the mothers ran to find someone, and a dilapidated old car came down the road driven by the father of one of the year-round residents, a particularly poor family with eight children. The man drove us to Doylestown Hospital where my brother was treated, receiving stitches. That weekend, my father went to their home to reward the man for his kindness, but he refused to take any money. He told my father that his daughter Betty was my friend, and that he could not accept money for helping a child. My father had his first peek into the house where we had played all summer. The next time he came for the weekend he brought shoes for all eight of the children and left them on their doorstep without knocking. My father imagined that an anonymous gift would be more easily accepted.

My mother blamed me for the accident. Though I explained to her I had tried to get Harold to move, she insisted it was my responsibility to care for my brother, and I had failed in doing that. I wasn't sure who I felt more anger towards, my brother or my mother. When I look back on it now, it is just one of several instances where I was to blame for something that was Harold's fault, but because he was younger, he was not held to account. Why was *I* to blame? Is this survivor behavior—the notion that the older or the stronger must, by necessity, look out for the younger and weaker? Is this my mother's guilt over not being able to save her siblings? Who knows. We never really talked about it when I was an adult, but I can remember my feeling of helplessness and indignation at being cast as the guilty one.

Whenever I meet one of the bungalow colony children, now all in their seventies, we reminisce about certain events. Remember when Jackie fell out of the tree? Remember when Morris broke his arm? Remember when Jerry aimed that crabapple right at Bonnie's head? Remember the movie *The Blue Gardenia* that we watched almost every Saturday night? Remember how the entrance shower at the Warrington Swim Club sprayed so strongly children were afraid to go through it alone? Remember skating at the rink, or learning the cha-cha, or the evening when the mothers got drunk and danced with glasses of whiskey on their heads? But most of all remember what it was like just to be children, without too much mention of what our parents had gone through.

The year we moved from the apartment above the store to a house with a lawn, there seemed to be no need to travel to the country anymore. Years later, I decided to try to find that place, but it wasn't there, at least not in the way I remembered it. The roads had been renamed and the farms that had surrounded us, supplying us with fresh fruit all summer, now sprouted McMansions in their place. No matter how I turned at the end of what I thought was Street Road and Elbow Lane, I could not figure out where the big old house had been. I couldn't see the entrance to the woods where we had spent so many hours or find the roller-skating rink on the highway. Even the Warrington Swim Club had become a country club, gentrified and members- only. And no matter how hard I listened, I could not hear the after-lunch call that meant it was time to go back to the woods and assume my alter identity of Maid Marian.

Gift

For my eleventh birthday in May 1960, my father bought me a house, or at least that's what he told me when he came home that evening. He had left on a mysterious errand by himself before closing time. My mother closed the store alone and came upstairs to our apartment. The three of us, Mom, Harold and I, ate dinner as if it was any other day, except that it was my birthday, and I was hoping for some sort of celebration. Nothing happened.

Then my father came home.

"I bought you a house. Happy birthday, Mamaleh!" (He only used that name when he was teasing me. I was my mother's Mamaleh).

He was grinning, his eyes dancing with mischief. He said this in front of my mother, who was as surprised as I was, perhaps even more so. She had never seen the house, but she knew my father was headed out to look at it when he left. She had probably expected a chance to inspect it before a decision was made, but my father, as decisive as always, had bought the house without her.

"Let's go! Let's go see Elaine's birthday present!"

Dad hurried us into our 1959 Chevy Impala—all aqua colored fins over cat's eye taillights, so we could see our new home before darkness fell. The journey to Anita Drive, two miles from our apartment on Castor Avenue, took only ten minutes. The prolonged light of the May evening allowed us to travel through streets whose trees were filtering the shadows of a spring sundown. Though the distance was short, this was a neighborhood I had never seen. Crossing Cottman Avenue in those days was like venturing into an unknown land.

"Dad, how did you find this place? How did you find your way back home?"

I turned my head looking for a familiar landmark, but I was lost. I thought when we would finally move to a house it would be in the same neighborhood as the store, one of the row houses of Oxford Circle. This was not what I had imagined.

As we drove down Whitaker Avenue, Dad informed us our new street took the form of a big loop. We would pass the far end of the street first, but not turn there, even though the sign read "Anita Drive." We would instead drive down the hill to where our house stood, at the bottom of the slope, just before the street leveled off and curved to the right. These were not the row houses I had passed each day on my way to school, imagining myself in one of them. Our new house was a rancher, all the living area on one floor with a recreation room, laundry room and garage beneath. It was all so *different*, perhaps not exactly what I had dreamed of, but a dream come true, nonetheless.

There were children still playing outside in the after-dinner light—girls jumping rope, boys tossing a ball, little ones on tricycles. The scene reminded me of what I had envied on television, a place where a girl could grow up without having to sleep in the living room of a one-bedroom apartment above her parents' shoe store. It was a house where we could sit on the front porch instead of climbing out the kitchen window to sit on the roof when we wanted some fresh air. It was a house where there was more than one bathroom, where there was a separate room for the television that would allow a person to watch without disturbing everyone else. It was a house with a kitchen and a separate dining room, and a garage for the car and the tools we would accumulate as we became the house-dwellers I wanted us to be. We would be able to keep our bikes in the garage instead of blocking the stairwell leading to our apartment.

The streets were not filled with traffic in this new neighborhood. Riding a bike, sledding on the hill, playing on the lawn, perhaps even getting a dog, all of these were possibilities now. My dad had responded to my yearning for a place where I could invite friends and not worry I was disturbing the customers in the store below. Though life would change for the better for everyone in the family, I believed the new house really was a gift for me.

Our new house was the only unoccupied one on the block, the only one with a barren front window. It was easy to spot among the others because it looked so empty. Dad pulled the car into the driveway, the first of many new home-dweller behaviors we would learn. He didn't have the key to the house yet. That would have to wait until the weekend, but Harold and I burst from the car and ran around on the lawn, *our* lawn, marveling at how much space there was between our house and the neighbor's. It was still light enough to peek into the sliding glass doors that led to the patio and back yard from the recreation room, although we really couldn't see much. Dad assured us we would each have our own room, and I imagined how I would be able to close the door and have some privacy. I could read in bed without being told to turn out the light or having to fall asleep in my parents' bed while they watched television in the living room, only to be awakened to go to my sofa bed when they were done. I would have my own furniture, a closet that held only my clothes, a dresser and mirror that would be all mine. It was dizzying to think of all the wonderful changes that awaited me.

We couldn't move in until August. I was too young to understand settlement and mortgage issues, but I did understand moving would mean I would be leaving my beloved Spruance School and all my classmates. I remember the day my mother came to school to affect the transfer. The secretary in the main office, who was a customer of my parents' store, told my mother she was sorry my brother and I were leaving. She knew I was often asked to be an office aide, and that I had proved myself to be very reliable. I enjoyed working in the office and had been one of the girls invited to come in before school started each September to help teachers set up their classrooms. Now I would be moving away before the start of the new school year even began. It was then I realized I would be an unknown person in my new school, not only to the children but also to the staff. Still, getting my own room was worth the dislocation. I told myself I would make new friends and that within six months I would be at Wilson Junior High with a chance to make a whole new group of friends. And in three years, my Spruance friends and I would meet up again at Northeast High School. Change was good, even change that was unsettling.

The month of July stretched out longer than seemed possible and the wait to move took an eternity. My room was to be papered in girly pink, and I was to inherit my parents' old furniture, which was being refinished while we waited. Our living room furniture was relegated to the recreation room while my parents decided what to buy for the new living room and dining room. Our old kitchen set was placed in the laundry room and a new dinette set was bought for the kitchen. Everything was either new, repurposed, or re-done.

Our family activity on many summer evenings was to take a trip to the new house to see what progress had been made on painting and papering, if the rugs had been laid, what pieces of furniture had been delivered. I introduced myself to my new next door neighbor Janice, and to the two sisters, Patty and Christine who lived two doors away. Several doors down in the other direction was another girl my age named Susan. And unbeknownst to me, a girl who lived across the street, Joyce, would be my classmate, but she was away at summer camp, and I did not meet her until the first day of school. There were five girls from my class who all lived within one street of each other. How different this was from the isolation I had felt on the busy commercial avenue where my brother and I had been two of only a handful of children in apartments above the stores.

Soon after we moved my mother came into my room and said, "This is a room for a princess." We were smoothing out the new bedspread I had asked for. It was pink with my initials monogrammed in black silk in the middle. There was a look on her face that let me know how proud she was of what she and my father were able to provide for us.

"Did you have your own room when you were a child?" I asked her.

"No, I always slept with my sister. We even slept in the same bed. I didn't want to be anywhere but with her.

I realized in that moment for my parents the new house was a particular achievement, one that they probably never imagined might be in their future.

Other than when I was away at school, I lived in that house on Anita Drive until I was married at twenty-two. My parents lived there for more than forty-five years, until a catastrophic accident changed their lives forever. When it became evident they could never return there, I put the house up for sale.

On my last visit I walked out on the lawn and stood next to the Japanese red maple tree we had planted in 1960 as our first effort as gardeners. At eleven, I had been taller than that tree. Now it towered over me, a living testament and symbol to the many years that my dad's gift had sheltered our family. It was time for another family to take over. The new owners had their own teenage daughter who would grow up in that house.

Recently, I drove past Anita Drive again. The windows have been replaced and the driveway redone, but the bones of the house seem the same. I don't know what the inside looks like now, but I could see that the trees are surprisingly full. My dad would have loved to see that red maple. For many years he worried it was not thriving; now it is breathtaking in its size and color.

So many scenes of our family's past flashed through my mind as I slowed down to absorb the full picture—my brother's Bar Mitzvah, my high school prom, graduation parties on the lawn, our German shepherd King, my parents' Saturday night card parties, my wedding, the *pidyon ha ben* for our son Joshua. I thought of all the people who had visited with us here, all the pivotal moments of our lives that house had witnessed, all the joys and sorrows we had known. In my heart I thanked my father for realizing how much his eleven-year-old daughter needed that house, how much we *all* needed it. It was the best birthday gift I have ever received.

Anita Drive

Regrets

I can see it in slow motion if I close my eyes—the red-hot buzz that fills my head, my face screwed up in anger, my hand closed into a fist, my arm extended toward his face. The heat descends from my head into my body, rising to a boiling point as my clenched fist makes contact with his mouth. One of my knuckles catches his tooth at exactly the right angle and I feel the tooth break against my force. My jaw drops as he screams. Neither one of us knows exactly what has happened until he opens his mouth, and I see the broken tooth. I am frozen in place for a moment and then I begin to run, not waiting to see what comes next, knowing whatever it will be will not be good.

How did I get to this point?

My little brother had a bad habit of wanting to do everything I did, aggravating my own bad habit of reacting with anger, and at times physical force. In my opinion he had no business doing what I was doing or going where I was going. If I had permission to stay up late to watch TV, he wanted to do that as well, even if he had no interest in the TV show I wanted to watch. If my friends were playing in the street, he would stand on the sidewalk and pretend he was playing along. He just wanted to be where I was, trailing behind me, asking my parents if he might go with me whenever I had permission to do something special.

I had resented his arrival from the moment he was born. What had been an ideal situation, two parents doting on me, had been overturned by this intruder who demanded and received what I felt was an unfair amount of my parents' attention. Now I was an older sister with responsibilities I had not volunteered for, but whose compliance was expected by the two people who ruled my world. I wanted to be away from Harold not only because he was younger and I deserved to experience the world years before he did, but because being away from him meant being out of my parents' jurisdiction, with no one to rat me out if I did anything I shouldn't. My parents usually sided with him, insisting I should let him tag along. They didn't seem to understand the stigma of having this little brat trailing after me. My friends would pout and ask if my brother had to come with us. By the time I was eleven, and he was eight, it was clear, at least to me if not to my parents, that what was going on was unfair.

One day my brother was doing his usual thing, asking my parents if he could tag along when I decided to walk home from visiting friends of our family, rather than wait for my parents to leave. It wasn't that walking home was going to be exciting. It was just that whatever I was doing enticed him. My parents saw it as his devotion to me, as a desire to spend time with his big sister. I hated that it was portrayed that way—the loyal brother versus the unloving sister. Before he was born, I was the golden child. Since his arrival, I was the selfish one, the one who did not love her devoted brother enough.

That day, I wanted him to stop whining and to shut up about going with me, and when he wouldn't, I punched him in the mouth.

Though we had often tussled with each other, I had never wounded him in any way. In fact, as he was growing bigger and stronger, I had determined we should stop the physical fights all together. It wasn't that I was such a good person; the truth was he was starting to gain on me, and I didn't want to get hurt. Now I had done what I feared he might soon have done to me. The only thing I could do afterwards, the only way to punish myself sufficiently for my mistake was to run away from home.

I did not wait to see how my parents might react. My mother was always yelling at me about how I should love my brother more. "When we are gone, you will only have each other. Remember he is your flesh and blood."

Yeah, I thought, that's true for the future, but he was so annoying in the present. While you are both still here, Mom and Dad, I can't stand him. Of course, I never said this out loud.

Now I had committed the crime of not only wanting to be as far away from my brother as possible, which went against everything my parents were always preaching and which hurt his feelings, but of hurting him *physically*. I had no choice. I had to leave. I set out on foot. I had no money, and no idea where to go or what to do when I got there. I was certain my brother would run directly to my parents and my father would probably come tearing after me.

That is exactly what happened. When Dad looked for me and couldn't find me, when I wasn't just standing there waiting for my punishment, he jumped into the car and started driving towards home. Given my lack of an escape plan it didn't take him long to catch up with me. I was foolish enough to be walking on the most obvious street. He pulled up beside me, rolled down the passenger window and yelled.

"Get in the car!" I could see that his face was in a grimace, flaming red with anger.

"No!" I continued walking, thinking I could get away if I could only get to the corner.

"Get in the car. Right *now!*" My father's bad temper was flaring, his anger evident. I was frightened.

"No!" I yelled, still thinking I could get away.

"Don't make me get out! I'll throw you into the car and you'll be sorry!" I knew he would do this. I had no doubt he would leap from the car and grab me if I did not comply.

I opened the back door, trying to avoid being near him. I was crying those deep heavy sobs that make your chest hurt. I had been crying the whole time I was running, sorry for what I had done, sure my father was going to beat me, although he had never done that before. I just assumed my punishment for physically hurting my brother was going to be something beyond the typical shouting, angry disappointed sighs, and shaming my parents usually employed when either my brother or I had done something wrong. My mother would probably have smacked me and then spent the rest of the day loudly bemoaning her fate at having such a disrespectful and unkind daughter, but my father worked differently. He exploded and then calmed down very quickly. I feared this time the explosion might involve physical contact. He had never hit me, but what I had done had escalated the situation. In all the little skirmishes with my brother before this, I had never really hurt him. My father had sometimes threatened to beat us with his belt. He would loosen his buckle and give us a withering look, and we knew to stop whatever it was we were doing right then and there. This might be the time when the belt finally came off.

Much to my surprise, my father never put a hand on me. In the car, he narrated what was going on at home, that Harold's tooth was broken, and he was standing in front of the bathroom mirror, shocked and crying. My mother was crying too.

Dora with Harold and Elaine, circa 1963

"Mommy is so disappointed in you. How *could* you hurt your brother like that? You have *one* brother, *one* person who adores you without reservation. He only wants to be with you and look how you react! You punch him in the mouth! If someone would have told me my daughter would act like this, I would have called him a liar! My Elaine? *Never!*"

By the time we reached home, I was more distraught than any of them. I wanted to make the situation right, but there was nothing I could do. I was confused by my own behavior, distressed I hadn't managed to run away, and even more upset knowing I deserved to be punished for what I had done. When the punishment never came, there was no opportunity for repenting and for forgiveness. My mother did rant a bit, but somehow it never amounted to the storm that I had expected. I wished there had been some sort of punishment, some way of ending the whole thing.

For a long time, Harold's chipped tooth was a physical reminder to me of my uncontrolled anger. Years later, when his tooth was capped, I would notice how the cap didn't really match his other teeth, and when he would smile, I would have that guilty feeling all over again, that pain of having hurt him in a permanent way.

I know he forgave me, but it has always remained a mild source of friction between us. Sometimes when we are reminiscing about our childhoods, he will remind me of what I did, and I remember with shame the strength of my own anger. He is and always has been a more devoted brother than I am a sister. If the situation had been reversed, I probably would have chided him about it forever. He only brings it up out of a kind of mocking amazement that I hit him at just the right angle and with just the right amount of force. I had never imagined how much we could hurt each other. This was a sad way to find out.

Bernie, Elaine, Dora and Harold toasting Harold's Bar mitzvah, 1965

A Jewish Treasure

When she turned thirteen my friend Janet was given a Star of David that had belonged to her grandmother. It was gold with pearls and a ruby in the center. Janet wore it to school one day to show it off. It was not the kind of necklace you wore to school, but she was proud of her inheritance and made sure every girl in class had a chance to see it. After that day I remember her wearing it only on Rosh Hashanah when we went to teen services. At Passover, Marcie received a tablecloth that had been used in her family for more than a hundred years. She was told to put it in her hope chest and to use it at her first Passover seder as a married woman, carrying on a tradition that had started in the old country and crossed the ocean to America. That same year, the twins, Missy and Ellie, received candlesticks that had belonged to their grandmothers from both sides of the family at their Bat Mitzvah. The candlesticks were held up for all to see as the twins stood on the bimah after reciting their haftorah. The silver gleamed in the sunlight and created sparks of light on the walls of the synagogue. Their parents beamed with pride at the girls that day as the guests watched. Several months later, during that year when all of us were turning thirteen, Alan wore his grandfather's tallis at his Bar Mitzvah. Much was made of this continuation of tradition, and even though Alan was short of stature and the tallis was much too big, there was something magical about the moment that his parents wrapped him in it, as if he was receiving a hug from the past ushering him into the tribe.

At each of these events, I was a spectator to something I would never experience. My family had no heirlooms to pass down to me as I came into adulthood. Everything our family had owned had been destroyed or looted during the Holocaust. There was no jewelry, no Judaica, nothing that had ever been touched by one of my ancestors.

"Mama, mir hoben gornisht fun deine elteren?" (Mother, we have nothing that belonged to your parents?)

"Nein, mine kind. Mir hoben nor unsere gedenken." (No, my child. We have only our memories.)

"Ich hob nisht vos tzu geben miner kinder, eppes fun zeyer familia." (I will have nothing to give to my children, something from their family).

"Du vest zey datzellen vos is gesheyn. Dos is deyn yeruchah." (You will tell them what happened. That is your inheritance).

It was in my late twenties I first realized that I *did* have an inheritance many of my contemporaries did not possess. I had my Yiddish. My parents did not speak English when they came to America, two months before I was born. They spoke Yiddish to me, and even after they learned English and felt comfortable with it, they still spoke to me and to my brother in Yiddish. For the first years of my life, I spoke only Yiddish. It was not until I was old enough to play outside with other children that I became bilingual. I had heard English on TV and understood it, but there was no one to have a conversation with until I encountered the world outside my door.

Once in school, I barely spoke Yiddish anymore. My mother would continue speaking Yiddish to me, but I would answer in English. As I grew older, I used the language even less. I could understand a joke or drop a word or two into my conversation, but it was never more complicated than the usual phrases, like *kinahora*, (a word said after someone compliments you that will ward off the evil eye that might appear when something good is said about you) or *shayna punim* (beautiful face, the ultimate compliment for a child.)

When I telephoned my mother each evening, she would warn me that I was forgetting my Yiddish, and she was right.

"Mamaleh, du vest fargesson alles. Red a bissel Yiddish. Sis gut far meir und far dir." (Mameleh, you will forget everything. Speak a little Yiddish. It's good for me and for you).

I should have listened. As my mother aged, she began to lose her English, and in the end of her life, reverted only to Yiddish when she spoke to me. My Yiddish began to improve again as I was forced to understand and reply. After traveling to Israel, I revived some of my vocabulary when meeting Holocaust survivors, and while traveling in Germany, I was able to understand more German than I had anticipated. When Jim and I were in Paris, a cab driver turned to us while taking us through the garment district and said,

"*Schmattes*" (the Yiddish word for rags, used to refer to the garment industry). We roared with laughter, wondering how he knew we would understand. Still, I did not realize even then the precious treasure that I possessed.

Now, I lament I did not practice more when my mother was still alive. She spoke a beautiful *Litvishe* (Northern European: Lithuania, Belarus, Northern Poland) Yiddish that had a musical quality to it. There were phrases that were part of her dialect that were not part of my father's *Galitzianer* (Southern Poland) Yiddish. To keep peace in the family, my father "converted" to Litvak Yiddish and even modified his Hebrew so that my mother would stop correcting him in synagogue. The endless debate over *kugel vs. kigel* and other Yiddish mispronunciations were part of my childhood, enhanced by my mother's ability to come up with just the right phrase for every mistake or misstep I ever made. I can still hear her voice in my head as she complimented someone's baby and then said, "*pooh, pooh, pooh*" to ward off the evil eye.

I don't know if Janet still wears her grandmother's necklace, if Marcie ever set the Passover table with her heirloom cloth, if the twins use their candlesticks or have handed them on to their grandchildren, or if Alan wears his grandfather's tallis. I do know not a day goes by that I don't try to squeak out a sentence or two in Yiddish, just for my own enjoyment, to remind me of who I am, who my parents were, and the inheritance they left me.

Beauty

My mother came from a full-figured family, known for their height and their ample size. From the one photo we have of my grandmother, although she is wearing a heavy fur coat, I can still recognize she is a buxom woman. My mother often told me my grandmother never got out of bed without putting on a full corset that was laced tight. She had back troubles, according to my mother, but I think the tight undergarments were also an attempt to control and shape her well-endowed figure. My mother inherited this womanly form from her mother, and during my childhood I watched her struggle into unforgiving girdles and long-line bras. They were the first things she removed when she came home from work or a party, and the indents in her shoulders from the bra straps were permanent features of her body. I remember going to the corset shop with her when she was ordering bras that had to be fitted and reworked with thicker straps to accommodate her. In her older years she could no longer fasten the hooks on the back of her bras, and I was sent on an endless search for front-closure bras that would allow her to dress herself. When that was no longer possible, it was the first task of her aides each morning to wrangle her into her bra. I watched in horror whenever I witnessed the struggle, glad the gene pool had spared me such discomfort.

I guess I took after my other grandmother. From what my father told me, she was slender and not very curvaceous, although being a boy, he did not pay too much attention to his mother's figure and was unfamiliar with her undergarments. I knew I was a disappointment to my mother. She had expected a mini-me, and she had received instead someone who grew much taller and who was much less full-figured than herself. Still, the Hollywood of my teen years prized a bosomy look, and my mother was determined to make me fit that image, the only shape of beauty that she recognized.

From the time I was about ten, padded bras suddenly began to appear in my underwear drawer. I had no need for them, and her purchases were always several cup sizes larger than those I might ever achieve. She would tell me my clothes would look so much better if I would wear these undergarments. I tried to reason with her, explaining you couldn't just suddenly blossom into these well-rounded shapes overnight, and that it was embarrassing to even talk about this with her. I kept assuring her my time would come, but she was impatient.

I think I was the last one of my friends to get her period. I was thirteen and wondered if it would ever happen. In the summer after 8th grade. I was sleeping at my friend Doris' house when it happened, and I had to rush home because I had stained my underwear. Luckily, I had not stained the sheets of the bed at Doris' house.

My parents were away in New York for a wedding. Not able to ask my mother where the necessary equipment might be, I rummaged through my mother's bureau looking for sanitary napkins. Although she had emphasized wearing a padded bra I did not want or need, my mother had never made provisions for me for what was the inevitable, the onset of my period. I finally found what I needed in one of her drawers and equipped myself, eager to impart the news to my mother when she came home.

I remember standing in the kitchen when I told her. I waited till my father was out of the room. My mother looked at me and as I delivered the news, she suddenly smacked me across the face, a blow that sent me reeling against the kitchen counter. Tears immediately came to my eyes and then ran down my cheeks.

"Why did you *do* that?" I cried.

"Because you grew up behind my back," she said, and then grabbed me to her, consoling me for the wallop.

She explained this was an old Jewish tradition, that a mother punished a girl for attaining puberty. I didn't understand the tradition then and don't understand it now. I went to my room and cried some more. Why hadn't she prepared me for what she was going to do? Had my grandmother smacked her in the same unexpected way? We never talked about it again, but I did swear to myself if I ever had a daughter, this was one tradition I would not continue. I have since spoken to other Jewish women about this. Some of them had similar experiences, some did not. None of us who had daughters repeated the custom.

My mother's campaign about bras had ended when I finally agreed to wear a lightly enhanced one. Then she immediately started in on urging me to wear makeup. She loved makeup and had a cosmetics bag she carried with her everywhere she went. We called it "The Factory" and it was a standing joke that even though my mother went to work with my father every morning, she spent the first hour of the workday in the bathroom fixing her hair and makeup. If The Factory was ever left behind, either at work or at home, an emergency trip would have to be made to retrieve it. It was filled with bottles of foundation, blush, eyebrow pencils, tweezers, her hair-teasing comb, and many tubes of lipstick. Everyone who worked in the store recognized the importance of The Factory and made sure to keep it from being knocked over into the bathroom sink where it was left during the day after my mother had finished her toilette. At one time there were two Factories—one that traveled with Mom if she went on vacation and one that stayed home.

My mother thought I should start wearing makeup to attract the attention of boys. This was a constant theme of our conversations, dating and attracting dates. When I was only ten or eleven, she began insisting I should stop wearing my glasses all the time, since, according to her, I was getting too used to them. When I explained I really did not see well without them, my mother countered that no boy would be interested in me if I wore glasses. Since she had achieved a bit of success with the bras, she now went on a serious makeup and no-glasses campaign. I adamantly refused. There was very little she could do, but she never missed a chance to tell me how pale I looked, and that a little makeup would certainly add some color to my naturally wan complexion, making me more attractive.

I know now she was living her teenage fantasies through me. She had missed out on her own adolescence, having spent the time from when she was thirteen until she was eighteen in a ghetto or concentration camp. But I was *me*, not her, and I was not ready or willing to become my mother's Barbie doll. Whatever the beauty topic, whether it was underwear, makeup or clothes, whatever it was my mother liked, I seemed to have the opposite opinion. Loud prints—not for me. Tight clothing, no thank you. High heels, I'm tall enough. Makeup—not ready for that yet.

During adolescence, most girls worry if they are pretty. I always knew I was bright, but I wasn't sure about beauty. If I measured myself against my mother, I could not compete. She had the look of a particular time, the kind of beauty one associates with Gina Lollobrigida, a sort of sexy allure of tight clothes and bouffant hair. I was not that. I was tall and thin. I was pale with very dark thick hair. My greatest attribute was my blue eyes, but until I got contacts, they were hidden behind my glasses. In my early teens I did not want boys' attention, nor would I have known what to do with it. My mother's focus on this brought about a lot of strife. I can still hear my father asking me to be nice to my mother, to stop arguing with her. I promised him I would try, but she always found a way to make me break that promise.

"Your mother needs your love. Can you just bend a little?"

"Can you tell *her* to bend a little? She's always riding me about everything. She pulls my glasses off my face when I am reading! Can you get her to focus somewhere else?"

"She only wants the best for you."

"My best and her best are not the same." Little did I know this would be the theme of my relationship with my mother for the rest of her life.

When a more natural look became the vogue, my mother finally eased off. She couldn't tell me to wear makeup when everyone else was fresh-faced. She couldn't urge me to have a perm when everyone else was letting their hair grow long and straight, and she couldn't insist on a padded bra when many of my contemporaries weren't wearing one at all. She never changed her own look, however. Until the end of her life, she insisted on dying her hair a dark red and wearing a full face of makeup. She applied it even when she was blind. When I would come to visit her at the assisted living facility, I would have to hold back my laughter when I saw how much blush she had applied, I would rub her cheeks to try to get some of it off.

"Too much?" she would ask.

"Mom, you look like your face is on fire." I could wipe away some of the blush, but there was no way to easily remove the eyebrows she had drawn almost to her hairline. I would have to ignore those and tell myself if it made her happy, what difference did it make.

I Bleed All Over

I do not know when the following fragments were written. I found them after my mother died, tucked away in her notebook on loose pieces of paper that had been folded and unfolded many times. It is my belief they were written very soon after the war, although they were in English, which might mean they were written when my mother felt more comfortable with her command of the language. Or perhaps, as with some of her pieces, they were translated from Yiddish or Polish. Since I have no evidence they once existed in another language, I assume she wrote them in English.

These pieces are among the most angry and desperate of any of her writings. I was astonished by them. For so much of my life, my mother refused to engage in the kind of anger that fueled my father's retelling of his experiences. When she was interviewed, she remained stoic in her retelling. I believed for a very long time that perhaps the hurt had evaporated a bit. This is not to say the effect was no longer there, but rather that some distance meant she could tell her story in a more matter-of-fact style. These pieces belie that theory. Unconnected to a particular event in the camps, they are brimming with anger, not only at her captors, but at those who, after the war, never tried to understand what she felt, and at herself for being paralyzed by her shame, a shame she may never have been able to overcome.

The first piece is a terse, heartbreaking explanation of her sadness:

I bleed all over. I bleed for lack of love, for lack of family, I bleed for lack of everything. I bleed because of atrocities committed against me. I wanted to die, so as not to live in pain for the rest of my life. That's why I wanted to die—to be free of pain, because nothing can cure this pain.

In the second fragment, Mom wonders about the persistence of life in the face of such horrors in Auschwitz and subsequently in Ravensbrueck:

You would have expected mass suicides or at least a great number of suicides, but there were hardly any suicides at all, because we felt nothing but hunger. We knew no other reality, except the reality of death. Nothing else was real, but the first reality was hunger, even

171

when the chimneys belched fire, your thoughts were only occupied with hunger. Hunger kept us alive.

I believed at first that the world was ignorant of what was being done to us, that as soon as they will learn about the horror, it would move heaven and earth to rescue us. But the world knew, and it didn't give a damn.

We had harnessed every ounce of energy to scrounge for food instead of to think. It was one or the other. So, we blindly followed our instincts of self-preservation. Thinking was suspended and hunger took over. It made us fight for food. Nothing else mattered – it is insane – but hunger kept us alive.

The next fragment is the one that shocked me most. When I read it for the first time, I misread the first sentence and thought my mother was writing about being raped. I was horrified. It was only when I went back to read it again that I understood she was comparing what had been done to her to a kind of emotional rape. I believe from this analogy the piece was written later than the first two. There seems to be anger at what occurred, intensified by disappointment at the lack of reprisal and retribution visited upon the perpetrators by the victims or by the victorious armies. What was pride in the first days after the war at the knowledge that most Jews did not seek revenge for their suffering turned into an ever-deepening shame at the inability to strike back.

I am ashamed of what they did to me, to us, as if I was raped in broad daylight in the middle of the market and they all watched and leered.

If just one of them would walk up to me and say, "sorry," acknowledge that something has happened, that's all.

As it is, they pretend nothing has happened, they saw nothing, they did nothing, So what's all the fuss about.

We were murdered, maimed, robbed. But nobody did it.

Where must I turn, whom must I confront. There is no one – no one to even acknowledge witnessing the rape. It didn't happen, they say. But I am left with the shame and the pain.

And do you want to know what I did after I was liberated. Nothing, I did absolutely nothing.

Was I embarrassed to do what others did to me? Too cruel, too crude, or what? Was I simply a coward? Then again, maybe I was stupid enough to think of right and wrong in the middle of the jungle.

I felt like dozens of sharp needles scraping through my insides and tormenting my guts.

I wished I could be alone somewhere to howl from the agony. If I could scream till my vocal cords snapped, or my brain exploded, or my heart burst, surely then, I thought, the pain would ease.

In this final fragment Mom seems to come to terms with the enormity of her sadness, realizing she is experiencing an uncharted kind of despair, perhaps one never felt by anyone before. It is not only the loss of family that saddens her, but the need to relearn every human emotion to cope with her new present. She understands what she has experienced has happened outside of the realm of normal human existence, and she is unequipped to mourn properly, and even less capable of making her way in the world where she must now live.

Our past left a void which can never be filled, never recaptured. Never! Only we, the survivors, can keep the past from total dissolution. There is no past without us, and contemplating a future is beyond our scope right now. Beyond our strength too. Yet the present is an agony. That's why we turn to our past, simply to survive. Anything compared to the past pales, in fact comparison becomes unbearable.

We've lost everything we've ever had. To go on living we now must relearn everything from the beginning. We must learn to feel and ache and love and trust and judge and think in a new way. We must create an entire system of thought and feelings and discover new ways of expression. When we'll have learned all that, perhaps we'll be ready to mourn. Until then everything hurts all the time, brutally endlessly.

I knew she was affected by the losses and by the brutality. I knew it from her screams in the night, from how she covered her tattoo with long sleeves, from her begging my father to stop talking about the war years. I knew it from her insistence that we eat every bit of food on our plates, from the Yahrzeit candles that burned on our kitchen counter in remembrance of her lost family, and from the scar on her shin that came from the boot of an SS soldier. I knew it from the way she caressed the faces in the photographs of her family that only existed because they had been sent to America before the war, from her fear of doctors and the police, from her insistence we could not go to overnight camp, and from her mistrust of anyone outside her circle of fellow Holocaust survivors.

What I could not have fathomed was how deep her trauma was. It was only in my late teens that I began to piece together her behaviors into a pattern of anxiety and depression that would not begin to be documented and understood by professionals until sometime later—the identification and diagnosis of post-traumatic stress disorder that afflicted both of my parents and shaped my personality. Much later, it was recognized that trauma alters the DNA and can be passed to the next generation. I have no doubt this is true.

Rosh Hashanah: New Year's Resolution

Services are over for the teenage congregation, but my parents are still in the sanctuary. How much longer will this take, I wonder, as I sit on the low brick wall outside the annex to the synagogue that houses the religious school. The sun beats down on me. There is no shade around the synagogue, and I do not dare cross the street to sit on the steps of the houses on the shady side. We have been told by the school principal and reminded by the rabbi that we are not to upset the neighbors during the High Holidays, even the Jewish ones. No loud laughing, no large groups. Though Rosh Hashanah is a joyous holiday, we must maintain decorum while we wait for our parents.

Those children who live close by have walked home. My family lives far from the shul (the Yiddish word for synagogue), and my brother and I cannot get home easily. There is no way to get word to my parents inside the sanctuary that Harold and I might walk home and not wait for them. If they come out and we are not there, will they be worried? Will they be angry they must drive all the way home to get us before we can go to Toby's for lunch? There is no best choice, but the path of least aggravation is to sit and wait for the service to be over. I wish I was somewhere else, which is a constant feeling for me—the desire to escape the present, to be somewhere else or someone else.

The great wooden doors open, and the congregation descends the stairs to the street. Everyone must stop to greet the rabbi and cantor. Everyone must compliment them on the service. My parents must wish a happy new year to their customers. It's good business after all. The crowd eventually thins, and I see my father and mother. I wave and my dad nods. He tilts his head in a way to indicate we should go to the car.

It is our tradition to eat lunch at Toby's on the first day of Rosh Hashanah. Toby works in my dad's store, but she and her husband Chaim had been my parents' friends for many years before that. Their children, Sandy and Stevie, have been raised, along with Harold and me, in the Family Group. We weren't really cousins, but we considered ourselves as such. Much of the Family Group will be at Toby's for lunch.

By the time my family arrives most of the others are seated at the crowded table. The men have loosened their ties and shed their jackets. Toby's window air conditioner is straining to cool the jampacked dining room.

"What is it with your rabbi? What takes so long at your synagogue?" they inquire. "We've been waiting for a half hour already."

"Our rabbi always squeezes every minute out of the service. He has a full house, and he loves to talk," my father explains.

"Sit down already. Let's eat."

"Oy, it's so hot in here. Let me take off my jacket before I sit down."

The crowd squeezes in so my parents can take a seat in the dining room, but Harold and I are relegated to eat in the tiny kitchen. Some of my "cousins" stand while others sit. Sandy, Toby's sixteen-year-old daughter, is washing the first set of dishes in the sweltering kitchen. She treats me like a kid sister. I am the youngest of the first-born children of the Family Group, most of them were born in Europe right after the war and are three years older than I am. My brother is part of the younger group, three years younger than I am. I don't fit with either group—not old enough for the older ones, and as the oldest to have been born in in America, too old for the younger. The sixteen-year-olds are learning to drive this year, or having attained driver status, are asking for the car keys so they can say "Good Yom Tov" (Happy Holiday) to all and go home. They want their parents to arrange a ride with one of the other families. They have made their obligatory appearance and long to get out of their dress clothes, to be free to drive around the neighborhood on this day off from school, to see their friends and show off that they have the car. The parents object, time stops as requests are denied, and everyone settles in for the afternoon. The older boys go out to sit on the front steps with the young boys trailing behind, the women carry the plates to the kitchen where Sandy washes and I dry, some of the diners go for a walk, straining in their uncomfortable dress shoes and sweating in the new fall outfits that are too warm for the late summer day.

The menu at Toby's is always the same: egg salad, tuna salad, tomatoes from Chaim's garden, challah and then the blueberry cake, Toby's specialty, the recipe for which she has promised to give me when I get married. She keeps her promise, but that is nine years into the future. Right now, on this mid-September day, I am thirteen and I don't belong anywhere, not even in my own body. I want the older ones to include me in their plans. I want to ride in the car one of them eventually wheedles away from his father. But they chuck me under the chin and pass me by.

"You're cute," they say as they leave. "Maybe next year we'll take you with us."

Will that ever happen, I wonder. They file out the door and rush to the car, eager to be out of their parents' sight. The younger boys fill the seats their older brothers have vacated. They have full command of the TV set if they want it, but they opt for the front steps and a bit of cooler air.

I stay behind and find myself at the dining room table, listening to the conversation that the holiday and food and perhaps a schnaps or two have liberated from the speakers' memories. I realize that I have been handed a gift, a chance to listen to the stories the elders are telling in Yiddish. The mood in the dining room shifts from present to past. As the sun illuminates different sections of the wall during the long afternoon, the invisible podium shifts from one speaker to another. Each story prompts a cascade of replies—the Nazis, the Poles, the ghettoes, the camps, family, survival, loss. The adventures are heart-warming and bone-chilling. These people, whose appearance might fool one into thinking they are just like everyone else, have lived through terrifying times with death always near at hand. Each one speaks with a distinct and personal storytelling style. Each story is accompanied by laughter or tears, and often by both.

I want to know what happened to them and to their loved ones. I ask questions, trying to clarify who, what, and when. They call me an "alte kop," an "old head," because I stayed to listen. I have been called this before by my mother when I was too young to hear these tales. Now she no longer worries the stories are too much for me.

Years later I will gather with the same crowd, only now the "kinder" are married with children of their own. The grandchildren are loud; Toby's house is too small for so many people, but that does not stop us from congregating there on this Rosh Hashanah afternoon. The elders are at the table, but the kitchen cannot accommodate the kinder. We eat in shifts, as someone finishes and stands up from the table their place is quickly filled by someone from the second shift. The sofa in the living room is crowded. Some of the men, first and second generation both, are nodding off, squeezed together on the sofa and full of food and schnapps. The television is on, perhaps the World Series captures the attention of some. Rosh Hashanah can happen any time from early September to October. The Jewish year is a lunar one and the sports on TV vary accordingly from baseball to football. The din of voices makes the conversations almost undecipherable, and the light and heat in the room combine to lull me into a reverie of another time.

For a moment I am lost in memories of past lunches. I remember I felt alone, even in the crowd. I remember wanting to grow up, wanting to be part of the older group of kids. Then I remember that when I was finally old enough for the kids to offer me a ride as they left the lunch the following year, I stayed behind by choice. And that has made all the difference. Sitting at that table opened a world to me I had previously glimpsed only through my parents' experiences. It made me realize history is made up of stories about what happened to ordinary people. If these stories mattered to me, then they might matter to others as well. I became determined to remember the stories and to retell them, and they became the foundation of my career in Holocaust education. My work was to champion survivor testimony and to engage students in the lessons of the past. I found my calling on a Rosh Hashanah afternoon. It was "bashert." It was meant to be.

Visit to Israel

Throughout her life, my mother maintained a correspondence with her cousin Velvel Shwartz, and with her camp sisters Shoshka and Nina. I can remember the thin Aeropostale letters that arrived regularly from Israel. They were usually written in Yiddish, with perhaps a dash of Polish. These were people I knew only by name and through photographs. They had established themselves in the new land and had families, children of about my age, growing up there despite the dire warnings about the lack of milk and the dangers of war that had kept my parents away.

In 1964 my mother decided she and I would visit Israel in the summer. My father could not leave the store, and my mother did not want to travel alone. My brother was almost twelve and would spend the days either at home or in the store with my dad. We also had a housekeeper who could look after him. He was promised a trip to the World's Fair, and tickets to some Phillies games, and he was happy with that.

I was not particularly interested in this trip. I was fifteen, and if you had told me I was going to England so I could immerse myself in Beatlemania, I would have jumped at the chance, but Israel seemed distant and foreign. I had exchanged a few letters with my cousin Chaya, Velvel's daughter, but I had no pressing desire to meet her or any of the others my mother was longing to see. For my mother it had been almost twenty years since their last face to face, and I am sure as I look back on it now, she wanted to see them again before it became too much of a burden to travel. It was never expected they would be able to come to America.

Arrangements were made, passports obtained, the list of shots necessary were secured including a second smallpox vaccination, and presents were bought for everyone and anyone we might see during the three weeks we would be there. The list of presents is very revealing about the differences between the US and Israel in 1964. I remember we brought clothing, linens, shoes, and several transistor radios. It was assumed whatever we brought from the US would be of better quality than anything that could be obtained in Israel. I was outfitted with new dresses and shoes to match all my outfits. My mother planned to carry a great deal of cash to give to my father's aunt who had been in Israel for several years and to his cousins, newly arrived in Israel from the Soviet Union and living in very poor circumstances. We were like a United Nations delegation; everyone had been informed of our arrival and everyone, about twenty-five people in all, showed up at the airport to meet us. There was a fight over who would drive us to Velvel's house, and my mother and I were eventually separated into two different cars so the honor could be shared among as many people as possible.

My first visit to an Israeli bathroom was memorable. The bathroom had all the modern necessities, but on the roller where toilet paper should have been were strips of newspaper. At first, I assumed they were for reading, and I looked at them and hung them back up. I looked around for the toilet paper and couldn't find any. I was confused and when I came out of the bathroom, after giving myself some time to dry, I whispered to my mother that there was no toilet paper. I was ashamed to say anything to our hosts. My mother walked me back to the bathroom to look around. When she saw the strips of newspaper she began to laugh. Of course, she knew what they were there for, but I didn't. When she explained I was horrified. Using newspapers as toilet paper had been common in Europe, my mother explained. The amenities of the United States, things I took for granted and could not live without, set me apart from who I might have become if my parents had come to Israel instead of the U.S.

The next morning, we went to the supermarket and purchased American toilet paper, a real luxury in Israel in 1964. Most of the toilet paper I found in public restrooms or in other people's homes was a kind of waxed paper a bakery might use to serve a donut or a vendor to hand you a hot dog. It was certainly a far cry from even the cheapest brands in the States. Even more embarrassing was the need for sanitary napkins during my time of the month. They were like huge wads of cotton covered with cheesecloth. I remember being extremely self-conscious during that week, and not knowing how to dispose of them, although I was assured that it was okay to flush them down the toilet!

My mother's purpose in coming to Israel was to see old friends, and we did more of that than of anything else. I would have loved to see some of the country, but most of our days were taken up with visiting. I was constantly being paraded about as the "American child," as if there was some vast difference between me and Israeli children. As I look back on it now, I realize there was, but at the time I felt like a specimen. My mother might be living in America, but she was not an American. I *was*. My clothes were different, my haircut was different, my attitudes were different. When I spoke, it was not British English, but American English. I was being raised in a world that most Israelis could only dream about. And because we had come to Israel, it was also assumed we were extraordinarily wealthy. Everyone kept asking if we had a car, and how many televisions we had, and how many bathrooms we had in our home. Every outfit I wore was scrutinized, first by my mother's friends and then by their daughters.

During our time in Israel, I was able to meet Shoshka and Nina, my mother's dear friends. Shoshka lived only a few streets away from Velvel. Seeing her became an almost daily occurrence. Nina lived in Haifa, and this meant a train ride to the north. Nina's husband Efraim and her children Sarale and Micha were wonderful hosts to us.

Efraim had a pickup truck, and he was able to transport us to see some of the sites of the north and to visit my father's cousin Faigel in a new settlement. She had run away to Russia during the war to escape capture by the Nazis and had been forced to stay after the borders to the Soviet Union were sealed. My dad and his brother Sam had found her, or she had found them, and they were determined to help her. They had so little family left that they wanted to ensure she would have a decent life. Somehow, with their help, she had come to Israel in 1964 with her family, her husband who was not Jewish, her daughter and her son. They were relegated to a small apartment in an out-of-the-way place with very little hope of finding a job or improving their lives, and they must have hated what was happening to them. I remember the apartment complex, surrounded by sand, no trees or plants anywhere. Their daughter, who was a few years older than I was, spoke no Hebrew or English and we had no way to communicate. She eyed me with suspicion and even though I tried to act friendly, it seemed our visit only pointed out the difference between the haves and the have nots. We had brought money to help, but whatever we gave was not enough. My mother panicked, as it was clear Faigel's husband was drinking and was beating her, though she bravely tried to hide what was going on. It was a harsher reality than I had ever seen up close, and it was happening to people that were of my blood.

What was it like for my mother to see her friends again? Did she regret not having emigrated to Israel herself? Certainly, life in

1960's Israel was vastly different from the life she was leading in America. By 1964, my father's store was doing well. We had moved from the apartment above the store to our home on Anita Drive. We had a car, and my mother had learned to drive. She worked in the store every day, but she had arranged her schedule so she could go to the beauty parlor every Saturday morning, and she could drive home if Harold or I needed her. There was enough money that we had a housekeeper a few times a week to maintain the house, to do the washing and ironing, and to keep watch over me and my brother. My mother had a closetful of beautiful clothes, a mink stole and some nice jewelry. My parents were part of a social circle that met every Saturday night for cards and chatter, and they belonged to a survivor organization that held regular balls and festivities. Would she have had all of this if they had gone to Israel? Would she have missed something she never had?

The real question, of course, was one of security. Living in the United States, my parents were not confronted by the dangers of the Arab states that plagued the Israelis daily. If they had gone to Israel in 1948 or early 1949, my father would surely have been drafted into the army and would have had to serve during the war then and again in 1956. Who knows what might have happened?

My mother and father loved America. They were grateful every day of their lives for what this country had afforded them. The only aspect of it they could ever find fault with was that people took advantage of their freedom in ways my parents might not have agreed with. That freedom of speech was guaranteed to people who promoted hate was something they could never come to terms with. My mother often said this was the best country in the world, and that people here could not appreciate it because they did not know what it might be like somewhere else. What America promised and delivered, especially to immigrants, could not be equaled anywhere in the world.

Would they have felt the same way about Israel? I know that my father would have been a proud defender of Israel. He had been brought up with the dream of emigrating there and had wanted to fight as a free Jew defending his homeland. But I think my mother would have preferred to be in America. I think she had had enough strife and needed to feel safe. As much as the Hebrew language intrigued her, and as proud as she was of being a Jew, she was also quite pleased to be an American.

That Girl

I'm not sure if this story illustrates a character trait of mine so much as it portrays my troubled relationship with my mother. That she was my harshest critic even into her old age is already clear. Her few kind words were so rare I am unable to construct a story around them. They were incidental, and most of them were about the fact I kept a well-stocked pantry or baked a good apple cake, or occasionally, that I was doing a good job raising Joshua. That one meant a great deal to me, but it never filled me with a feeling of being the daughter my mother wanted. Her most frequent and harshest words were about my appearance. Her disappointment in the way I looked started when I was a preteen and continued until she went blind in her eighties. At that point she could no longer see I had stopped dying my hair and allowed the gray to dominate, but she did feel my thighs when I came to visit to see if I had gained weight.

In my early years my mother managed my hair, and she was certain the look she created was perfect, since it mirrored her own hairstyle as a child. When I no longer wore braids or a high ponytail and could take care of my own hair, she lost control, and she continued to criticize whatever style I sported. At the first signs of gray in my hair she became apoplectic. It was not that I was getting gray as much as it made *her* look older to have a daughter who was going gray. By then, I had realized how much my mother's self-image was tied up in my appearance. I was more than a mirror for her; I was the Barbie doll she wanted to dress and fuss over. That I was not Barbie-ish was a huge disappointment.

An oft-told tale in our family is about the evening I gave a speech about Holocaust education at a local synagogue. I was a guest on the bimah, and my parents and husband were in the audience. I did not know that a particular exchange between my father and mother took place until after my speech was finished. At the close of services, I came down from the platform to find my family. My father was smiling and proud, but then he said this:

"Your mother asked me where you were. She wondered who that pretty girl on the bimah was. I asked her if she was kidding. I told her it was you. She said it couldn't be you because that girl was good-looking."

My father was laughing, not realizing what he was saying was hurtful. What he'd said also confirmed what I had known all along——nothing I ever accomplished mattered to my mother as much as how I looked. The fact she didn't even recognize me from afar should have been an indication that perhaps I looked better than she thought, but that was not the way this story went. My mother was surprised the girl on the platform, the one she was admiring, was me. Without knowing who it was, she could be complimentary. As soon as it was her daughter, she would deny it could be me.

That story was repeated many times, at family dinners, at Passover seders, when there was a chance to tell one on my mother. Though it was supposed to be funny, it always made me cringe. Even as I write this, I remember the chill I felt when it happened and when it was repeated.

Two Smacks

After we had moved to our house, my brother and I were expected to call my parents as soon as we arrived home from school. We had gone from being under the constant gaze of our parents to being latch-key kids whose comings and goings were unsupervised other than these check-in phone calls. These calls became such an ingrained habit that they continued through college and graduate school, and I made the tactical error early on in my marriage of maintaining these daily check-ins with my mother. If I didn't call her, she assumed something was wrong and called me instead.

I had not called my mother before Jim, Josh and I left for our ride that Saturday in the 1980's. I had a feeling of dread as we drove along that my mother was calling me, especially since it was my birthday. If cell phones had been available, I would have been in the clear. As it was, I just hoped we would get home in time to allow me to call her before she could get hold of me. Don't ask why we didn't stop at a pay phone; we were just enjoying the day, but I would beat myself up over that mistake for a long time.

Josh was still young enough that Jim and I could drag him along on a celebratory car ride out into the country with lunch somewhere along the road. As usual, Josh was reading comic books in the back seat, totally oblivious to the world outside his imaginary adventures.

"Could you look out the window and enjoy the scenery?" we asked him. His obsession with comic books was keeping him from noticing the beauty of the early spring day.

"I'm so bored. Even my teeth are bored," said eleven-year-old Josh, dropping his nose back into the book. If I turned discreetly towards the back seat, I could see that every so often he would glance at the passing view. I was certain I could get him into one of those car games he had loved to play like out-of-state license plates or misspelled road signs. He was still young enough he wasn't completely against joining in an activity that made his mother happy. I knew the teenage years would make that willingness disappear, at least for a while. Enjoy him for as long as you can before all of that happens, I reminded myself almost daily. I taught high school and knew what teenagers could be like.

It was a bright and sunny spring day, and the car windows were open to let the breezes blow. I had always enjoyed being born in May, and the lovely weather felt like a personal gift to me. We stopped at a Bucks County roadside stand for burgers and fries, and ate at wooden picnic tables, sharing the space with others who were also enjoying the chance to be outside. We shed our jackets and soaked in the sun.

"Mom, I feel the need for a milkshake, and I believe your birthday should be celebrated properly. Milkshakes all around?"

Josh offered to get in line at the stand and bring back the birthday treats. I watched as he walked away. He was almost as tall as I was. The doctor had predicted he would be 6'6" when he reached his full height. Still, he was my baby, my sweet boy whose company I so enjoyed. On the way back home, we laughed about other car rides, particularly the ten-hour trips my in-laws would subject us to when we visited them out west. Before long we were home, and my boy had disappeared up the stairs into his room. I was filled with the warmth that comes from spending a beautiful day with people you love.

But the day was not over. I noticed the answering machine's red light blinking. My mother had indeed called. And she had called many, many times, and in each of her messages her voice became more distressed.

It was her habit to talk to the answering machine as if I was there listening to it. She would start out saying, "Mamaleh, pick up the phone," and then go into an extended monologue.

"Mamaleh, I am calling to say Happy Birthday. Pick up."

"Mamaleh, I called ten minutes ago, and you didn't pick up. Maybe you were in the bathroom. Pick up."

"Elaine, I called a half hour ago. Call me back. Are you okay? Is Josh okay?"

"Elaine, this is Mommy. I am getting worried. Call me!"

She continued calling for as long as the machine would record. Her messages, each recorded about thirty minutes apart, became more intense and frenzied than the previous one. "Where *are* you?" she kept asking. "Why don't you *answer*?" What's *wrong!*"

I had listened to five of the seven or eight messages and had tried calling her back with no answer when the downstairs doorbell rang. I ran down the steps from the kitchen and opened the door. My mother stood on the doorstep, her face twisted into an angry snarl. Without saying a word, she extended her arm and with an open hand smacked me across the face. I reeled back, clutching the door frame. My father was a step behind her, watching this scene. He grabbed my mother by the shoulders and pulled her away, back towards their car.

Shaking, stunned, and off balance, I slammed the door on them both. My husband and son, who had heard the doorbell and come down the steps right behind me, had witnessed the whole thing. Jim was furious, but Josh was shocked. He had never seen his Bubbie so out of control. I had the red imprint of my mother's hand across my cheek, each of her fingers stretched in an obvious pattern across my face.

"I swear that I will *never* speak to her again," I shouted. "She is crazy, and she is making me crazy!" I began to shake with anger.

Jim held me and Josh watched as I screamed and ranted. What I felt was more than anger. I felt humiliated and exhausted, worn down from the hysteria that drove my mother to this kind of behavior. It had been this way for my entire life. Her irrational fears had driven our relationship to an untenable place. I was aware what I was saying would have a profound impact on Josh's relationship with his grandmother, so I tried to control myself, but the sobbing continued, my chest heaving and aching. I had never lifted a hand to Josh, and seeing my mother's actions must have shocked him. I wanted his relationship with his grandmother to be free of the strain I had experienced with my mother. What she had just done and the way in which I responded had not helped.

I think a whole week went by before my mother and I communicated in any way. My father tried to talk to me, but I wasn't in the mood to relent. After three or four days of my silence my father finally called.

"You know your mother. She worries about you so much. She lost everyone and so she always thinks the worst. She was sure something bad had happened to you."

"Something bad happened all right. And *she* did it. She can't come to my door and smack me. I am not a *child*. I'm a grown woman! I don't care what she was worried about or why. I cannot forgive her."

"Don't talk like that! You will regret it. No matter what, she is your *mother*."

As far as I was concerned and no matter who she was, there was no excuse for what she had done. I was tired of having to live my life on her terms, tired of always compensating for the anxieties that were fueled by her losses. Keeping tabs on me while I was living in her house was one thing; keeping this close a watch when I was a fully functioning adult who was raising my own pre-teenager was something else again. The anger was not only mine. My husband and son were angry, too. Bubbie had stolen the joy of that day; our carefree ride into the country was tinged, once again, with the residual terror brought on by the Holocaust.

I was so tired of being the one who had to take care of my mother by deferring my own happiness to make sure she was okay. Yet, even in my righteous anger, I was guilt-ridden. I could not forgive myself for not having called her in the morning before we left. I could have avoided the entire disaster by making that one call. Was I being the rebellious teenager who went out for a joyride?

Many years earlier, in the summer before my senior year of high school, I had spent the evening at my friend Marion's house, just around the corner from where we lived. My parents had instituted a strict phone call policy about being out in the evenings. I had to check in to let them know where I was. The truth was I was always at Marion's. Marion's house was always filled with teenagers, the friends of her older brother, our mutual friends, and her younger sister's friends. At Marion's house there were no rules. We could do anything there. We would play records, dance, cook, paint the rooms wild colors, and just hang out.

That was not the case where I lived. There, the plastic slipcovers on the living room sofa told the whole story. Everything at my parents' house was in perfect order, as if no one inhabited it. The carpet looked as if it had never been stepped on, the lines made by the vacuum cleaner lasted from one week to the next without a footprint marring the perfect rows. No wonder I wanted to be at

Marion's and not in the French provincial palace my parents had furnished and so pristinely maintained.

On one night, about a week before school was to start, I was introduced to a boy named Michael. He was already in college and was tall and handsome. I was enchanted and wanted to appear cool and sophisticated. I did not want him to see me leave the room to call my parents to tell them where I was. I was afraid my mother would insist I come home, and that was the last thing I wanted to hear. The time passed quickly. Before I realized it was well after 11:30. I knew I had better get going. Michael offered to walk me home, and I don't think my feet touched the sidewalk as we made our way around the corner.

We came up the steps onto the porch that led to my front door.

"May I have your phone number?"

"Yes. I'll just get a pen and some paper for you." *He likes me*, I thought.

Michael stood so close behind me as I put the key in the door that I could smell his cologne. The key clicked in the lock and the door opened. A hand flew out and hit me in the face, a smack that sent me flying back, almost into Michael's arms. He, of course, ran down the steps as fast as he could.

After the initial shock, when I realized what had just happened, I stormed into the house screaming and sobbing.

"How could you *do* that? There was a boy standing right behind me! How could you embarrass me like that? He's probably telling everyone right now how crazy you are! I will never see him again because of you!"

My mother shouted, "I warned you" and then she was gone, down the hall to the bedroom.

"You knew where I was. You knew I was at Marion's. Why would you *do* that?" I stood in the kitchen rubbing my stinging cheek and then threw myself into a chair at the kitchen table. I could not stop crying. I don't know if I was more hurt physically by the smack or if the humiliation was the greater pain. I feared that Michael would go right back to Marion's house and tell the crowd what had happened. I also knew I would probably never hear from him again. Why would anyone want to get involved with a girl who had a mother crazy enough to do something like that?

Even more, I was railing against my mother and her irrational, unwarranted fears. She knew if I wasn't at home, I was at Marion's. There was nowhere else I would be. She also knew I would never do anything even remotely dangerous. I was a responsible, almost fearful kid. And she was aware she had done something unforgiveable by hitting me in front of someone else.

My father came into the kitchen.

"Go to bed," he said quietly. Then he turned and walked down the hall to their bedroom. He never addressed what had happened. Neither did my mother the next day or ever again. It took me a long time to calm down enough to leave the kitchen and go to my room. I lay on my bed that night feeling sorry for myself, hating my mother.

While doing research before writing about my mother, I came across a testimony she gave in 1996 to a psychologist who interviewed Holocaust survivors about their relationships with their families. In the transcript my mother mentions not wanting to let me go away to college. She says that I "belonged to her," that I was the only thing she had she hadn't lost. She also says my brother and I were brought up to behave in a way that would make my parents happy. We were never to give them any reason to feel ashamed of their children or to make them mad. She says, "they knew (meaning my brother and I) that there is something different about us, and they tried to be good children, ... to satisfy us, that we should not have more anxiety." Later she adds, "I think they knew that we went through bad times, and they wanted, in a way, to save the parents and bring them good news." She comments on her protectiveness and that she always felt it more with me than with my brother. This was not a surprise to me. I always felt it, just as I always knew that the world inside of our house was very different from the world other people were living in. I knew my parents' war experiences colored every interaction they had.

This expectation, to make up for my mother's losses, weighed on me my entire life, even after her death. I knew that I was everything to her. I carried out my responsibility even as I resented being her "everything." I knew, especially when I was a teenager, that she was living the life she lost through me, and yet I also knew our lives and our hopes and dreams were very different. I was not like her, but she wanted me to be. Any time I defied her, she told me she would never have behaved that way to her mother. I knew this was untrue, especially given that she never had a chance to defy her mother at all. What should have been her rebellious teenage years were spent in the ghetto and in Auschwitz-Birkenau. Her own mother was dead by the time my mother was sixteen. And as a result, the mother-daughter relationship was crystallized, almost sanctified, which made it impossible for me to have a relationship with my mother that could ever satisfy her needs without completely subsuming mine.

I was never allowed to show anger. I was told I had no reason to be angry, no reason ever to cry. I had no reason to be sad. I had everything because my parents were alive and provided everything I needed. What could possibly be missing? In her testimonies, my mother reveals something interesting about her own parenting. She says many times that she did not spend very much time with us after the purchase of the shoe store. She needed to be at work and could not be at home with us. She adds she tried to make up for that by buying things for us. She mentions buying me clothes and pocketbooks, and though I cannot hear her voice, as I read the transcript, I know she must have told the interviewer this with feelings of both pride and regret. I think she realized no possessions could ever make up for the time we lost with her and my father. Yet she prided herself on being able to buy those things. She had succeeded in achieving the American dream, but she had sacrificed something along the way—the establishment of a relationship that would allow me to grow into being an equal with her. My role would forever be to carry her burdens, to "be good, to lessen her anxiety."

But by necessity, I would become the one that *defied* her wishes, especially because they seemed so contrary to the person I was. Every act that would have pleased her and cemented over the cracks in our relationship, I performed grudgingly or completely refused to do. I knew it pained her, but I also realized I had to be my own self, despite her overwhelming needs.

These two overreactions and violent responses are some of my most vivid memories of my mother. How unfortunate they have lingered for so many years. Though I can retell the story now with some empathy for her, I cannot forgive my mother entirely. Her curse, that I might have a child that defied me as much as I defied her, never came to pass. My son and I weathered his teen years with a sense of humor and a great deal of mutual acceptance, overlooking the occasional slips of the tongue that might have escalated into something more serious. I would like to think his stories about me will not be tinged with the sorrow I feel as I write these words today.

Despite the Differences

It was a given that I would marry someone of the Jewish faith. My parents were not Orthodox, but they did bring us up with certain strong beliefs. We kept a "kosher-style" home, eating only kosher meat, not mixing milk with meat, but we didn't have two sets of dishes. We weren't observant enough to keep kosher outside of the house. We attended services on the High Holy Days of Rosh Hashanah and Yom Kippur, but we drove to the synagogue rather than walking, as more devout people did. My brother and I both went to Hebrew school, although I would suggest that this poorly conceived institution did nothing in the way of making us more religious and might even have sabotaged any interest in Judaism we could have had. We did not eat bread during the eight days of Passover, and we never celebrated Christmas or had a tree disguised as a Chanukah bush as some of my Jewish classmates did. Ours was a complicated mix of beliefs and practices, but that Harold and I would marry a Jew was a primary tenet.

The first question my parents always asked about someone was if they were Jewish. This applied to friends, teachers, and especially to boyfriends. The neighborhood we lived in was mixed with Jews and non-Jews, but most of my friends were Jewish. My parents always cautioned it was a mistake even to date a non-Jewish boy—better not to let your heart get hold of your head. I obeyed this rule until I was in college. By then, I felt I had become a good enough judge of character to make decisions about who to date, not based on religion, but based on shared values.

In my sophomore year of college. I became infatuated with a very WASP-y fellow from Chester County. We had absolutely nothing in common, and the whole thing ended very quickly as each of us realized that what had attracted us was the exotic nature of what we each represented. What followed were long relationships with "nice Jewish boys" and proposals of marriage from each I rejected when I realized none of them was 'the one."

I met Jim Culbertson on my first day as a high school English teacher, which was also his first day as a high school History teacher. He was not my type for several reasons, or so I thought then. In fact, I disliked him intensely, which should have been a clue there was more to our relationship than I realized. He pursued me repeatedly and I put him off him repeatedly. Eight years older than I was, he had already lived on his own for quite a while, including a three-year stint in the Peace Corps in Nigeria. The first time I went to his apartment, I noticed he had a colander in his kitchen. He was not a child like my other beaus had been. Only a grown man had his own colander.

Our relationship moved forward in secrecy for two reasons. I did not want people at school to know we were dating because I had been told by my work mentors, two more veteran teachers than I, that "you don't shit where you eat," meaning you don't do anything to foul your workplace with personal problems. But the real reason I kept Jim a secret was that he was not Jewish. If he had just been a fling, it wouldn't have mattered, but my feelings were intensifying, and it soon became more than a fling.

Jim would call my house, and I would drive to our appointed meeting place, the parking lot at the mall, so we could spend time together away from work. And as we became serious about each other, I dated other people to create a distraction and to hide what was going on from my parents. I could not begin to imagine how I would introduce Jim to my parents. I knew they would be offended and angry, and their disappointment in me would never dissipate. In strict Jewish families when someone marries outside of the faith, the family acts as if that person has died, *sitting shivah* (mourning) and never speaking their name again. Would my parents go that far, I wondered? My close friends had all met Jim by this time, and so had my brother, Harold. Though my friends were watching the development of the relationship, my brother was away at school and had no idea how serious Jim and I were becoming about each other.

I realized after several months the sneaking around was harder on my conscience than the pain of confronting my parents might be, so I made the decision to tell them that I was dating a non-Jew and that we loved each other. My parents were apoplectic. My father summoned his wrath and crafted elaborate stories about what the future held in store for me.

"You'll see! One day when he is angry with you, he'll call you a dirty Jew! He'll hit you!

Because that's what they do! They beat their wives. He'll drink! And when he's drunk, he'll turn his anger on *you*. And your children, as far as I'm concerned, they will be bastards!"

My mother acted as if I had done this deliberately to cause her pain. She told me, "You can control who you love! Rein in your heart and come to your senses!"

The more they yelled, the more adamant I became they could not tell me what to do. I was no longer living at home, nor did I depend on them for income. All I wanted was their blessing, but not only would they not give me that, they would not even agree to meet Jim. Much of what they said centered on how ashamed they would be in front of their community of friends and relatives, as if they had done a poor job of raising me and now it would be evident to all. Shame was the primary emotion behind their anger. For some reason, this hardened me against them even more. Their reaction was not so much about me but about what others would think.

My father would call me and tell me I was killing my mother. My mother would call me and tell me I was killing my father. One evening, I received a phone call from my brother. It must have been on a weekend when he was home from college. It went something like this:

"I'm calling because Mommy and Daddy are very upset. They want me to talk you out of seeing Jim. Dad says that Mom cries every night. She's going out of her mind. If you care about them, you should think about what you are doing to them."

"What are you? Their little *agent*?" I yelled, enraged they would put him up to this and that he would follow through. "I cannot believe you are taking their side! Don't ever do this again! Don't call me with their bullshit! You are *my* brother. You must be on *my* side, no matter what. When they're gone, it will just be *you* and *me*."

I turned to Bernie, (the more adult version of his childhood nickname Benny), the son of Tillie and Jack, my parents' best friends. Bernie and Jim had developed a close relationship. When I asked for his help, Bernie suggested he could go to my parents to talk with them. I agreed any intervention that might possibly help was worth a try, but I doubted anything would come of it. I was wrong. I don't know what he said, and I have never asked him, but Bernie's visit eased the way for the eventual meeting that took place between Jim and my parents.

I was particularly wary of what might happen when we were all finally together. We sat at the kitchen table where my parents served tea and Entenmann's coffee cake. I don't think anyone touched a piece of it. We were all uncomfortable. My parents remained cordial, as if Jim was an insurance agent or an accountant stopping in for a visit to check on a policy or an investment, but I knew there was a lot more going on in their heads. The conversation was stilted, but everyone remained calm, and after the visit my mother told me that she thought Jim was very nice. She noticed that his shoes were polished, which, given their work, was one of the measures of how acceptable a potential suitor might be. This acknowledgement of his well-kept shoes was as far as she could go in admitting that he might be appropriate.

Jim offered to convert to Judaism to motivate their acceptance of the match.

"I'm not asking you to do that. It might make things easier, but I can't honestly require that of you," I told him.

"My interest in Judaism goes back before I met you," Jim said. "Ever since I was an altar server and lay reader in the Episcopal church, I had an interest in religion. I've been reading about Judaism for years, thinking about the connections to Christianity. I've always admired the ethics of its teachings."

"I can't promise that will have any influence on my parents. They're upset. I'm the first child among all their friends that will marry a non-Jew. I have disgraced them."

It was about the outside community's approbation. But this is who they were, so I had to deal with and overcome their fears of loss of face.

It was the rabbi's job to dissuade me from marrying a non-Jew, and to make the conversion process as uncomfortable for Jim as he could. The rabbi failed on both counts. Despite himself, he took a liking to Jim, even calling him "Jimmy" (the only other person who did that was Jim's grandmother). I believe he came to understand why I loved Jim, and our sessions with the rabbi took a philosophical turn as we began discussing the ethics of the religion itself. All the while, I was teaching Jim to read some Hebrew. His first public appearance as my fiancé would be at the Passover seder with Tillie and Jack's family. It was the test for whether people important to my parents would accept him. As he stood to recite the Hebrew blessing over the wine, I could sense the ice melt in my parents' hearts. He might not have been their first choice for me, but he had redeemed himself in their eyes through the dedication and hard work he had put into this moment. Jim converted to Judaism, and we were married a few months later. As I write this, we will soon celebrate our 54th wedding anniversary.

Jim became not only a son-in-law, but my parents'son. In the early years of our marriage, he helped my father with home improvements and mowed their lawn regularly. He raised Joshua to love Judaism and to honor his grandparents. As my parents aged, Jim transported them to doctors' appointments, helped with chores around their home, and spent every Sunday with them while I refilled their pill containers and paid their bills. In every way, he respected them and valued them. He was never an outsider, but a cherished member of the family.

A Fish Story

"Mom, I want to learn how to make gefilte fish."

"So, come over and we will make it together."

"Do you have anything written down, like a list of ingredients?"

"When you know how to cook something you have the ingredients in your head. I don't have to write it down."

"Yes, but I don't have it in my head. I'll bring a notebook and write as we are cooking."

"Don't make a big deal out of it. It's just gefilte fish."

"Okay, Sunday? Do you want me to help you shop for the stuff we need?"

"No, I'll take care of it. Just come on Sunday."

I did not know how much of anything was needed to make a batch of gefilte fish. My mother and I had never cooked anything together. Nor had she ever invited me to learn any cooking techniques from her. My only kitchen experiences in her house had been dishwashing, figuring out on my own how to make cheese omelets and a few instances of baking that I initiated. To get an idea of what was involved in making the fish I looked up a recipe in one of the cookbooks I had received as a wedding present. Some of it seemed familiar, but not all.

Joan Nathan had developed a recipe to make gefilte fish so that skeptics might learn to overcome their dislike of the Ashkenazi Jewish staple. She offered the addition of trout, or salmon or striped bass to the traditional ingredients, pike and carp, that most of us who grew up eating it associate with gefilte fish. I read the list of ingredients and marveled. What would my mother think? Trout? Salmon, striped bass? Tarragon? Fennel? Radicchio and endive as serving decorations? My mother didn't even know what those were! Her decorations were the carrots and the fish jelly, which we hoped would congeal in time for the meal. I promised myself I wouldn't mention the Nathan recipe. I was open and eager to learn Mom's way

I arrive at my parents' home on Sunday mid-morning.

"That's what you wore to cook fish?" is my mother's greeting. She is in a housedress and bedroom slippers, but underneath she is fully armored in her long line bra and panty girdle. I am wearing jeans and a T-shirt that somehow strike her as disrespectful to our enterprise, but no matter what I would have worn, it would not have been right. We are off to a not-so-happy start.

Mom brings out the grinder which she attaches to the kitchen table. My job is to grind the fish meat into the wooden bowl. She has already prepared the pot with carrots, onions and celery. When I ask how many carrots and how many onions, she shrugs. Also in the huge pot is the carcass of a fish whose meat I am now grinding.

"I am trying to write down a recipe. I need to know the amounts. How many carrots? Onions? Celery? How much fish did you buy?" My questions seem to annoy her.

"Enough carrots and onions and celery to cover the bottom of the pot. A big enough fish to make about 20 pieces of fish. The man showed me the fish, I liked how it looked, shiny and fresh, and I bought it."

"Is that what I should write in my recipe? Ask the man to show you the fish and if you like how it looks, buy it'?"

"Elaine, stop! You're making me nervous. Just do what I tell you and you'll write it down later."

Just do what I tell you—the refrain of our relationship.

I have my Cuisinart in the front seat of my car. I thought I might coax my mother into the 20th century by suggesting we use it instead of the old-fashioned grinder.

"It won't work. It will be too mushy." She fends off my suggestions without so much as a trial run. I grind the fish for what seems like hours. When I make gefilte fish, I think to myself, I will use the Cuisinart, but I still don't know how much fish to buy or any of the other specifics. My notebook is on the floor in the dining room next to my purse. My mother cleared it off the kitchen table as soon as I came in.

Where did my mother learn to cook gefilte fish? She told me that most of the cooking in her family home was done by the maid, a Christian girl from a village not far from Mom's small town of Pruzana.

"Who taught the Christian girl to cook gefilte fish?" I ask this in all seriousness, but my mother dismisses me with a wry laugh.

"What do you mean? Probably my mother or my grandmother who lived with us. In those days, the old people didn't live on their own or in nursing homes. My father built a room onto the house, off the kitchen for my grandmother. She used to sit in a rocking chair near the big stove to keep warm. When we came into the house from playing outside, we would put our cold cheeks next to her warm one. She would scold us with fake anger and then hug us, kissing the tops of our heads and pinching our cheeks."

"So, you knew your grandmother." I say this with a bit of jealousy. No grandparents in my life except for the Zayde that all of us in the Family Group shared.

"Of course, she lived with us until she died. That's why Cousin Lola would come from Lodz to stay with us during vacation. She wanted to be with Grandmother too."

"It sounds nice. What was her name? Did you call her Bubbie?"

"Zlateh Bayleh was her name. I don't remember what I called her. It was a long time ago. I can't remember what she looked like. To tell you the truth, I can't remember what my Papa looked like. If it wasn't for the picture of my mother that Uncle Abe gave me, I might not remember her face either. It's like I am talking about a different world, a world that vanished."

With the fish cooking we continue to talk about her childhood while I wash the dishes. My parents have a dishwasher, but it is never used. My mother thinks it's too much trouble to load and unload it, and so she washes everything by hand. As I am washing, she comes up behind me and pushes me closer to the sink. This has been a running argument for years. Even though I am married with a home of my own, she doesn't approve of the distance I stand from the sink when I wash the dishes. She wants me closer, more involved in the task. To ward her off, I stick out my backside and push back against her. This time, she laughs and moves away. She has lost the battle this time and she admits defeat, at least until the next time when she will feel compelled to criticize my stance once again.

"Who washed the dishes in your house when you were a child?"

"The *shiksa* (Christian girl) who worked for us. My mother was not home. She was at the bakery at the cash register during the day. Christina took care of the house and us. She cooked and cleaned."

"Did you ever cook? Did you bake cookies? Did Christina teach you how to cook?"

"My father owned a bakery. I could have all the cookies I wanted. We did not bake in the house. Papa brought home bread and rolls and sweets every day."

"Girls usually like to cook, especially to bake. Remember when I bought the baking pans and made a layer cake? You were amazed that I could do it. You said I must have the baking gene from your father. But then you told me that your father really didn't bake. He had people working for him who were the bakers." Before I had been informed that he himself did not bake, I had had a brief moment when I had felt a connection to my grandfather.

My mother is suddenly struck by a memory.

"I never cooked or baked at home. I got in trouble once for peeling potatoes at a friend's house. It was something I never did at home. I was having so much fun I peeled about five pounds of potatoes. I didn't realize it was food the family needed for the week. Papa had to buy potatoes for them to apologize for my being so thoughtless." Mom's expression moves from embarrassment to remorse. I watch her to see if there is more to the story, but she stops, lost for a moment in the past. I love this story, not only because it takes place in the before times when she was a child, but because it is one in which she was an imperfect child.

"You were rich, weren't you? Sam Kaufman says you were a spoiled brat." Sam is a family friend who grew up in the same town as my mother.

"Sam Kaufman was a little *pisher* that I wouldn't even have looked at. We were rich, I guess. We had everything we needed and more. We went to camp in the summer. We had ice skates and sleds and skis in the winter. My father insisted we learn to read and write Yiddish and Hebrew, so a tutor came to the house for me and my sister. We had new clothes for Pesach made for us by a woman who came to the house and custom sewed them. It was a good childhood." She sighs with what must be longing. These memories may be too painful for her, but I want to know everything about her life, hoping that the more I know, the more it will bridge the gap between us.

"A good childhood." I toss this phrase around in my head.

The aroma fills the kitchen, and my father comes upstairs from the recreation room where he has been watching a ballgame on TV remarking on how good the food smells. This is years before he starts his downward spiral into dementia. He is still the father I choose to remember—alert, smart, strong and generous.

"So, did you learn how to make fish?" He stands in the entryway of the kitchen, in his undershirt and boxer shorts, his typical Sunday attire that he wears before they go out somewhere to meet friends and play cards. His pants are hanging over one of the dining room chairs, his ripple soled shoes sit next to the chair, a bad habit of his that my mother has been trying to break forever. Everything in this house is the same as when I was growing up, I think, and I bask in the comfort of it. I cannot yet imagine the changes that will upend their lives and mine.

"I'm not sure Mom is ready to give up her secret recipe. I have become very good at grinding though. Perhaps that is my destiny. I won't be the chef, just the chef's helper."

"When I'm gone, you'll eat the fish from the jar," Mom muses.

She is right. I have Joan Nathan's recipe, but it is not the method my mother would have used to make gefilte fish. There is no mention of the sugar she would add—a Litvak tradition that sweetened the fish just the way I liked it. I will never undertake the gefilte fish project and I will never find out how she learned to cook gefilte fish.

Years before her death, my mother falls and breaks both of her arms. This catastrophe handicaps her for the rest of her life, and she never cooks anything again. On Sundays in her assisted living quarters, I bring my notebook and ask questions, not about cooking but about her family. Sometimes she is comfortable answering and other times she tells me, "Not today." The information I am unable to retrieve cannot be told to me by anyone else. Mom is the last of her European-born cousins to die. Their children, my second cousins, look to me now with questions about our shared relatives and the events that occurred before and during the war. My little notebook comes in handy. I am the only one who knows the grandmother's name, the only one who can reel off the names of the cousins who were killed in the Holocaust. I may not be able to prepare the fish, but I can tell a bit of the story of the family that we lost. I can always buy fish in a jar.

The Strawberry

"That must be removed right away. You must take the baby back to the doctor. Or better yet, to a cancer specialist." My mother's voice was insistent and filled with panic.

"Mom, he was examined by a doctor in the hospital when he was born. No one said anything about it. "

"They have probably never seen it before. We have. Don't play around with this. It must be looked at right away. It took months for you to heal from the procedures. Why has God cursed us like this again?"

I held my baby and tried to shield him from my mother's eyes and from her words. To my loving eyes he was perfect in every way, beautiful and abundant dark blond hair, lovely bright eyes, his ears situated close to his head. Why did my mother have to focus on the one slight imperfection? Not a surprise. This was who she was, the one who saw the glass half- full. My father called her a *schwartzzayer* in Yiddish, the one who sees the dark side and the doom in everything. Even in this happy moment of seeing her first grandchild, she found something to be worried about. Even as she had defied the odds, surviving the death camps, marrying and bearing her own children, welcoming a new generation, even now she found the darkness.

Josh was born with a hemangioma—a collection of small blood vessels that form a lump under the skin, sometimes called a strawberry—on his shoulder right above what I lovingly called his wings. It was bright red and slightly raised, like an oval of tiny red bumps clustered together. Had it been the first time my mother had seen it she might not have concentrated her anxiety on it with such intensity. But I had been born with the same kind of birthmark on my rear end, and the doctors had advised my parents, then only two months in America, that it must be removed. They told my parents that it might be a precancerous condition, and although their English was limited, the urgency of the word cancer was not lost on them. This mark had necessitated many trips to the Skin and Cancer Hospital in Manhattan, a long punishing ride on public transportation from our home in Brooklyn, especially for a new mother who was also new to this country. The saga of these procedures, which I was too young to remember, had been imprinted in my mother's memory and retold to me many times during my childhood. The journey, the remedy, and the recovery were painful and frightening for both of us.

The hospital I had been taken to was part of Sloan Kettering, and the procedures to which I had been subjected were applications of dry ice to the affected area to burn the birthmark and cause new skin to regenerate. Each time the application was performed I was left with open wounds on my rear end which were irritated by the urine in my wet diapers. What had been a small strawberry turned into an inflamed and very sore backside that my mother had to clean constantly, watching it heal only to be reinjured by the next procedure. For my mother, it was agony to see her baby in such pain. But she feared cancer even more. The procedures went on for months, leaving me with a hideous scar on my rear, a large burn mark of rippled uneven skin. It was only visible in the scantest of bathing suits, but I was conscious of it all my life. I had never expected the mark was hereditary, that it might reappear on my baby.

Josh's pediatrician, Dr. Widerman, was a legend in our neighborhood. This disheveled and shabby older man with Albert Einstein hair shambled into my hospital room the morning after Josh's birth, asking me if I wanted a glass of wine. I had no idea who he was or why he was offering me a drink. He was wearing a white coat and had a stethoscope hanging around his neck, but he didn't look like any doctor I had ever seen. The offer of wine was his way of telling me I was to take no pain killers for the episiotomy, but to drink wine, which would not only help my discomfort but also calm my nursing baby. When he offered to perform the circumcision, I explained that it would be done by a *mohel* in a *bris* (someone trained to perform the traditional Jewish circumcision rite).

Dr. Widerman laughed, apologizing because he had assumed from the last name Culbertson that we were not Jewish. He had examined the baby, found him perfect, and suggested that I go home as soon as I felt able. He also advised me I could take the baby outside for a walk as soon as I wanted to, because Josh was a healthy nine pounder. It was July and the warm weather would help the baby sleep and be refreshing for the new mother.

When I finally got a peek at the name embroidered on his ratty lab coat, I realized that he was the famed doctor everyone had told me about, and I was pleased we had been assigned to him. So many of my friends had grown up under his care. Some of them were still making appointments with him well into their twenties. His no-nonsense manner allayed everyone's fears. In each of his examining rooms he had posted a sign that said, "Let 'em yell." He believed that crying helped babies ease their own nervous tension and developed their lungs. Mothers should sit on the front steps out of earshot when babies were fretful and crying. This was good for both, Dr. Widerman advised.

I followed Dr. Widerman's advice just as I had been told. I didn't ask about the strawberry while I was in the hospital, but my mother continued to question why I had done nothing to address the issue. It was on the first well-baby visit to the pediatrician's office a few weeks later that I asked the question whose answer I feared.

"What about the red mark on the baby's shoulder? "

"That's nothing. Leave it alone. It will be gone by the time he is two."

"But I had a similar birthmark on my behind and they burned it off. My mother insists that it must be removed."

"Where did you grow up? New York, by any chance?"

"Yes, I was born in Brooklyn, and the doctors sent us to ..."

"Let me guess! Sloan Kettering? Dry Ice? "

I nodded, amazed that he would know.

"I was a resident there in pediatrics. We did these procedures on infants, this burning that caused terrible scars. It was all about a cancer scare. We are not going to do that to this young man. Leave it alone."

"You're sure of that? My mother is driving me crazy. She insists it must be removed."

"This beautiful boy is perfect. Let's not mess with Mother Nature. By the time he is two, there will be nothing there. "

I loved him for that answer, and I came to love him even more as the years went by. I even brought my mother to his office so that he might explain to her that no procedure was necessary. My mother was shocked by the doctor's crumpled clothes and wild hair, but she was soothed by his confidence. Despite believing the doctor was right, she checked Josh's shoulder every time she was with him. I knew what she was doing, but I also understood her not so secret peeks into his onesies reassured her that the mark was indeed fading. And Dr. Widerman was right. By the time Josh was two, there was no evidence of the strawberry mark. He was spared the pain, and I was spared the anguish of having my baby burned and scarred.

Was my mother's fear of cancer the only thing that made her so insistent the strawberry mark be removed? I have never thought about this until now, but I wonder if she feared that any imperfection would somehow make Josh stand out, make him vulnerable. How deeply ingrained was the concentration camp mentality that weakness and imperfection meant certain death in her mind? Was this another remnant of her camp experience that the years of safety here in America could not erase? No wonder she had seized on the strawberry and insisted it be removed. How lucky we were we had happened upon a doctor who was familiar with the mark and the cure.

Food

Unlike a lot of other survivor families where home cooking was prized, our family went out to eat quite a bit. Some of this had to do with my mother's work in the store, and some with the finicky appetites of my brother especially. I won't say my mother was a bad cook, but she was not a very accomplished one.

The war years with the deprivations of the ghetto and concentration camp certainly did not add to my mother's culinary skills. When they first met in 1946, my father marveled at the fact that the Litvaks had very peculiar eating habits. When my mother and my aunt Basha prepared a meal for their beaus, my dad and his brother Sam, the men were served the main course right away. Having been raised in a different part of Poland with a different tradition, they looked around for the soup and decided there must not be any. They ate the meat, only to be surprised that the next course was soup, the Litvak way. By the time I came along, Mom had figured out the soup was served first in most households. We always joked that the habit of meat first must have come from a long history of pogroms. Eat the main dish first, because you never know if a war might break out!

Mom had a few stock items she could cook, but most of them tasted the same, and most of them involved meat. We never had a salad, we never had a light evening meal, there was no pasta, no green vegetable except for frozen string beans, just meat and potatoes, and the only dessert was apple sauce. Given the menu, it was a relief to go out to eat. Our favorite haunt was Horn and Hardart, a Philly staple and now a fond memory. There were two options in our neighborhood, the restaurant where you ordered from the menu, or the cafeteria where you could see what you were getting as you pushed your tray along the rails. Both had amazing vegetable choices that I loved, and both had wonderful desserts. Horn and Hardart was the place I first tasted macaroni and cheese, buttered carrots, broccoli, and stewed tomatoes. When the shoe store closed at six, our parents would put us into the car and take us out to eat. On the nights when the store was open late and we still lived in the apartment above the store, Mom would supervise our meal first and then bring dinner down to Dad. Once we moved to the house on Anita Drive, my brother and I were pretty much on our own for dinner on nights when the store was open late. Neither Mom nor

Dad was home, and it was then we discovered TV dinners, sandwiches, and junk food.

On Sundays, if we did not go to H and H, we were dragged to the Ambassador, a Jewish restaurant on Girard Avenue that served only dairy. We hated it as children, but my parents loved it, and I must admit that as I grew older, I loved it as well. It closed many years ago, perhaps because Jewish customers feared traveling to the neighborhood where it was located, or maybe our tastes as an ethnic group changed and the traditional foods no longer had the same appeal. I remember the Ambassador had the best potato latkes I have ever tasted, and the desserts were made with real cream. My brother could never find anything to eat there, and he would be miserable until he could have a salami sandwich at home. That was what he ate for the first ten years of his life, and he ate it for every meal. To this day, the smell of salami makes me a bit sick as I recall the mornings when I watched him eat his sandwich at 7:00 a.m.

The Ambassador was in a neighborhood that was changing from being very Jewish to being almost entirely African American. It had an African American busboy who spoke Yiddish, which delighted my parents as well as all the other customers. If you went there today, there would be no Jewish dairy restaurant. The area has become a place for high-priced condos populated by young hipsters who have been part of the regentrification.

Given my mother's limited cooking repertoire, I thought everyone had meat and potatoes every night. I did not realize that meat was costly or there were other foods that might be served. I remember when I was about eleven going to a friend's for dinner and being served mac and cheese, not as a side dish, but as the main course. I was delighted, and I enthusiastically blurted out how lucky they were because we had meat every night. The look on the parents' faces gave me a clue what I had just said was very stupid. But I was a kid with very little experience of eating at any house other than my own. And there were certain foods that my parents did not know about because they hadn't existed in Poland. I remember when I persuaded Mom and Dad to try pizza for the first time, and then Chinese food, and when we were first allowed to drink Coca-Cola in a restaurant, because there was no way we would have that at home. I never even tried peanut butter until I went to college.

To Jews, food is a way of communicating. What you fix when someone comes over to visit indicates how much you care for them. If you've gone out of your way to cook something rare and exotic, that is a sign of respect. My mother would prepare herring and potatoes, a weird combination, for her friends in the card group, according to a specific tradition from her part of Poland, and it made her card game a special occasion. It was more than just opening a jar of herring, although in her old age even the jar would suffice because it approximated a taste from her childhood.

My mother never taught me to cook. Most of our interactions in the kitchen were like the gefilte fish experience. When I asked how to make chicken soup, she told me to boil the chicken parts in water until it was soup. I knew there was more to it than that, but she would never articulate the rest. I attribute this kind of reluctance to be the teacher to my mother's lack of role models. I had no choice but to find these things out on my own through cookbooks and trial and error.

I remember my mother telling me that when she and my father were living in Germany, an older woman in their apartment building told her that the secret to cooking was a low fire and a long cooking time. My mother took that to heart. She overcooked *everything*, especially meat. Part of this was the old kosher rule of making sure there was no blood visible when the meat was served, and part of this was just following a bad piece of advice. When my parents retired from the store, my mother spent more time cooking, but by this time my father's stomach, always a problem, had gotten worse, and everything he ate caused stomach upset. Mom cooked a very bland diet for him, but on Sundays when my husband and I would come over to do what I referred to as "bills and pills," we would go out to the deli for brunch. Dad would order an omelet and potatoes, but he would snack on the onion rings we ordered with our sandwiches and the pickles that were on the table. Mom would usually split something with me, and if she ordered her own platter, we always had to bring the leftovers home. We used to joke with Dad and ask if we should pack up the ketchup bottle and the salt and pepper shaker that were on the table. Even as I laughed, I understood that the years of privation had left their mark, and food was never to be wasted.

Why is it the foods of your childhood have the most lingering tastes, spoiling everything you eat as an adult? Why doesn't a hotdog taste like the ones from Lenny's across the street from my dad's store? Why doesn't the corned beef taste like what we used to get at the Castor Deli? Or the lox my mother would buy and hide from me because she wanted it for herself? How come the Milky Way I would buy on the way to Hebrew school had a much more delicious flavor than the ones I buy now?

Food is one key to my past, one way I have of remembering the idiosyncrasies of my family, their special history, and the geography of their lives. I am an amalgam of Poland and America, of pierogies and pizza, of *flanken* and *falafel*, of blintzes and burgers. I am the child born into the land of plenty, who could never truly understand the deprivation of their past. Food was the gift they were able to give us every day. It was the visible accomplishment of their hard work. To not eat every bit of what was on our plates or to turn our noses up at what was offered was a sin. We could never appreciate food as they did. Thank God for that.

The Past is Always Present: Part 1

The countryside of Germany is too beautiful, too lush. Could I
be forgiven if I want it to be barren, overgrown with twisted roots
and gnarled trees that defy any attempt to cultivate the land. Am
I being vengeful if I want the fields that crisscross each other in
precise geometric patterns to be sterile, the smooth roads to be rut-
filled and impassable, to be lined with broken down hovels where
haggard mothers struggle to put thin gruel on the table for their
skinny starving children, children whose feet are unshod, whose
clothes are rags hanging from scrawny underdeveloped bodies,
whose unwashed faces and greasy hair smell of sweat and the kind
of cheap fuel that permeates every crevice in their dark and dingy
dwellings and scars their lungs. I am beset with the feeling this is
what they deserve for what they did to my family. This desire for
vengeance is a part of me I am not proud of, but I want to reflect
and forgive myself for considering such horrible thoughts.

I am faced with the reality of clean streets, fertile fields, rolling
green countryside, well-kept farms and orchards, and people
glowing with health from the chemical-free foods they eat. Every
home we pass is being refurbished with new windows, fancy doors
festooned with decorative hardware, awnings, and shutters. Solar
panels rest on top of newly stuccoed houses and satellite dishes dot
the skyline even in the most remote rural areas. The autobahn is
crowded with fast expensive cars that pass our bus as if we are
standing still. Germany is prosperous and verdant.

The young girls on the Kurfürstendamm in Berlin might as well
be strolling in Paris or Milan. Their mini frocks barely cover their
beautiful bodies, so stylish as they teeter on the highest heels,
laughing as they window-shop the most expensive stores. I am
surprised to see Cartier, Gucci, Prada lining the sidewalks,
surrounded by outdoor cafes where the tables are filled not with
tourists but with natives enjoying a cappuccino or a wurst in the
dazzling summer sun. Around the corner from all this glamour, just
steps away, is a monument to the resistance heroes of World War II,
those who fought against the policies of the Third Reich from
within the country. No one in the cafes seems to notice. Only my
group of American teachers stops to photograph it before we move
on to the next memorial. We are not here to shop or enjoy the
afternoon warmth. Our mission is remembrance, not the casual

amnesia that a languid afternoon sitting in a café promotes. We are marked by an aura that says we are not your ordinary tourists. Perhaps it is our notebooks that give us away as we scribble references to each monument and plaque we visit. The natives pass us quickly, averting their eyes. We remind them of what they have been working to forget for the past seventy years.

I am in Germany facilitating a program that brings American secondary teachers to Europe to study about the Holocaust. The 35 members of the group have been carefully selected from among hundreds of applicants. They will spend more than two weeks together touring the actual sites of this dreadful history, with the expectation that it will change the way they teach. The trip is funded by the American Gathering of Jewish Holocaust Survivors and Their Descendants, and I work for them as a curriculum consultant and seminar leader. This is not my first time in Germany, but it still has the power to upset me. All day long I have struggled to keep my own emotions in check as I am confronted with a place I have been taught to fear.

In the evening, after a long day getting on and off the bus and a dinner of stewed beef and potatoes much too heavy for the torrid July, we debrief in a room the hotel has assigned us. I imagine this room usually holds engagement parties or important business dinners where potential partnerships are formed and victories are celebrated, but tonight and for all the nights we are in Berlin there will be no frolicking here. I am mindful that the teachers must get a few hours off or they will be useless the next day. I watch the setting sun through the panoramic windows and promise myself I will release them in time to grab a beer and sample the night life for which Berlin is so famous. But for now, we sit in a circle and talk about what we have seen.

"What will you tell your students about Berlin?" I ask and wait for responses. "We have seen so many things today. What stood out?"

The teachers look at one another, each one hoping someone else will break the silence and offer an answer to satisfy me, showing they have been paying attention, that they have absorbed the contradictions between then and now.

One of the men in the group says. "The memorial to the murdered Roma and Sinti (gypsies) was very beautiful. The setting in the park, the way that one flower rises on that pedestal out of the pond is quite effective. And I liked the panels that explained the history of how the Nazis treated the gypsies. Those panels were beautiful. They did a good job."

"Who is 'they,'" I ask. "Was the memorial put there by the government?" No one answers. "That's the kind of thing you need to notice. Make sure you can distinguish between private and public memorials. Who funded the memorial and how did it come to be placed in this particular spot? Is this an act of contrition by the German government or a private commemoration by a particular group? Is it an accident the Roma and Sinti memorial is so close to the Bundestag? And when was it erected? In our travels, we will see monuments from different eras. Not only will they look different, but they will identify the victims in different ways. In what was once East Germany, how are the victims labeled? Be aware, because it makes a difference. Always ask yourself, where and when and how? By whom?"

"Why the gypsies? Why did the Nazis despise the gypsies?" One of the middle school teachers from Ohio asks. We talk for a bit about the history. Heads go down as they write. Some of them have used up half of their notebooks and it is only day four.

"And what about the memorial to the homosexuals? A black booth with a peephole! Is that supposed to show remorse or just disapproval, then and still?" This from one of the gay men in the seminar. Is it just coincidence four gay men have applied and been accepted to the seminar this year? How will their presence, half of the eight men in the group, affect what we see and how we parse it? "You look inside and see a film of men kissing each other. What was that supposed to be about?" Eyes meet each other across the circle and then turn to me, looking for answers. I am not going to respond unless I must. I will wait to hear how this memorial has been interpreted.

"And the area around it was filled with litter. Candy wrappers and cigarette butts! Disgusting!" This from a modest midwestern woman who could not bring herself to investigate the peephole and had stood off to the side watching as others stepped up. She does not condone homosexuality, and she feels strongly about littering.

"Why the gays?"

"Was Hitler secretly gay?"

"Was it all about self-hate?"

I wait again, hoping the conversation will broaden. It always does; it just takes a while. We are new to each other, these teachers and I, and it is only our second day in Germany. We have only been to one actual site, Bergen Belsen, but we arrived too late to the hotel last night to have our debrief. Today was a focus on memorials. Germany is filled with them. As it should be.

"Who put up that memorial? Where is it placed and why?" I realize they need a push. "The memorial is in the park where gay men would meet," I say. "They were hiding from the police. The black booth represents the public toilets. Does the memorial make you think about the experience of those who were persecuted? That's the issue, does it make you *think*?" I am lecturing reluctantly, but I can't let this teachable moment go by.

Berlin is now a city with an openly gay mayor. It is known for its acceptance of LGBTQ+ people. Yet, the memorial is hidden within in the park. No one is satisfied with the booth or its location. There is animosity brewing between those who are gay and those who are troubled by their existence. We are in a transitional era when acceptance of homosexuality has become more commonplace, but there are still those who cannot abide it.

The topic everyone is avoiding is the Memorial to the Murdered Jews of Europe. A square city block of the most expensive Berlin real estate, filled with stone cubes of varying heights. It has become a playground for Berlin youth, a place to play hide and seek, to jump from one stone to another, to lie in the sun atop one of the cubes, to make love in the dark. Underneath the memorial is a museum detailing the history and destruction of Europe's Jews, which most visitors never visit. The few signs at each of the four corners explaining the memorial are ignored, for the most part, as passersby search for a cold drink and some shade at the cafes facing the square on one side or escape into the greenery of the park fronting it on the other. Some people are more intrigued to follow the signs to the bunker where Hitler committed suicide. It's safer to look at that than to confront this memorial to six million dead.

"That design won a *contest*?" A teacher from New York voices her disdain. "What are those cubes supposed to represent? Are they gravestones? Is that what we are? The only good Jew is a dead Jew! Let's have a whole city block in the center of Berlin filled with Jewish gravestones. No live Jews here, just dead ones."

No one asks, "Why the Jews?" No one questions that. They seem to accept that Jews were the appropriate victims, that Jews have always been the objects of ridicule, of suspicion, of hatred, not worthy of life. I want to scream, but I hold my tongue, waiting for the right moment, when their own feelings burst out of them, when they have seen enough to make them disgusted and angry. They are not there yet. We still have other questions to ponder. We will get to it, if not today, then on another day.

"We saw a lot of monuments today. I can't make sense of any of it." A young teacher from California begins to weep quietly. "I felt like crying at each one of them, even the ones to the good people, the rescuers, the ones on the right side."

"Not me," says an older man from Washington, D.C. "Am I gonna cry at a monument that I think is disrespectful? Or one I can't even make sense of? Have they no idea of what the world thinks of them? Of what they did? Of how many people died to defeat them?" Ah, one of the classic American points of view—our boys were sacrificed to a war we had no reason to be fighting. It was a European problem, not an American one. How many people in the group still have that opinion? He is the oldest participant. Perhaps his father was in World War II? The rest might as well be studying ancient history; anything that happened before 1960 is like the Peloponnesian Wars for them.

Here it comes, I think. The opening to the question: what constitutes the appropriate reaction to the Holocaust from the government that was the perpetrator of it? What can the Germans do to show their remorse? How can they atone for what they did to the world? Will anything they do ever be right? Will anything ever be enough? The richest country in Europe, Germany can now throw money at its problems, but the stigma cannot be washed away with cash. The discussion on this night produces more heat than light. The teachers don't know each other well enough to be able to share their true feelings. Caution tempers their words, but some lash out—at Germany, at antisemitism, at intolerance in general.

"What is the best way to commemorate what happened? How can a country prove it is truly sorry for what it has done?" I ask. The question hangs in the air.

"Okay, think more about what you have seen. Tomorrow is another day—a long day. We're headed to Ravensbrueck, a camp that was primarily for women prisoners of the Reich. Read the selections I prepared for you to be ready. Our guide is a historian of the camp. He expects good questions from you."

I watch as they file out; some of them are looking for some nightlife to clear their minds, but most will go back to their rooms. They may want to connect with their families or write in their journals. They are learning that this is not a pleasure cruise; it may also be more than what they had bargained for.

I head back to my own room and hope that I can fall asleep. I will need to be rested to face the following day. My mother told me that Ravensbrueck, the destination on the death march from Poland to Germany, was worse than Auschwitz, if that can be imagined. There was no food at all, there was no work. It was the end of the war. The Nazis were losing, and the more prisoners who died, the fewer witnesses were left to testify to the atrocities they had suffered. She and Basha, the woman who would become my aunt, shared a piece of wood as a bed board. They secreted it inside their clothing. One slept while the other kept watch, lest someone steal the only protection they had from sleeping directly on the frozen ground.

What will I feel when I see this place? At what point will I share my mother's story? I try to bargain with myself for some sleep. If I can fall asleep now, I will have six hours before I must wake up. I stare at the ceiling, waiting for the wake-up call that arrives with typical German precision at 5:45 a.m.

Ravensbrueck sits on a scenic lake across from the town of Furstenberg. The contrast between the two locations could not be more dramatic, a picture postcard spot with a church steeple rising above the red tiled roofs, a concentration camp with a crematorium that the Furstenberg residents swore they thought was a chimney for a bakery. The fact that many of the residents worked at the camp, even vied for prized positions there as guards or attendants, contradicted the lies they hoped would exonerate them from the horrors they had perpetrated. When I finally see it, I feel almost dazed, wandering from the exhibits inside the cement block prison cells to the grounds. There is very little left of the original structures, but my imagination reconstructs every building and its purpose and peoples every corner with the specters of skeletal women and children. My mother was only eighteen when she was here, standing in this same place, clinging to life.

I hate everyone is what I think. It is an unreasonable but emotionally satisfying feeling to have at this moment. I sit on the steps of the crematorium and let the tears come. I don't care who sees. How much of who my mother became was generated here? How much of who I became?

Instead of the historian we were promised, we are met by a young woman who will be our guide. She has brought with her pieces of testimony from prisoners, highlighting each spot we stand on with the words of someone who experienced this place in its most active state. The teachers are mesmerized by the words of the witnesses. They are tearful. They are angry. They stare at the town across the lake and mutter under their breath. *Good*, I think. This is what should happen. We are not at a pretty memorial in the park. We are on a trip to hell.

The comments start when we board the bus back to the hotel. Some time goes by as the horror sinks in. And then the questions begin.

"How could they *do* such things?"

"How can human beings hurt others like that?"

"They were monsters."

"No!" I say from the front seat of the bus, grabbing the microphone away from our guide. "If we think of them as monsters, then we let them off the hook, we let *us* off the hook. They were *people*, just like us. *People* did this. Not monsters, not aliens from outer space, not some other creatures. *Us!*"

Silence and shame follow. We stare out the window as we roll through the countryside, doing what we can to come to terms with what we have seen. It is, of course, an impossible task.

We stop for lunch before our next site visit where I will spend the time looking at the locals, wondering how many of them are descended from Nazis. It is a masochistic pleasure I have adopted on my visits to Germany. I can't stop myself from imagining each person that passes in full Nazi regalia. I want to ask, "What did your *oma* and *opa* (grandma and grandpa) do during the war?" But what they will answer is what Oma and Opa told them: that they saved people, that they hid people, that it was others, not them. If all this saving and hiding was going on, how did six million Jews die?

The debrief that evening is contentious. The anger infects all of us.

"I couldn't believe the beauty of the lake and the horror of the camp. Heaven and hell," says one of the middle school teachers. "That place might be too terrible to even tell my students about."

"That's a decision you will have to make for yourself," I say. "Only you will know what is right for your classroom. My purpose is to show you everything, with nothing held back." I watch as this thought enters each of their minds.

"I want my students to know the facts. I especially want them to know that that place was a training ground for guards. And the commandant's house was right there. His family lived with him! Children growing up in the midst of that, witnessing that cruelty. What kind of parents would allow their children to see that?" Disgust twists the faces of those who are raising their own children as they contemplate this reality.

"Why did Ravensbrueck affect you this way?" I ask. "You spent your first day in Germany at Bergen Belsen. You were sad, but not angry. Why the anger this evening?"

One of the younger teachers, just married, looks up from her notes. "It's been building. The anger, I mean. At Bergen Belsen there was a kind of serenity. It was all green and felt a bit like a park. Only occasionally was there a mound with a stone wall that said there were people buried there, but you had to imagine the place as it might have been. Ravensbrueck had actual prison cells. And the town across the lake! Belsen was in the middle of nowhere. Not so today. The people *had* to smell the burning skin and hair from Ravensbrueck. There is no pretending about what happened there, either then or now."

Others nod in agreement. Though many more died at Bergen Belsen, this second camp has disturbed them deeply. Even the mock graves of Anne Frank and sister Margot at Belsen, a ploy I find in remarkably bad taste given how many others died there, but which are often the focus of much photography and admiration, did not elicit the emotion that is on display this evening. At Belsen we spent time with German teachers talking about how they portray the Holocaust to their students. Germany is no longer the monocultural society it had once been. Immigrants, particularly Muslims fleeing poverty and oppression, believed that Germany would provide them with safe haven in a largely antagonistic Europe. These immigrants have no connection to the events of the Holocaust and teaching them about German history presents the teachers with an interesting set of problems, complicated by the rising tide of nationalism and support for closed borders that newcomers are facing. Is another Reich rising as neo-Nazis win elections promoting isolationism and targeting "others"? Is another rising in America, too?

"At Belsen, we thought about teaching more. Today I thought about people more," an anxious young woman from Texas adds. "Maybe because it was mostly women prisoners. I imagined myself having to exist there. The torture those women endured, the cruelty of the women guards. I had never thought about women as perpetrators. But they certainly were."

The hour grows later. We are all weary. "Go get some rest. There is a lot to take in tomorrow. And remember, your suitcases must be on the bus when we leave the hotel because we will go directly to the airport for our flight to Poland in the afternoon. We are not coming back here." That idea is met with palpable relief.

I think about the piles of worn and battered suitcases they will see in a few days when we reach Auschwitz. Some made of leather with brass hinges and fancy handles, others made of cardboard now rotting after almost eighty years, despite the conservation attempts to maintain them. The suitcases that were labeled with the names and hometowns of their owners, suitcases that will reach their destination but never again be in the hands of those to whom they belonged. Each suitcase will be pillaged for its contents, and everything that is stolen will be sent back to Germany. I go to my room and look at what I have packed. What if I never saw any of it again? What is in there I couldn't live without? I am ashamed of my "necessities," the bulging suitcase I can barely lift. Things can be replaced, people cannot.

The next day we are at Sachsenhausen. This is the first time we see the infamous *Arbeit macht frei* ("Work will set you free") sign that we will encounter again at Auschwitz. The death toll here is greater than at Ravensbrueck, not specifically Jews, more Soviet POW's and political prisoners. Are we engaging in some cruel kind of arithmetic, counting the dead and measuring the hatred by statistics? More of this group dead, less of that one. I shudder at how the numbers can so easily replace the faces, obscure the fact that each statistic was someone's mother, sister, father, brother, child. Stop the counting and focus on what happened to one person, then multiply by millions—a horrific kind of algebra.

The mood today is somber; the teachers are prepared to face the mounting evidence of Nazi guilt. This time, the camp sits right in the town. There is no lake to buffer reality. Our guides are relentless in relaying statistics and stories. There is no escaping what went on here, and there is no denying that the surrounding populace was complicit. This will be the pattern for all the places we will visit next, other than Treblinka. That place will be deep in the woods of Poland. The locals will spend years after the war coming from their farms and villages, unearthing gold teeth and other valuables that may have been hidden inside the body cavities of the Jews who were killed upon arrival there. These Polish peasants will mine the spot with little regard for how the riches got there. No slave labor ever at that death camp, no sham of possible survival, just a train that brings its victims to the slaughterhouse and leaves behind bits for the scavengers to pick through.

But today, Sachsenhausen does not disappoint. We are witness to the daily sadistic practices of the SS at each stop of the tour, the dehumanization that made it easier to kill those imprisoned. Even the executions are done with the utmost cruelty, wringing every bit of humanity out of both guard and victim. High walls loom over us on one side. When we leave, I realize that there are houses built right next to the camp, abutting this wall. What kind of people live next door to a concentration camp? I will ask this question of the teachers again at Majdanek and at Auschwitz-Birkenau. The children's swing set that is just steps away from that death camp is forever emblazoned in my mind. From their back window this family can see the infamous gate into Birkenau. What do they tell their children about the place next door?

Sometimes we see people walking their dogs through a former concentration camp, or children joyfully riding their bikes, oblivious to where they are. Are they wrong to do that, or am I wrong to judge? For me, this is sacred ground, but not everyone feels that way. My shock at the casual acceptance of these places, the ability to live with them amid the mundane, is something I don't have to lecture the teachers about. They come to it on their own and are horrified at the nonchalance with which people ignore the past and desecrate the resting places of the dead.

We leave Germany and land in Krakow. The beautiful university town was not destroyed during the war. Its central square, the amber market, the horse drawn carriages, the puppeteers and street musicians combine to make us forget why we are here. Almost. It would be easy to sit in a café and people-watch, to hear the different languages being spoken at the tables around the square, to spy a student reading *I Know Why the Caged Bird Sings* and strike up a conversation in English. I could let myself relax, have a time out, but the schedule demands we cram each day with the murderous, blood-stained past. We are in Auschwitz territory, only an hour away by bus. There are signs around the square advertising tourist trips to the camp. You can go there or go to the salt mines. I wonder how I, if I were a normal tourist, would want to spend my day.

We eat pierogies at a tiny mom-and-pop restaurant that can barely hold our small group. My father adored pierogies. My uncle often regaled me with a story about how my father once ate twenty-four potato pierogies in one sitting! He was so stuffed that he fell asleep, fell off the bed, and was found underneath it in the morning, unaware that he had spent most of the night on the floor in carbohydrate coma. I love that story of my dad as a boy, before the beginning of the end, before everything changed, when everyone in their family was still alive.

Auschwitz awaits us the next morning. It is everything that I fear and despise. My mother hates that I come here. She would never return to Poland, never want to see this place. For her, it represents only suffering and death. For me, it represents mourning and a kind of revenge. You may have killed most of us, but not all. I am here despite your brutal plans.

The first part of the day is spent in the army barracks which have been converted to museum blocks, each building representing one aspect of what happened here. I have been here before, but I never lose the anxiety that comes with each visit. It twists my insides with the same intensity each time. I have been here in blazing sun, and I have been here in rain so strong that the mud traps our feet and our soaked jeans grow in length and weight as the day goes on. I prefer the rain because I want the teachers to get a glimpse, albeit small of how physically miserable this place was. I know it can never ever approach what the victims experienced, but I want visitors to have a sense of both the harshness of the climate and the vulnerability of those imprisoned there.

Mom once told me that every blade of grass that grew here was quickly eaten by the starving inmates. There are flowers growing now, and thick, dark green grass. Everything is tidy. There are souvenirs to purchase and a cafeteria where you can slake your thirst and feed your hunger. The parking lot is filled with tour buses, and the lines are long for each exhibit. Auschwitz is a success. Poland has turned its shame into an attraction. How easy to pretend that you did not abet the perpetrators, that you were victims of the Nazis, that you wept for your murdered Jews. That you didn't turn them in for a kilo of sugar. That was someone else. You didn't ransack their houses after they were deported, wrapping yourself in their clothes, using their Sabbath candlesticks to light your tables at Christmas and Easter, their gravestones to pave your dirt roads. Pretend you miss the Jews, especially when you sell those caricatures of them in the market, the ones in the traditional Chasidic dress with the cartoonish noses, holding a penny to bring you good luck. Jews were always about money. Everyone knows that.

The Past is Always Present: Part 2

I don't know if my crying makes me angry or if my anger makes me cry. I walk through Birkenau with tears that are always at the ready. I wonder if I am walking the same path to the gas chambers that my grandmother and her young son and baby daughter walked in 1943. I talk to myself, each step a word of encouragement laced with anger, "You can do this. You must do this. They didn't succeed in killing all your family. Your mother survived and now you are here." I remember that my father once placed a notice in a journal published by my mother's hometown memorial committee where he called them Nazi "basterds," misspelling the word. No one at the printers caught the error. I was only nine or ten when I saw the printed page but even then, I knew the word was misspelled. I wondered though, if it was a different word, a word I had not learned yet, a word that was even worse than bastard, a word coined to describe people who murder other people's children. If so, then yes, basterds.

The teachers from the seminar are perusing the ruins of the gas chamber and crematorium, looking closely at the huge chunks of concrete that testify to the explosion that almost succeeded in disguising its nefarious intent. It was destroyed before the camp was abandoned in another attempt to hide the evidence. They walk around it, snapping photos with their cameras. I have spoken to them about hiding behind their cameras, forsaking or denying the emotion for the photo op, distancing themselves through a lens. What is the compulsion that makes people want to take a picture of everything?

"When you show this to your students will it look like anything more than a pile of broken cement? Will you be able to tell them what you *felt* when you saw it? I doubt it, if you have spent your time looking for the best angle for each shot. I have seen too many of our participants attempting to achieve the art house photo of the dandelions with the barbed wire, ignoring the guide whose information will illuminate the moment." Some have heard me, others cannot stop themselves. They are addicted to the visual, and only a photo will suffice.

I cannot look at the remains of the broken girders and rubble. I have stopped instead at a shallow pond of black water that holds the ashes of those cremated after being gassed. There are more than one of these ponds on the grounds, but this one is identified with signs and small tombstones have been placed beside it, each inscribed in a different language offering explanations of what the visitor is seeing. Perhaps my family's ashes are here. I will never know. I say the *kaddish (a prayer of mourning)* silently, lost in my mourning. Some of the teachers stand near me and one puts her hand on my shoulder. I am not sure if I want sympathy or if I want to infect everyone with the rage that is pulsing through me. What would make me feel better—if everyone cried or if everyone howled at the sky? Keep it to yourself for now, I counsel myself. They must come to the anger on their own. It happened that way in Germany when this group visited the camps, and it will happen here, perhaps with even more fervency.

The trip is filled with opportunities to hate the Nazis and to wonder about the ability of humans to devise and carry out unfathomable evil. My anger shapes and reshapes itself by the hour. Do I hate the Nazis more than the Poles? How can I measure? Who was worse, the SS who did not know my family when they killed them or the years-long neighbors who watched as they were taken away? The anonymous political prisoner who beats another to save her own life, or the girl from one's hometown who hoards her food as she watches her childhood classmates starve in the barracks. I don't know how to do this math, where to divide, where to multiply my disappointment and hatred. Depending on the moment, I experience animosity for an entire nation or dismay at the desertion and betrayal by an individual. I caution myself not to blame the victims. Whatever they did under these circumstances is forgivable, in my opinion. This place, all these places, forced the victims into choiceless choices. No rules apply for them. Not so for the perpetrators, the collaborators or the bystanders. There is no judgement or punishment harsh enough.

Walk away for a moment and clear your mind, I tell myself. Auschwitz always leaves me headachy and breathless. It will be hours before I can see clearly again.

At Belzec where my paternal grandmother and her three children were killed, I am stunned by a host of butterflies that arrive as if from nowhere. They alight on the wildflowers that eke out an existence between the stones covering the killing ground so thoroughly it seems impossible that there can be enough soil to allow a living thing to flourish. Even in the foulest places, nature recovers. Will I do the same? A butterfly lands on my jacket, then flits onto the jackets of the women who have come with me to say a special prayer for my family and for all the mothers who died alongside their children in this place.

I think back now to the moment when my father told me I looked like his mother. It was just one time that he said it, and I can remember the feeling of warmth spreading through me, my blood coursing as if it felt the connection, as if it had been repurposed that day to honor my grandmother, to sustain a granddaughter she never knew. The butterfly refuses to leave us. We watch, transfixed, as it binds us together with its fragile flight, moving from one woman to another, weaving a bond those of us who were there that day will never forget. The butterfly sisterhood to which we now belong is a symbol of what we experienced. When we tell the story at the evening debrief, the men are unhappy to have been excluded from such a magical moment. I understand their jealousy. There has been so much sorrow in the past few days. The butterfly gave us a respite and a moment of wonder. But I explain it as a moment for women, a moment when women acknowledged our ability to nurture life and our inability to protect it against such enormous evil.

The last place we visit in Birkenau is the sauna. It is not a spa, but a place where stolen goods were fumigated before being sent to Germany. One room in this building holds a display of photographs that were found in the suitcases the deportees brought to the transports, thinking they would need the contents at their destination. Such a deception! Now the photographs are a testimony to the lives that people lived before they were the targets of the Nazis. Every possible sort of photo is on display—baby pictures, first days of school, summer vacations, ski trips, piano lessons, picnics, teens with their buddies, sweethearts on their engagement day, and brides and grooms looking into each other's eyes with love and promise. There are family portraits with grandparents seated amid their progeny, graduation pictures in cap and gown, toddlers clutching beloved stuffed animals, Passover seders, birthday parties, and class pictures with teachers standing proudly with their students. A human being treasured and chose to pack each one of these photographs.

These were real people whose lives meant nothing to their torturers and executioners. Someone in these pictures might have gone on to find the cure for cancer, or might have composed the most beautiful symphony or made the most expressive art. And the most ordinary man or woman among them still deserved to live his or her life to its fullest. All of them, *gone*. These images are the evidence of the lives they lived, proof that they once existed, that they loved and were loved.

I spend time with every photo, honoring the lives captured forever in one dimension. We all have photos like these, and most of us would rescue them from a fire or some other disaster. That is exactly what these people thought, only they did not yet know that the whole world was on fire, and that it would burn them whole. Now only their photos can speak for them and tell their silent stories to me across the years. My father had a photo of his mother he concealed in his shoe until almost the end of the war. Somehow, although he has no idea how, he lost it. It broke his heart not to be able to see her face again. And it breaks my heart too. I will never know for myself if I really did look like her, or if it was only my father's wishful thinking that made him think so. I want to believe that it was true.

We have walked the length of Birkenau. We have lit candles and said the Kaddish. Now we must retrace our steps and leave. The vast expanse of the camp lies before us, the outlines of the many barracks now just rectangles of land that suggest the immensity of this place. Only a few structures remain. After so many years weather and time have taken their toll. These poorly built structures were never meant to last but letting them fall into ruin is controversial. Do we still need physical proof of the Nazis' crimes? Do we still need places to visit to believe what they did was real? Yes, I think as I walk out. Because people *don't* believe it, even when the proof is in front of them. If we let the buildings sink and the grass grow over the fields of barracks, will anyone give credence to the testimonies of the survivors?

I walk through the gate and board the bus. All the way back to the hotel I am lost in thought. Each visit to Auschwitz calls up a memory of something different from my childhood. Today, I think about my mother wanting to commit suicide after the death of her sister, how she wanted to throw herself at the electrified fence to end her misery, to end the loneliness that was destroying her sanity. My childish response was, "But Mommy, if you did that, I would never be alive."

"Yes, Mamaleh, but I didn't know you then, did I?"

No, Mom, you didn't know me, and I wonder now if I will ever know you fully. These painful places are my search to find you and, in doing so, myself.

Reunion with A Stranger

The elderly man stood waiting for me at the bottom of the stairs as I descended from the women's balcony of the Nozyk Synagogue in Warsaw. It was a July Shabbat in 1995. Earlier that morning I had shepherded about twenty women into the balcony as we separated from the men in our group who, by virtue of being male, were allowed take seats on the main floor.

I was attending services with that summer's group from the Holocaust and Jewish Resistance Teachers' Program. For fifteen years I was the director of this program that brought American teachers to Europe and Israel to study about the Holocaust with the purpose of dispelling the myth that the Jews went like sheep to the slaughter. 1995 was my first year in that role, and much of what happened each day was startling and disturbing. Today would be a bit different I thought, perhaps a bit of sweetness rather than the endless bitterness I confronted at every place we went.

Although attendance was not mandated, most of the forty teachers had chosen to wake up early and join me on this day off from our usual touring schedule. The majority had never been in a synagogue, much less an Orthodox one that adhered to the principle of separation of men and women during prayers. As the group divided at the door and the women trudged up the narrow steps, I felt a certain nostalgic chill. I hadn't been in this kind of shul since my childhood, and even then, as a little girl, I could still sit with my father. It was only when a girl reached puberty that she was relegated to the balcony.

This separation of men from women is an important precept of Jewish orthodoxy. It helps ensure that the focus is on prayer and not on the opposite gender. Orthodox Jews believe women and men are very different beings—that they are not only physically different, but that they have different thought processes and emotions. This is because women's souls are believed to be different from men's and to come from complementary but opposite sources. The prayer experience is an opportunity to be with your true self, to communicate with your soul. Men and women need space from each other to help them become one with their higher selves. Though I was not Orthodox, I had told the women in the group that we would be sitting in the balcony and that they would be somewhat removed from the action on the floor below. I didn't like the separation, but I had learned to accept it out of respect for those who believed.

There were four hundred Jewish houses of prayer in Warsaw before the Holocaust. These served 350,000 Jews, which was one third of the entire population of the city. The Nozyk synagogue is the only surviving Jewish house of worship in post-war Warsaw. Those numbers tell the story of the destruction of everything Jewish in the city, which is why it was so important for the teachers to visit this place on a Shabbat, to celebrate life after having seen so much death.

The synagogue must have been quite grand when it was built, but during the occupation, the Nazis had used it as a stable, defiling every holy aspect of the place that they could. After it was almost destroyed during a bombing, donations from Jews all over the world helped to rebuild and restore it so it could be used for services, which began again in 1983. But the building no longer gleamed with the sacred objects of silver and gold that had once decorated the bimah and the ark where the Torah scrolls were held. Still, its tall, stained-glass windows refracted the light into tessellated patterns on the floor of the sanctified space.

Now, as one of the few in my group who could read Hebrew or who had any familiarity with the order of the Sabbath service, I tried to orient the women, using the mismatched prayerbooks that were available, most of them lacking the accompanying English page that partnered each Hebrew page in the *siddurim* (prayer books) I knew. We fumbled along, searching for the right prayers, but mostly we peeked over the balcony wall to observe the men on the main floor of the sanctuary, just as women have done for a thousand years.

The men from our group were being helped by other Americans who were sightseeing in Warsaw and had come to experience Shabbat services in Poland. They were given skullcaps and those few who were Jews donned *tallesim* (prayer shawls). In the corners of the shul by the tall windows stood a few more devout supplicants who had pulled the *tallesim* over their heads to establish a private prayer space, a practice I had only seen in old photos or in artistic interpretations. It was as if this place had one foot in the past and one in the present, depending upon where you chose to look, whether it was up at the segregated balcony of women, or down at the tourists in short-sleeved shirts, or into the corners where those immersed in their prayers stood in the same postures as their ancestors had done for generations.

The women in the balcony buzzed with subdued conversation, gesturing toward the men on the ground floor and looking around in a kind of bewildered curiosity. There was no attempt by the rabbi to connect with those in the balcony as there might have been in a less orthodox synagogue in the States. I was beset with fear at the prospect of being in Poland, as I thought of it as the belly of the beast. That had been my first time visiting the places whose names my family had indelibly marked on my heart, and I was doing my best to maintain a professional demeanor as I led the group into a darkness that almost paralyzed me. A trip to the synagogue that morning was a reprieve. There was nothing here but a variation of what I already knew. Or so I thought.

A woman seated next to me whispered in my ear that an elderly man seated on the main floor was staring up at us with great intensity. I thought he was looking at her, but she insisted he was looking at me.

"Pay attention to the service," I whispered back. "We're setting a bad example with all this yakking. What will the *goyim* (non-Jews) think?"

"I'm not wrong," she insisted. "He is staring right at you. Do you know him? Does he look familiar?"

I stared back brazenly, thinking that a modest woman would never have done this even a generation ago. But rather than deter him, my gaze seemed to encourage him. He continued to look straight at me. As the service ended, he motioned with a nod towards the door, indicating that he would wait for me there.

I had never seen this man before, although he looked like so many of the men I had grown up with. He fit right in with my parents' friends and the few relatives we had left. He was stocky but not tall, and it was clear that in his youth he had been quite strong. But now, as a man in what was likely his late seventies, the outline had stayed but the muscles had withered. His skin showed signs of time in the sun, and I wondered if perhaps he was a friend of my parents from Florida who had seen a picture of me in their apartment there. Maybe he was from Israel and knew my mother's cousin. I made these assessments and assumptions in the few seconds that my eyes spent adjusting to the bright sunlight of the courtyard where we now found ourselves.

He asked if I spoke Hebrew, to which I shook my head *no*. He offered Spanish, I offered English, to which he shook his head. We settled on Yiddish, and he smiled at our agreement, amazed that a woman of my generation could not only understand but could speak to him in his first language. His name was Moshe, he said. He was a Holocaust survivor, which had been immediately obvious to me because of the number I could see under the short sleeve of his shirt. He asked my name and, realizing that it was my family he was trying to ascertain, I answered "Freilich," which is my maiden name. The answer did not elicit any positive response, and he went on to tell me why he was looking at me with such interest.

"*Ich bin fun Pruzana, fun Poleyn.*" (I am from Pruzana, from Poland). He offered this as a possible connection.

"*Vart a minute. Mein Mama is fun Pruzana. Sie hut geven Dvera Golubowicz, tochter fun Itzhak and Chava Golubowicz.*" (Wait a minute. My mother is from Pruzana. She was Dora Golubowicz, daughter of Itzhak and Chava Golubowicz).

He smiled and nodded. This was the connection he had been hoping for.

"*Dein Mama is de shvester fun Fradel. Ich chub yir geliebt. Dein punim iz yir punim. Ich chob dir gezen und ich chub gechollemt as Fradel zitst in galleria.*" (Your mother is the sister of Fradel. I loved her. Your face is her face. I saw you and thought I was dreaming that Fradel was sitting in the balcony). Now his expression was one of both delight and heartbreak.

I had been told many times that I looked like my mother's sister. We were both pale- skinned with dark hair and blue eyes. My mother's coloring was entirely different. That Moshe had recognized Fradel's looks in my face was astonishing.

"*Zie is gestorben in Auschwitz. Mein mama is de ein in eintzege fun de familia.*" (She died in Auschwitz. My mother is the only one left from the family.) As I said this, I noticed he cast his eyes downward. It was not the news he had hoped to hear, but it was not a surprise either.

"*Ich chob gegangen tzu Argentina noch de milchama. Yetzt cum ich tzurik aff a reize tzu Poleyn in mein eltere yoren.* (I went to Argentina after the war. Now I have returned to Poland on a trip in my old age.) This explained the Spanish and the suntan.

"*Ich vil clingen mein Mama heint benacht and dartzellen yir vus hut geshen.*" (I will call my mother this evening and tell her what has occurred.) I knew my mother too would be overcome with a mixture of joy and sadness. Someone remembered her sister, someone had known and loved her.

"*Zug yir as ich chob geliebt yir shvester. Zug yir as a grosse nes hut heint geshayn.*" (Tell her that I loved her sister. Tell her that a great miracle happened today.) He looked at me directly, charging me with this important task. He took my hand and kissed it, then turned and walked away. No attempt at exchanging numbers, no further contact requested. I looked at the other teachers and some of the women had tears in their eyes. Without understanding Yiddish, they had pieced together that something amazing was taking place. We were no longer in the realm of six million nameless, faceless dead. We had just put a face and a name on that destruction. My mother's sister, the girl who would have been my Aunt Fradel, was suddenly made real to them. She was a girl who had lived a life. And that life had been taken away from her and from those who had known her.

That night, in a phone call across many miles, I told my mother what had happened. She could not remember this Moshe and I had never asked his last name, so she had little to go on. She told me her sister had had many suitors, which made me smile. Was my mother bragging or had Fradel been the kind of girl who caught the eye of more than just Moshe? It might be that this Moshe had been a schoolmate, or simply someone who had loved her sister from afar. It didn't matter. What happened was still a miracle. So many *what ifs* went through my mind as I lay in my hotel bed that night. In one of the only photos we had of her she was about eight and not yet old enough to attract a boy's attention. I wondered what she looked like as a teen, what hopes and dreams she had had for the future. The soft hum of the traffic outside my window played background music to my thoughts as I tried to picture that eight-year-old as the object of Moshe's affection.

As I began to fall asleep, I marveled again how this Moshe and I could both be in the synagogue on the same Shabbat. What if Moshe had never glanced up? What if I had never looked down or had ignored his gaze? That this man, who was targeted for destruction and had miraculously survived, had met a woman who might never have been born had her mother not also survived, was bashert. And so, the story goes on

Dora's and Bernie's Life Lessons

Mom: Don't tell me what someone else's mother said! I don't care what other people are allowed to do. If they jump off the roof, will you do that too? Some mothers let their children do anything they like. In my house, you will do what I think is right.

Dad: Life is not a bowl of cherries!

Mom: Stand closer to the sink when you wash the dishes. Put your arms in the water. You are getting the floor wet because you stand too far back. Dishwashing is not poison, get closer!

Dad: You can love a rich boy just as easily as a poor one. (Self-explanatory.)

Mom: Stand up straight. You will be permanently hunched over if you don't listen to me. (Whacks me on the back as she says this. I was sure that I would have a permanent black and blue mark from the daily whacks).

Dad: You should never let anyone know how much you earn. Don't show off your money by buying expensive things. If I drove a Cadillac my customers would think I was charging too much for the shoes. They don't need to know how much I have.

Mom: Stop wearing your glasses all the time. Your eyes are just getting weaker from them. No one will marry a girl with big heavy glasses. Make your eyes strong by exercising them. And don't read so much! Who needs to know so much!

Dad: Be a teacher. You'll be home by 3:30, you'll have the summers off, and you won't work that hard. It's a good job for a girl.

Mom: You must wear a padded bra. You are too tall and thin, and your clothes do not hang correctly. Don't come out of your room until you put on the bra I bought for you. (The bra is a 34 C. I try to explain that you can't go from nothing to a 34C in one day, but she does not want to hear it. I wear the bra and a very loose sweater to hide the "sudden growth spurt").

Dad: Don't trust anyone. No one is here to do you favors. There is always a motive. If it seems too good to be true, it is. Foolish American children don't understand this. You have no idea what the world is like. You think everyone is nice. No one is nice.

Mom: Go out on practice dates. If a boy asks you out, even if you don't like him, go out so you can learn how to act on a date.

Dad: Don't sign anything. Never put your name on anything like a petition. They can change the top of the paper and then you have signed something against the government, and they will come for you. I don't want to tell you this more than once. Watch out!

Mom: Don't talk back! Don't argue with me! I am the mother, not your friend. If my mother would have lived, I would have kissed her hands every day and thanked her for her words of advice. You are disrespectful. God will pay you back. I hope He gives you a child who talks to you like you talk to me.

Dad: Stop fighting with your mother. She is trying her best. (Really?)

Mom: I expect you to call me the minute you come home from school. I need to know where you are. I want to hear from you if you are going to stop at someone's house on the way home from school. I don't care if your friends don't have to check in; so what if their parents don't care where they are! Your parents care!

Mom: Say hello to everyone in the room. Greet each elder personally with a kiss and by name. Don't just yell "hi" from the other room or pass by and wave. Show respect. (Once in a fevered dementia brought on by a urinary tract infection, she insisted I say hello to people in the hospital room that only she could see. There was no arguing with her even in her weakened state).

Mom: Go ask your father what he thinks. You won't listen to me anyway. (If I play my cards right, I can get Dad to agree, but different tactics will be necessary with him).

Dad: You are killing your mother!

Mom: You are killing your father!

Elaine: Then we can have a double funeral and only sit shiva for one week! Call Goldstein's!

Mom and Dad: Such a mouth! Only in America! In Yiddish: Ich gib der a patch, klepts zach arein in vant! (I'll smack you so hard you'll stick to the wall!) What did we do to deserve such a disrespectful child?

A Religious Experience

I felt G-d's presence not in a synagogue, as one might have expected, but in a death camp in Poland. There were many serious and sorrowful moments in my travels there, times when I reflected on what I felt about this whole G-d idea. I never could summon His presence when I imagined it should be evident to me. It was not there when we were reciting the Kaddish over the candles we lit at each place we visited, though I sometimes felt a chill come over me during the sonorous chant, causing me to shiver despite the heat of the blazing July sun. It was not there in the gas chamber I entered and then backed out of, afraid to walk through lest I might be stuck there, either emotionally or physically, unable to reach the exit. This was a place where I found myself wondering if G-d could even exist given what I was seeing. His presence was not there as I stood in front of the display of victims' shoes—when I spied the white baby shoe next to the red high heeled sandal and wondered if their owners had arrived there at the same time and if they were related. It wasn't there even as I stood by the window of the room filled with hair from victims of Auschwitz, fixating on one set of dark braids that I hoped was not the hair of my mother or her sister. None of the physical evidence of death and destruction brought me to G-d.

On that morning, I stayed back near the bus as our group of teachers followed our guide and my colleague Stephen down through Majdanek, into and out of the barracks and storerooms, into the "medical" room where tortures were performed, and eventually up to the monument built over the ashes of thousands of victims killed in an autumn "harvest." I had been to this camp many times before and I had nothing to add to the facts and stories that Stephen and Waclaw would relate so well. I needed time alone, time to steel myself for the visit to another camp. We were to go to Belzec the next day, and then on to Auschwitz soon after. I was gathering strength, musing over what I would say to the teachers when they witnessed each of those places, wondering what it would take out of me this time, and expecting the impact of raw emotions I knew was waiting for me. And then something extraordinary startled me out of my self-imposed contemplation.

I found my cellphone in my backpack and called the States. It was 10:30 in the morning in Lublin, Poland, and in my haste, I paid little attention to what time it was in Philadelphia. It was the middle of the night back home, but what I wanted my mother to hear would not wait until morning reached her on the other side of the ocean.

I gazed down at the camp from my perch on the hill, waiting for the phone to connect, watching as a group of Israeli men and women marched in carrying Israeli flags, dressed in full uniform. They stood at attention on the parade ground that had once been the center of Majdanek. At the signal, their voices rose and the sound of Hatikvah floated over the still-standing barracks and gas chamber, buildings that looked like they could be restored to their evil purpose at any moment. These young people, perhaps the grandchildren of Holocaust survivors, were defying the fate that had been planned for their ancestors just by their presence in this terrible place. They stood there, alive and free, proof of the resilience of the Jewish people.

I wanted my mother to hear them. I wanted to share the spiritual exhilaration of that moment with her. She could not see them, but as I held the phone up to get stronger reception, I hoped that she could hear them.

"Mom, do you hear this?"

"Yes, Mamaleh, I hear it. Who are they? Listen to how strong they sound."

"They're from a police battalion. Young men and women. Mom, they are so beautiful in their uniforms, and they are standing so straight and tall, with Israeli flags."

When I put the phone back to my ear, I could hear her singing along, a death camp survivor herself, in the middle of the night in Philadelphia, laughing and crying and singing Hatikvah all at the same time.

"Thank you, Mamaleh."

That is when I knew there was a G-d. I still had issues with Him that would never be resolved, questions that were unanswered, complaints about what He had allowed to take place. Nevertheless, those young lives, defiant in their very existence, made me believe in Him.

The Family Smile

Just by looking at us one could see that I was my mother's daughter. Though our coloring was different, my mother and I shared the same dimples and the same high cheekbones. Though she colored her hair a bright red to mask the gray, she had once been a brunette like me. The few pictures of my mother that were sent to America before the war bore evidence of our similarity. Those survivors from her hometown who had known her as a child would always remark on the resemblance and compared me to my aunt Fradel as well. Even in my adult years people would tell me how much I looked like her. So much so that strangers, like Moshe, who knew her but not me, would tell me that they knew exactly who I was. Later, I saw my mother's face and mine in the face of my niece Emily, my brother's daughter, so it seemed obvious that there was a strong family likeness being passed on. With only one surviving picture of my maternal grandmother, wrapped in a big fur collar that almost covers her face and posing sans smile in a photographer's studio, and no photos of anyone at all on my paternal side, I relied on the perceptions of other people. It was important to me to have a physical connection to someone in the family, to belong to a line of people and to share something with them.

Having read a great deal about the psychology of second-generation Holocaust survivors, I know that we search for connections to those we never knew. Being on the branch of a tree that has been felled is a precarious place to exist. There are serious health implications—I cannot answer the questions doctors often have about diseases that run in the family. When asked what the cause of death was for my grandparents I answer "murder." It stops the health interview abruptly and underlines how little can be predicted about my own physical state. So, we second generation survivors look for any way to relate to the ghosts of our families, even a hint of resemblance attested to by others.

Every day I pass the rows of pictures of my husband's family in our hallway, some dating back to the 1800's. I can see the line of Jim's mouth in many of the people in these frames, the outline of his jaw and nose in some of the men. I am grateful that he can connect to these faces and saddened that there are very few photos where I might find a likeness.

Lately however, when I pass a mirror, I can't help but notice how much I look like my father. I have his blue eyes and his pale skin, but there is something more than that. We share a way of holding our heads on an angle when listening to people, a way of placing a hand under the chin that is particularly distinct. I have found myself covering my mouth with my fingertips the way my dad did when he was thinking through a problem, biting my lip in times of stress. This is not learned behavior, but something intrinsic that I do, unconscious of my pose until I am suddenly very aware of how similar it is to my dad's.

I am startled yet gratified when I notice these similarities. I catch a glimpse of my dad's smile on my face when I am combing my wet hair after a shower. With my hair flat against my head, I am struck by how much I look like him. Why did everyone think I looked like my mother? Were they mistaken? Or is the process of aging one in which we move through stages, resembling each of our parents at different moments along the way.

When I look at pictures of my dad taken in his early twenties, I see the face of my son Joshua. From the time he was born and even to the present, everyone has always seen the strong resemblance he has to Jim, as if I had nothing to do with the genetics that formed my own child. In Josh's first formal portrait taken on his first birthday, he could be mistaken for Jim's twin at the same age. Yet as he matures, I see my father emerging in Josh's face. If I look like my father and Josh looks like my father, does this mean Josh looks like me? And who else might Josh resemble from my side of the family? Those who might have been witnesses are gone, so I have to assume that the genetic dice keep rolling, giving us a different outcome over time. The possibility makes me smile to myself, and I know now that it is my dad's smile.

The "Golden" Rule

Years ago, after dinner was finished and our kitchens were tidy, I enjoyed a regular evening walk with my then neighbor Regina. Despite certain differences in our family geographies, my family from Poland and hers from France, we had both grown up in Holocaust survivor families. That we lived next door to each other was a serendipitous coincidence. The similarities in the way our families had raised us allowed us to share stories and anecdotes without misinterpreting or passing judgement on either our parents or ourselves. We understood each other and empathized with the daily conversations and confrontations that being part of immigrant families who had survived the Holocaust entailed. Our evening walks were a chance to debrief and counsel each other, taking a collective breath and licking our wounds when warranted.

On this evening Regina was waiting for me on the sidewalk. I could see her through my dining room window, lighting a cigarette that illuminated her face in the dusk. I finished with the dinner dishes and met her for our "therapy session." As we walked, she related this anecdote:

Brian, her nine-year-old, had been given a school assignment to write about the Golden Rule. Since Regina and her husband Ronnie were at work and the babysitter was a teenager whom he didn't trust to help him, Brian had called his grandmother to ask what that was. Grandma V had told him the Golden Rule was "Honor your father and mother." When Regina came home, Brian was eager to read his essay to her.

"I almost choked holding back my laughter." Regina smiled as she told me the story. She knew she had the right audience since our parents' interpretations of American life often intersected.

"I asked Brian how he came up with this version of the Golden Rule. That's when he told me he had called my mother for help. Of course, my mother, born in the old country and with definite ideas about what was most important in a child's upbringing, would never think of the Golden Rule as 'Do unto others as you would have them do unto you.' Not on her list of what comes first!"

We roared with laughter in a somewhat rueful outburst that only the two of us could appreciate. I had no doubt if I called my mother at that moment and asked her what the Golden Rule was, she would give me the same response as Mrs. Talis.

If you want to talk about rules, the one that has circumscribed every part of my life is Honor your father and mother. Everything I have done from the time I was born to this very moment has been to honor my father and mother. Every action I have taken, every decision I have made has filtered through the sieve of how it might affect my parents. Would they approve? Would they be proud? Would they understand? Would it bring shame on the family? Though I may not have avoided certain actions or always curbed my desires, and though at times I have forged ahead despite knowing my actions would upset my parents, I cannot remember ever being able to ignore them when making a decision.

I remember once asking my parents to come to school to see me perform in a play. I was in first grade and cast as an elf in *The Shoemaker and the Elves*. I desperately wanted them to be there to see me on stage. But my father had warned me that the only reason he would ever come to school was if I had done something wrong. The expectation was that I would never disgrace the family by doing anything to warrant that.

And he never did come to school, other than when I wanted to transfer out of AP in tenth grade. Knowing that I had made myself sick with worry about my grade in Chemistry, my father agreed to sit down with the principal and advocate for a change. He never saw me in a show, never saw me win an award, never heard praise from my teachers. Praise and doing well were *expected*. By taking care of my schoolwork, I was honoring my father and mother. Transferring out of an honors class was disrespecting their expectations for me, but it took physical illness and a doctor's advice for my parents to realize that this time they had better show up at school and advocate for me.

When I wanted to move out of the house after finishing college and grad school and getting a job to support myself, my parents were baffled, angry, and ashamed. They thought my actions were dishonoring them. What kind of unmarried girl would live on her own? What must I be planning to do that I could not do in my parents' house? What would their friends say? I could not make them understand; the only solution was to leave and to hope they would calm down, that they might eventually understand I did not intend to shine a negative light on them. My actions were my attempt to come into my own and should reflect only on me. But they could not see it that way.

Until they allowed themselves to know him, my parents felt that marrying Jim was the ultimate form of dishonoring of them. It took them a while to realize his qualities and to recognize his devotion to me and to them. He eventually became more a son than a son-in-law in their eyes, but first they had to overcome the feeling that they had lost face in the eyes of their community. I had broken their ultimate Golden Rule, and it took time for them to recover from that.

I can only imagine my parents were raised with the same version of the Golden Rule that they espoused. And do not get me wrong, they understood and respected the *other* version. They even lived by it, but it was not what they found paramount in the way they raised their children. For them, their children were on this earth to honor them. The *do unto others* version, as far as they were concerned, was secondary.

A Living Memorial

Jewish rituals for burial are precise. There can be no funeral on the Shabbat, but the deceased must be buried as quickly as possible, usually within twenty-four hours from the death. It is traditional to guard the body until the burial, to wash the body and dress it in a simple shroud. Most Jews do not include any items that belonged to the deceased in the casket, adhering to the belief that we came into this life without possessions, and so we should leave in the same way. Traditionally, Jews are buried in a casket made of soft wood, sometimes even with holes drilled into the bottom to assist in the decaying process that will return the body to the earth. Jews do not favor cremation, particularly since the Holocaust, but especially because they believe the body should remain in its human form. For a week after the burial, Jews sit shiva to mourn, segregating themselves from daily tasks and accepting food and visits from extended family and friends. They cover the mirrors in the house to avoid focusing on themselves. They allow others to take care of household responsibilities, keeping themselves separate from the mundane. The men refrain from shaving, and everyone prays each evening. None of the prayers are about death or the deceased; rather they are about extolling the name of God to whom we owe thanks for the rhythms of life and death. After sitting shiva, the mourners then "rise up" to begin their lives again. A mourner, a direct relative or spouse of the deceased, says the Kaddish daily for eleven months after the death. Jews visit the grave site and leave small stones to signify their presence atop a tombstone that is erected not at the time of burial, but eleven months from the day of the funeral.

With such a circumscribed set of rituals, what do you do when you are not able to bury the dead properly, when you have not had the chance to sit shiva, and you don't have a cemetery to visit to honor your dead? How do you accomplish this integral part of the obligations of Judaism? My grandparents were all murdered in the Holocaust, as were most of those who would have been my aunts and uncles, had they lived, and so in my early years there were no funerals to attend. Everyone who was left was too young to die. But there was a need to commemorate what had happened to those lost families, and so the Pruzaner Memorial Service for my mother's hometown of Pruzana, organized by the *landsmanschaft* (members of the community), was held at the end of each January in New

York starting in the 1950's. There, my mother would find the remnants of her destroyed community.

The date was specific. The service coincided with the Sunday closest to the three days in 1943 when the town was "liquidated," meaning when the bulk of the population was taken in cattle cars to Auschwitz Birkenau. The attendees were people who had survived the war, either in camps or in hiding, and people who had immigrated to America before the war but still felt a strong connection to their place of birth. During the arrival of the guests, a kind of social atmosphere prevailed. There was always someone who was attending for the first time, and their presence might represent the first sighting of this person since the dissolution of the ghetto in early 1943. The crowd marveled that this new person had in fact survived the war, as if they were witnessing a miracle, as if someone was returning from the dead.

The service was entirely in Yiddish. Survivors from the town would stand and give speeches about what had happened during the last days of Pruzana—how the ghetto had been formed and then emptied, how the *Judenrat* (the Jewish council formed by the Nazis to administer the Jewish community) had operated, who had stood up against the oppressors, and finally, how the deportations had taken place. There were a great many tears shed as the story was told and retold. After my first time there, I knew that my parents would be in a solemn mood once the program began. Even though this was not my father's town, he joined in the community of mourners.

Though not an actual funeral, the memorial service had many aspects of one. There was a recitation of the Mourner's Kaddish, and there was an air of solemnity which led to full-on grief as the service went on. Men wore *kippot* (skullcaps) and everyone was dressed formally; even the children, who were kept outside of the auditorium, wore their best clothes. This was traditional as well; small children were rarely brought to funerals or cemeteries. Perhaps it was superstition that drove this practice of keeping them away from death for as long as possible.

In the first years I attended, I was too young to understand why we were there. The kids stayed in the outer hall, running around, looking for something to do. We only entered the auditorium if we wanted to annoy our parents by asking how much longer the program would take, or by whining that we were hungry. There was never any good resolution to these interruptions, and they were most often met by a threat to *behave or else!* and a promise that there would be an end to the program sooner rather than later.

For a religion with *so* many specifics concerning death, there is very little information about Jewish afterlife. Good deeds are said to be rewarded in the world to come, but there's very little written regarding what that world looks like. Some Jews believe that the soul goes to a paradise. Some Jewish mystics believe in resurrection and even reincarnation. But there are no promises. The bottom line of Judaism is: Do your best while you're alive, and don't worry so much about the rest. Surely these people who suddenly seemed to return to life at this memorial were proof that the dead, or those we believed were dead, might somehow find their way back to us.

When I was about seven, I saw the Shirley Temple movie *Heidi* in which Heidi is separated from her grandfather and then miraculously reunited with him later. I was sure that my grandfather, who had jumped from the train on the way to Auschwitz, would appear at one of these meetings, surprising us all. I was sure he would know me right away because I looked so much like the childhood photos of my mother and her sister. Of course, it never happened, but I had worked out a scenario in my mind that he had seen the advertisement for the event in the *Forward*, and had come to the meeting hall, hoping against hope that someone from his family would be there. I fantasized that he had suffered from amnesia—a common plot element in those early days of television—and that he had just recently regained his memory after all these many years. I wished so strongly for this to happen, and I wonder if that same wish was in my mother's mind as well— the hope for a reunion, a miracle that would restore some small part of all that she had lost.

When I was old enough to stay home and not have to attend these events, I was relieved. I did not want to be reminded of the losses my family had suffered. I did not want to undergo the scrutiny of those who remembered my lost family. I wondered how it made my mother feel to have someone who looked like her sister in her presence every day. When my mother looked at me each day, did she see Fradel's face? When we argued, as we did often, did it hurt her that a Fradel look-alike was talking back?

After Jim and I married, we attended one of these memorials to show respect to my parents and for Jim to meet some of the people who had become our substitute family. Standing there, I realized that the crowd was thinning out. Those who had emigrated before the war were well into their senior years and were slowly dying off, and some of the younger ones, the survivors my parents' age, had died as well.

I had been asked to speak at the service, to talk about what these meetings meant to me as part of the second generation, as the American child of someone who had experienced the War. I felt my grandparents hovering over me as I spoke, listening to my words, and was reminded again that the Nazis had not been entirely successful in their attempt to destroy the Jewish people. My grandfather, the man I had hoped would surprise us at one of these meetings, was there in my thoughts and he had been for as long as I could remember. The people I had never met, those who had been so senselessly murdered before I was born but whose existence had impacted mine so heavily, were all present in that hall. They were being remembered, if it is possible, by a granddaughter who had never known them when they were alive.

Birth and Death

One summer night almost forty years ago, my father and I were working in his shoe store. I was not a regular employee but was continually drafted and was there that night to help. I don't remember why I was needed that evening. Perhaps my mother was taking some time off, or maybe Toby was on vacation. There were no customers, and the usually vibrant shopping street was deserted. The movie theater three doors away was not showing a crowd pleaser that might have brought foot traffic. There were even empty parking spots available, and the meters did not have to be fed after 6 p.m. But still, my dad insisted on keeping to the posted hours.

"Dad, no one is out buying shoes today. Let's close early. You can go home and watch a ball game."

"The sign says we are open until 9:30. You never know who might need a new pair of sandals."

Though I hoped he would send me home, I was reluctant to leave him alone. With shoes on three different floors, he would have to leave the front of the store to bring stock from the various rooms, depending upon a customer's needs. Leaving the front of the store with no one watching was asking for trouble. The cash register sat on the front counter and there was plenty of merchandise available for someone to grab. I settled in for a few more hours.

My dad was reading a paperback, bending back the cover so he could hold it in one hand, a habit that annoyed me as I could never treat a book that way. He did everything with full force, and this strong grip was the way he lived his life—all in, all the time. He was ready to spring into action if a customer came in and was seated in the chair closest to the counter where he kept the tools he used to adjust the shoes for his customers. I sat at the end of the row of chairs, marking time, as far away from a potential customer as I could get. I was eager to get home to my husband and young son, to enjoy my summer vacation from teaching school, to be anywhere but inside the store on a beautiful summer evening. Keeping my eyes on the clock that advertised Esquire shoe polish, I willed time to speed up and waited for liberation.

Out of nowhere, my dad looked up from his book and started talking, and this is the story that he told me. Some of the details were not clear until years later when I watched to my father's *Shoah* interview.

In my father's words:

Father and Sam (his older brother) and I were in hiding. It was 1942 and our town was under the Nazis and had been for more than eighteen months. We were working, making shoes for the commandant, grateful for having a skill that made us valuable and kept us from being deported. The Nazis knew that my father was the most skilled shoemaker in town, so that kept us safe. Sam was also very good at his work, and I watched and learned and improved because I wanted to live.

The Nazis had declared an "aktion." They were rounding up Jewish men. Even though we had work cards, we knew that it was best to hide. We went to the forest. We left Mom and the younger children, my two sisters and my little brother, in the apartment. Mom was pregnant. The pregnancy was a surprise, one of those things that happens when women go through the change. She was probably in her 40's but I don't know exactly how old she was. Sam was already 21 and I was 19. My sisters, Dora and Bronia were in their teens, and my little brother Feivel was 10 or 11. We thought they would be safe since only men were being taken.

Our neighbor was a gynecologist. He had offered my father the option of an abortion when the pregnancy was determined, a secret one of course, to protect my mother. With food being rationed the doctor advised that a pregnancy would be difficult for my mother. It was widely known that the Nazis would show no mercy to pregnant women or to babies, and the doctor tried to persuade my father to allow my mother this chance. My father refused. He told the doctor that it was bad enough that the Nazis were killing Jews. Did Jews have to kill each other as well?

We stayed in hiding in the forest for several days, waiting for things to calm down. We had a bunker where we hid. During the day we remained as quiet as possible, lying down in the cramped space. At night one of us, usually me, would go out to search for food. We knew that the farmers would let us buy eggs and cheese from them, sometimes a bread. It wasn't much, but it kept us alive. After a few days, we thought it might be safe to return to the town.

When we came to our apartment, no one was there. The Christian neighbors told us what had happened, that my mother had gone into labor and had been taken to the hospital. In my mother's absence my two sisters and my little brother had been hiding in vacant apartments in the building that had once belonged to Jewish families, hoping to avoid capture. Months before we had constructed secret spaces for them, behind the walls or in closets, not easily detected in a cursory search. We had taught them how to go into hiding quickly if they heard the loud banging and the shouts that accompanied these searches. This time our plans had not succeeded. With Mother gone, they were on their own. The girls were discovered in the raid and hearing his sisters' cries my younger brother had come out of his hiding spot and surrendered. All three had been taken away.

The neighbors told us that the baby, a girl, had been born only a day or two before. We ran to the hospital to see Mother and the baby, but we were too late. Everyone in the hospital had been taken away. We later learned that their destination was Belzec, a death camp.

I was so upset and so angry with my father. He had the chance to save my mother, or so I thought, if he had allowed her to have the abortion. I remember biting my tongue when my father forbade it. I knew it was against Jewish law to kill, but I also knew that one should do everything to save a Jewish life. If my mother had not gone into labor, she might have been home at the time of the raid and perhaps she would have been able to keep my sisters and brother safe. Who knows? We lost everyone. There was only me and Sam and Father left after that. We lost everyone.

I thought I knew all the stories about the family until that evening. I knew my grandmother had given birth to a baby in 1942, and that she had been taken to Belzec. What I did not know were the circumstances—the possibility of the abortion, and the capture and death of the rest of the family.

Why did my father tell me this story that night? I do not know. I did not ask. I only know that it sits in my heart like a shard of glass, stabbing me each day since the day I first heard it.

Not long after that summer evening my father and his brother Sam dedicated a memorial plaque for their family at a local cemetery where Philadelphia Holocaust survivors had established a sacred space to remember their dead families who had no real resting places. The brothers included the names of their mother and father, Malkah and Chaim Freilich, their sisters Dora and Bronia, and their brother Feivel. A name that I had never seen before was added, Sarah. The two surviving brothers had consulted our rabbi to ask whether it was appropriate to memorialize the baby sister they had never seen, one who had been killed quite soon after her birth, the one who had never been named. The rabbi instructed them that the child deserved to be remembered as part of the family and that she should be named Sarah, the traditional name for a Jewish girl who dies before she can be named. And so, Sarah became a part of the family. She was no longer nameless.

It is hard to find on a map because of its infamous past coupled with a national, perhaps universal desire to forget. Until a few years ago, it was a shallow ravine surrounded by hills covered with the same tall grasses that populate all the fields in that region. No trace of what had transpired there for those few months that it sizzled with the activity of murder and stank from the stacks of corpses being burned after the gassings had killed the victims. It was once served by a train line; the station is still there, although it is out of use now since the traffic does not warrant stopping as it did at the height of its utility. Only those who know what to look for come here, and once they disembark from their tour buses or cars, they are struck by the simplicity of the memorial and the complicated horror of the inhumanity that once made this death factory function day and night. It is Belzec.

A small museum details the destruction of the Jews of Galicia in 1942—almost 500,000 victims of the Nazi perpetrators and their Polish and Ukrainian collaborators, the third highest death toll in the camp system surpassed only by Auschwitz and Treblinka. Photographs of the roundups, some artifacts of prisoners' belongings including housekeys and eyeglasses, and some written excerpts of personal accounts testify silently, and yet somehow deafeningly, that this was a place where survival was not possible, where people were killed immediately upon arrival, and where the surrounding neighbors knew exactly what was going on, even camping out on the hills on Sundays to watch the executions.

The ravine, plowed under when the job was considered satisfactorily complete, when there were no Jews left to kill, has been covered with what looks like cooled black lava, rough and inhospitable to life, but where, like at Auschwitz, stray wildflowers manage to eke out an existence while butterflies flit about them. Nature will not let this place remain entirely dead.

There are two sides to this lava field, bisected by a path that leads to a stone wall at the back. As you walk down the middle path, the field of lava seems to grow higher around you, and you become smaller and smaller in relation to it as it engulfs you. At some point you can no longer see past the lava and cannot see light. You can only continue to walk into the dark, as those who suffered here must have walked, not knowing where they were headed. Once you reach the back wall, you are faced with the inscription from the Book of Job, *Earth, do not cover my blood. Let there be no resting place for my outcry.* You then turn to the left or right to face walls of a lighter stone. On these walls are etched the most common Jewish first names, Chaim, Eva, Rebecca, Israel—and hundreds more. Without hesitation you begin to look for names that are familiar, family names, names you have heard, even your own name, as macabre as that might seem. Since there are no records of who was brought here and died here, all evidence of the camp's existence having been destroyed, only seven survivors were left to tell exactly what happened here.

I find the name of my paternal grandmother, Malkah. And I find the names of her daughters, Dora and Bronia, her son Feivel, and Sarah, the baby girl that she gave birth to a day before the roundup in their town. I have brought candles, and I say the Kaddish for people I have never seen, but whose blood runs through my veins. I imagine what they must have looked like, a woman in her early forties, two teenage girls, a young boy of about eleven, and a newborn baby, if in fact the newborn ever made it into the trains that brought them to this place. I hope that none of them knew where they were going. I hope that death came quickly. I hope that they were together, but I fear that Feivel may have been separated from the women and sent to stand with the men. I am kidding myself that it made any difference.

The first time I visit Belzec I am so overcome that I spend the rest of the day in silence. During subsequent visits I make it a point to tell my family's story to my fellow travelers. I tell people in the States to visit Belzec, to witness what was done there, not to let this place of death remain unknown. I am performing a sacred duty. I will not let the earth cover up my family's blood, and I will not allow their voices to go unheard.

I am Malkah's granddaughter. I am Bronia's and Dora's and Feivel's niece. And I am Sarah's niece. She was born only six years before me. We might have had a special aunt and niece relationship—so close in age, we would be more like sisters. But that was not to be. Now I am the one who remembers them, who contains their story, who tells it to whoever will listen. I am the dutiful daughter whose evening in a quiet shoe store long ago changed my life in ways I could never have foreseen.

In the Cards

My father's booming voice rises from the basement recreation room through the air vents and into my bedroom. It is a Saturday night sometime in the 1960s. I am in junior high, too young to date or to be out on a Saturday night. I have said the obligatory hello to my parents' friends, endured the faux compliments and embarrassing questions, and made my escape to my bedroom, but I cannot get away from my father's shouts.

"Why did you play the jack? Are you an idiot? Don't you remember that hearts are trump? How can I play with you as my partner if you constantly make these ridiculous mistakes and cause us to lose?" I can tell from the tenor of his voice that he has thrown the cards down onto the game table in disgust.

"It's only a game. Stop hollering! If you don't calm down, we'll stop playing, because I won't be yelled at like that," His card partner's voice is not as loud, but being called an idiot has angered his target, one of the men in my parents' circle of friends.

"It might be a game, but you must play with your whole heart, no matter. You have to care. You have to *want* to win." My father keeps shouting. I imagine that he is standing now, edging away from the table to get a drink of water from the pitcher on the bar. All other activity has probably stopped. The other men are watching as my father and his partner continue yelling at each other.

"Nobody cares as much as you do about winning," his partner responds. "We're playing for fun. If you lose this game, you can win the next. This is not big money we are playing for. Your children will still eat this week."

"No, you must play like your food depended on it, no matter what the game! You are either all in, or not in at all."

I can picture exactly what is happening. My father turns away and faces the bar. He can see himself in the mirror behind the counter, his face is red. I have seen him like this many times in our home, at the park where the players meet on Sunday afternoons, and on the beach in the summer. To him, the game is not just like life, it *is* life. The lesson is always the same: you must play with all your faculties, you must read your partner's signals, recognize and act on your opponents' weaknesses and mistakes, and finally, you must triumph. There is no game that is simply fun or is played for laughs. Mistakes can be catastrophic, which means there is no room for indecision. This is how he does everything. This is how he teaches us, my brother and me, to face life. This is what he drills into us—give it your all, no matter what the circumstance, even something as trivial as a game of cards.

The weekly card games are my parents' recreational outlet. The ten couples in the Family Group met every Saturday evening starting in 1960 and continued for the next forty years, rotating from one house to another. The women play Rummikub or 14-card rummy. They gossip over their hands, not caring who wins or loses. They are there for the camaraderie. This is, after all, the group that understands them best, this is the place where they are accepted. Here their stories are never-ending, and no explanations are necessary. When the game is being held in our house, the women sit in groups of five, one set at the dining room table, and the other at the kitchen table, close enough for one group to overhear the other and to laugh at jokes or commiserate over the sad stories of how one's children have disappointed them.

"Girls, I have a problem. My son is dating a *shiksa*. She seems a nice girl, but I cannot accept her into my house. If his father finds out, there will be hell to pay!"

"It's our worst nightmare. That a child should go outside the religion! My parents would have killed me if I even looked at non-Jew."

"Who even knew a non-Jew in the old country? This is the danger in America. We live among them and soon our children will marry them!"

"Oy, God forbid a thousand times!"

The men sit downstairs in the recreation room. Their game, some crazy Polish one called *kapitsch* whose rules are completely mysterious and inexplicable to their American children, can only accommodate four players at a time. If there are ten men present, two groups of four play while two people sit out, snoozing on the sofa, or watching whatever sport is being played on television. For some of the men this presents no problem. They have no great interest in the game and would rather sit out. For my father, not being able to play is disastrous. My uncle tells me that my dad has always been this competitive. As a boy he played soccer with all his heart in every game. But it was the concentration camps that made him even more determined to best everyone, to win at everything, as if each game was still a contest of life and death. When he watches my brother pitch in little league, when we kick the soccer ball around on the lawn, no matter the level of competition, winning for my father is paramount.

My father's shouts travel up the steps to the dining room and kitchen. The women can hear him even over their chatter. He is the only one who takes the game this seriously, the only one who gets worked up. My mother is accustomed to his rants. He is impatient with anything less than perfection. His quick temper flares up and is spent in a few hot minutes, unlike hers which burns like a damp rag for hours. My mother is embarrassed, but reluctant to start an argument with him by asking him to calm down. I know the expression that must be on her face as the arguments coming up from the recreation room become more heated. The louder he gets, the more worried she gets. Rather than focusing on the game or the gossip, she cannot help but try to overhear the sounds from downstairs. Soon enough, she hopes it will be time for cake and coffee. The women will go downstairs and join their husbands, or the men will come up to join their wives. There will be idle chatter, a drink of schnapps to congratulate someone on a happy event, and then, if it is still early, more cards.

After the company leaves and while they are cleaning up, my mother asks my father the same question she always does. I am still awake, and my room shares a wall with the kitchen. I can hear her disappointment and his defense.

"Why do you have to get so excited? It's only a game. You'll see, no one will want to play with you if you keep this up. I don't want to lose our friends because you can't calm down. I could hear you. Calling them idiots! Oy! Why should they allow you to call them names? They are right. This is not a game you must win. Our children, thank God, have food to eat."

"I can't help it if they are idiots. Do you know how many mistakes Chaim made during that hand? We could have won easily, but he doesn't watch the cards. And Sam K.! He is the worst partner. He doesn't watch and he doesn't care. He would rather sleep on the sofa than play. It's not a challenge at all with him because he doesn't try!"

"Calm down. Promise me you will try to control yourself next Saturday. Don't shame me like this."

"If I have Sol for a partner, I can be calm. He plays smart. He plays to win. And don't worry. They won't throw us out of the game. They are our friends. They understand."

I knew my father was smarter than the other players. I knew that was why he criticized their card-playing skills. I also knew how much winning meant to him. It was the way my brother and I were instructed to face the world. B's were failures, A's were what counted. Second place was never good enough. His high standards for himself were the same ones he held for us. There were times when I resented his all-consuming drive, and it made me angry to have him tell me how disappointed he was if I was not the best in everything I attempted. Our battles over my lack of success in chemistry, a subject my father loved, made it clear that I should either lie about how well I was doing or not ever try to do things that he cared deeply about. Stay in your own lane, I learned.

My mother's attempts to change my father's behavior at the card game were repeated every Saturday night for forty years until my father's dementia made it impossible for him to play cards at all, and until it was impossible for him to follow sports on television, impossible to read even the front page of the newspaper. His intellect and survival skills withered to such an extent that the card game with its arcane rules began to baffle him just as it had baffled us for all those years. No longer sharp and determined to win, he became sweet and mellow, as if he had undergone a personality transplant. No cutting remarks would ever again pass his lips, and he went from being the loudest person in the room to fading into almost complete silence. I lost the man I grew up with—the man whose aggressive nature had driven him and compelled me to never be satisfied with "good enough." And I watched this metamorphosis with great sorrow. As much as my father's insistence on winning had irritated me, I missed the edge that had defined him. This gentle soul was someone I didn't know.

And so my father became someone else. The few friends that were still alive noticed that he spent time during the card games sleeping on the couch or pretending to watch the sports that he no longer could follow. Soon, he was too confused to attend the Saturday night card games at all. My mother shielded him from the prying questions and pitying looks by isolating them both. Rather than ask her friends for help and support, which they would have gladly given, she chose to remain at home with my dad, making excuses about not wanting to drive at night, pretending that she no longer cared to join the card games. In their last years in their own home, when it was clear that nothing would ever be the same, Mom pretended everything was fine.

I have often wondered how much of this denial of Dad's deteriorating condition was a part of Mom's camp mentality. She had learned never to show weakness, never to admit anything was wrong. Weakness meant certain death, meant being sent to the gas. Their fear of doctors played a part in this as well. Was this what made her reluctant to seek help for Dad when it was clear he was losing his mental abilities? Did some mechanism deep inside keep her from admitting that what was troubling Dad was not temporary, was not curable? Did she believe he would be taken away from her?

At times I attributed her attitude to selfishness. I thought she could not bear to have her life upset in any way. Admitting that Dad needed help might mean she would have to become more responsible for the everyday tasks he had always seen to. She would have to pay their bills, she would have to drive to the market or the beauty parlor, no longer being chauffeured there by Dad. She would have to make decisions, talk to their financial advisor, make the doctor appointments, hire someone to do small home repairs. No matter how much I helped with any of these things on the weekends, their lives were no longer the same. No matter how much I urged her to confront the reality of the situation, she accused me of exaggerating the level of his decline.

"He's all right. Don't make him into an invalid."

"Mom, you must be kidding. He doesn't know where he is most of the time. Face the facts. Your life and his are changing. We must do something to keep both of you safe."

For years I blamed her for the circumstances that eventually brought them both to the senior facility where they lived until their respective deaths. Mom would not administer Dad's medicine; she insisted that he could handle it by himself. She would not take away the checkbook from which Dad was writing checks to phony charities and paying non-existent bills. She told me that it would insult him if she took control of the money. She would not stop Dad from driving until it became clear that he was endangering both the two of them as well as everyone else on the road, and my brother and I finally had to take away their car. Most destructive of all was her inability to admit to her best friends that Dad was succumbing to dementia. Because she would not talk about the problem, her friends didn't either. And the result was that she was left alone when she needed her friends more than ever.

My father never would have had patience with the physical failings of old age and in some ways, dementia was exactly the kindest disease that might have afflicted him. Not being aware of what was happening to him was perhaps the gentlest way for him to go. Though it was painful for my mother and for the rest of the family to see him in his broken state, he was spared the agony of his own downward spiral—a diminishment he never could have tolerated.

Life is a Wonderful Gift

Written by Mom on March 21, 1981

Life is a wonderful gift. Never despair of it. Live, and if you can, love. I believe that life is good, and that man can be good, or at least better than their circumstances. I have known the worst that the world can do to me, and yet I have faith.

Do not linger with the dead. They must be left in peace. Do not forget what has happened, but do not live in bitterness. The past is the past, do not dig it up.

Look for the pot of gold at the rainbow's end, and even if you do not believe it is there, go on looking.

I was finished with the past. From anxiety, I passed to fear, and from fear to sorrow. Fear was a terrible wandering that destroyed my spirit, but sorrow was an arriving, a new beginning. I was not running away from something but going toward it.

Of course, one must always be on one's guard. Evil is not dead. It might break out again and again and that is why I must not forget. Why I must always remain a messenger from the dead.

Perhaps there is no God, whom I had promised to believe in forever, perhaps in time I will reconcile myself to a human God. Only time will tell.

The future remains a question mark.

Nothing Stays

My eyes dart from one side of the street to the other. The signs are in a language I can't read, not only foreign but in characters of an alphabet that I can't decipher. Is it Korean? Some other Asian language? The stores are indistinguishable to me, except for the ones with signs in Portuguese, which I fool myself into thinking I am translating correctly, given my four years of high school Latin. Does it matter what the signs say? I am not here to stay. I am merely driving by on my way to somewhere else. I once lived on this street and knew every doorway along it and the faces behind the doors. Now I have become someone else, and I am as unrecognizable as this place.

What happened to those landmarks of my childhood? Where is the Food Fair market and its competition, the Penn Fruit, on the opposite corner? My mother sent me there to buy "sconions," one of her many mispronunciations, this time of scallions, that had me wandering the produce aisle, finally asking the manager who laughed heartily, much to my humiliation. What has replaced the Castor Deli where my mother would buy succulent corned beef for our sandwiches, where the pickle barrel nearly overflowed in abundance, where the entire store was redolent with the aromas of Jewish appetizing? Has the new tenant of that space ever been able to rid it of those mouthwatering scents? Does anyone purchase fresh cottage cheese scooped by hand at a dairy store anymore? Or buy *lekvar* (prune filling) for *hamantaschen* (triangular pastries for Purim) by the pound? Those specialty stores have disappeared, or maybe others catering to a different clientele have sprung up in their place. I don't stop to investigate but continue on my way.

Can it be true that Fleet's Men's and Boys' has closed? For many years they published photos of boys in their newly purchased Bar Mitzvah suits in the *Jewish Exponent*. How we waited expectantly for my brother's picture to appear fifty-five years ago, and then many years later my son's when he became bar mitzvah. Where do boys get their Bar Mitzvah suits now, I wonder? And Fleet's next-door neighbor, the Mr. Bond Shop, where the latest in ladies' sportswear was sold? My mother had a charge account at both stores, not a credit card but a store account. Every week she would drop off a payment. I remember when I opened my own account. No one checked my credit status; they had known me since

I was seven, and my family name was enough of a guarantee of payment. But Mr. Bond is gone as well and the corner I once knew so well is strangely unfamiliar.

Lenny's Hot Dogs has gone out of business. How many of those hot dogs did my brother and I consume for lunch because my mother was working, and it was easier to send me across the street than for her to leave my dad alone in the store. Why did the hot dogs we cooked at home never taste as good as Lenny's? I think back to when my son would spend time with my parents at the store. If a Jewish holiday occurred during the week and his day school was closed, my parents would take care of him while my husband and I were at work. He walked the Avenue with my mother as I had done years before. A Lenny's hot dog was his reward for being good, and he was an expert at cajoling my mother into buying him two for lunch, even though when I came for him, I was told he had eaten only one. We all knew we were lying, but that was part of the fun of spending the day with Bubbie and Zayde.

The Frankford Trust Bank folded long ago. It's a discount drug store now and has one of the few signs in English. I remember walking to the bank with my mother to make daily deposits and to get change for the cash register. The tellers all knew her well, and the business she was transacting always ended with a recount of how everyone's kids were and whether the new shoes for fall or spring had come in yet to the store. It was part of my mother's daily stroll on Castor Avenue—stopping into the Shelly Shoppe to schmooze with the salesladies, picking up a steak sandwich for my dad at Dante's Inferno, buying ground meat at Potok's kosher butcher for her famous meatloaf, perhaps checking to see if her special order bras had come into the Castor Corset Shop. She might call into Leon's to say hello and to ask after fellow Auschwitz survivor, Fema, who operated a beauty shop in the rear part of her husband's barber shop. What stroke of fate had brought my mother and Fema together, owning businesses across the street from each other, so many thousands of miles away from the hell where they first met.

Perhaps Mom and I would be on a mission at S and H Hardware, a place so overcrowded with items that only Harold, the owner, and one or two trusted employees could find anything there. Has the hardware store gone too? Though it morphed into a luxury kitchen and bath remodeling shop to keep pace with the times, it was never as busy as in the old days. Those in the know still frequented S and H to buy the obscure hardware fitting. Was that enough to sustain it?

The red light turns green, and I drive forward, but my mind wanders back.

Castor Avenue was filled with wonders. Two blocks from my dad's shoe store there was a Woolworth's whose aisles held a miscellany of sewing notions, paperback books, Halloween costumes, school supplies and wonder of wonders—pets! There we purchased our first parakeet. We named it Jackie because we couldn't tell if it was male or female. Jackie learned to talk from my persistent repetitions of his name, which I would say over and over as I stood in front of the cage each morning while enduring my mother's vigorous braiding of my hair. One block further up the street was the Bushrod Library I frequented once a week, proudly leaving with my new stack of books. I longed to graduate from the children's section to the adult room, but the rules were strict in those days. One had to be in 6th grade, and by the time I reached that milestone, we had moved away.

Two doors from the shoe store and our apartment was the Castor Movies where the manager would let us in for free. When I was nine, the film *Gigi* was playing, but only in the evenings. I was enchanted with the poster drawing of Leslie Caron, the adorable French girl on the verge of womanhood. I convinced my parents to let me see the film. My father escorted me to the door, and the manager waited with me in the lobby after the movie was over until Dad came back to retrieve me. The pleasure of being by myself in the large auditorium surrounded by all the color and music of the film has never left me. As far as I can tell, the Castor Movies has become a furniture store. There is no cinematic magic there anymore.

One door away from our store was Flossie's Hat Shop where Flossie employed seven- year-old me and my four-year-old brother to pick up straight pins from the floor, each of us earning a quarter for doing so. We never figured out if she was too old to bend down to pick up the pins herself, or if she just wanted to give us some money for a treat. The hat shop no longer exists, having succumbed to the change in women's styles long ago.

Best of all was Lipton's Bakery right next door. Oh, the smells of bread and cakes that wafted into our apartment each morning! Is it any wonder that the whole family was cake addicted? No matter how hard I try, my chocolate cupcakes will never measure up to those of my memory. My brother and I reminisce about the bakery with longing, especially for the times when Mr. Lipton would beckon us over and give us cupcakes for free. We were just about the only children on the Avenue and were the darlings of so many of the shopkeepers, my brother with his red hair and freckles, me with my long braids flying as I played with my hula hoop for hours on the sidewalk, careful not to block the door to my dad's store.

Would my father cringe to know that his beloved shoe store had become, of all things, a halal butcher shop? Or would he have understood that change is inevitable and that he had taken everything he could from Castor Avenue and given back much as well. I set my gaze forward, determined to drive on. Relish the memories, I tell myself. Nothing stays.

Farewell

I knew my mother was going to die. She had been moved to a hospice to give her caregivers and the family a bit of a reprieve from the crisis mode we had been living in for several months. Mom had been in and out of the hospital with infections that caused a kind of sundown dementia that afflicted her at night. She believed she was back in Auschwitz, or perhaps awaiting deportation. I would call her each evening as was our routine, fearful of how she might respond as she sank more deeply into this state. Sometimes she would be her calm self, able to talk about the day's events and ask after family and friends. But more often, the calls were filled with desperate cries for help. On some evenings she insisted that she was in the wrong room, other times she was filled with dread and insisted that unless I came to get her immediately, she would no longer be there, and I would be unable to find her. She screamed that I would be sorry that I had not heeded her cries for help. On those nights, no matter what I said or did, I was not able to calm her. These fears seemed to evaporate in the morning, only to recur with the same intensity again the following evening. There was no point in trying to reason with her. I could only beg the aides and nurses to try to settle her and then weep each time I hung up the phone. This fate was too cruel. Why was she being forced to suffer through the Holocaust *again*?

Once she was moved into hospice, she was sedated around the clock. Though the surroundings and the staff were totally unfamiliar, she seemed more comfortable than she had been in the room she had occupied at the Watermark retirement home. When I visited her each day, the staff told me she had not eaten, but that she was still taking fluids, and then finally, the hospice doctor took me aside one afternoon three days into her stay and explained to me that she was actively dying. I did not know how to respond. I was losing her, but I was also aware her quality of life had diminished so much her life held no joy for her any longer. I was relieved I would no longer be responsible for her and guilty that I could feel that way. My friends often told me what a good daughter I was, how much care I had shown for my father before he died, and how devoted I was to my mother. I wanted to believe them, but I knew that at times I was going through the motions of the dutiful daughter, and my heart wasn't in it anymore.

The twelve years since my mother's accident had drained me, and despite my exhaustion, I was ashamed of my lack of compassion for her. All my life I had lived with the awareness it was my job to alleviate her suffering in any way I could. The last few years had brought back the feelings of being burdened unfairly. I was more abrupt with her and less tender than I had been at the outset of this phase of her life when she had been recuperating from her fall. Though we had always had a difficult, even fractious relationship, I had managed to focus on the positive, trying my best to make her as comfortable and happy as I could. But things had changed over the years. My later visits with her were marked by unending accusations about my lack of attention. No matter how long I visited, she criticized my impatience to leave, and most of our time together was spent with her insisting she wanted to die and my offering counterarguments that she had many reasons to live. I was lying to her, and we both knew it. She was unhappy, struggling with her blindness, trapped in her dependence on others for her most basic needs. She accused me of never hugging her anymore and she was right. I did not hug her. The most I could manage was a quick touch on arriving and a kiss goodbye when I left. My Sundays were taken up with these nightmare visits that left me angry with her and frustrated with myself. I felt my jaw clench from the moment I walked into the Watermark until I walked out again hours later. Our relationship had devolved into one of filial duty rather than love.

The last time I saw her she was asleep in her hospice bed. I sat in the corner chair, quietly waiting for her to awaken. After a long while she opened her eyes. She was totally blind and would not have known I was there, but seeing her movements, I spoke to her to let her know I was with her.

"Mom, I'm here. You were sleeping so peacefully I didn't want to wake you."

As always, she recognized my voice and beckoned me to sit on her bed.

"Mamaleh, I had a dream about Papa." Her voice was happier than it had been in months.

"My father?"

"No, *my* father," she replied and smiled. I was surprised. She had not spoken about her parents in a long time.

"How did he look?"

She had told me many times that her father was tall, bald, and very handsome. She had loved him for his playful nature and generous spirit and for how he had showered his children with affection and provided them a comfortable life before the Nazis. The last time she had seen her father was when he had jumped from the train, leaving his two daughters alone to face a terrible fate.

"He looked good," she said. "I thought I would not remember what he looked like, but he looked like my papa."

"That's amazing, Mom. You seem happy. I'm glad for you."

Her smile was beatific. A kind of calm radiated from her, a calm so different from the nervous anxiety that had marked her every moment for months. It was then I knew my mother would die. Seeing her father again must have been some sort of closure for her—the resolution to the mystery of what had happened to him, and a modicum of comfort for her in her last hours. It seemed to me, and perhaps to her, that it was as if he was beckoning to her, telling her he would be taking her with him this time on the journey.

She died the following morning.

After the Skokie March

This is from a speech Mom gave at several different gatherings after the 1977 Skokie, Illinois march by the Ku Klux Klan. She was asked to reflect on how a Holocaust survivor felt seeing the Klan have the right to assemble and air their hateful message.

My story is not a pretty one. Nonetheless, it cannot be forgotten. By remembering the Holocaust, we can prevent a universal holocaust from reoccurring.

I have learned through the years that some experiences cannot be shared, cannot be understood by those who were not there, still we must try to understand, we must try to learn the unlearnable and speak the unspeakable. Only our continuing concern for human rights and the awareness of the pain of others can prevent another Holocaust.

We are one people, we are responsible for each other, we will not stand idly by as the world once did. The holocaust should no longer be the painful private world of the Jewish people.

Through the years the Holocaust has been exploited through different media, Many books have been written about the Holocaust, many words have been voiced, and many questions have been asked and remained unanswered. And up to this day many learned men are puzzled if something like this could ever happen again.

As history tends to repeat itself, we must certainly be aware of what is happening in the world, for what happened is a warning. To forget it is guilt. It must be continuously remembered. It was possible for it to happen, and it remains possible for it to happen again, at any minute. Only through knowledge can it be prevented, but the message must be clear, and the truth must be revealed.

It is important to tell the world, especially the young people the story of the Nazis. It is to give meaning to the meaningless deaths of millions, each an individual, individuals with families, and hopes and dreams and fears.

It is a tale of an event so vile that it both attracts and repels us. It is an epic in history that defies imagination, yet this war of such destruction as never witnessed before in history, was thought of, planned and carried out by human beings.

The more enlightened Jews have learned that when we fail to speak out om favor of our fellow Jews then all Jews are in danger.

Today many sources of danger threaten the Jewish community. We have learned, if the world has not, that the virus of antisemitism is contagious. The Russians oppress us, the recent spread of antisemitic incidents in the West must not be ignored. The increasing isolation of Israel gives cause for concern for all thinking Jews. In America, "Death to the Jews" is preached.

The fires were extinguished, but the embers continue to glow. In Chicago, a band of men put the twisted cross back on their arms, and the supreme court deems it legal.

But to know is not enough. We must have the courage to stand up and be counted, whether it is by marching in Skokie, answering antisemitic remarks, to correct false information, or to communicate in a meaningful way, therefore it requires the basic truth and knowledge about our people, both from a historical and modern perspective. If we allow ourselves to be intimidated, guilty or ashamed, we have only ourselves to blame.

We must leave to our children an explanation not of the "how" of that period, but rather of the "why." That they may remain eternally vigilant against the flaws in human nature so horribly exemplified in the death of the six million martyrs.

The importance of the Holocaust is not the sickness of the few who led, but the normality of the millions who willingly followed.

The message of the Holocaust is that never again can mankind tolerate a group of people, no matter how small or seemingly sick, who believe that they hold the one and only truth for the world.

Amng the nations of the world there must come to be an understanding that free men must spill their blood and treasures in defense of human dignity.

A Letter to God

I found this in Mom's papers. She had written it more than once. This is the last version.

Today God, I need to reckon with you. Whether I am indebted to you for my life, or perhaps are you in debt to me? First, make clear to me God, give me an accounting for things as they are! Why are the best doomed to death and lesser persons permitted the breath of life?

Why didn't the world come apart and sink into nothingness at the unbelievable horror and monstrousness of the mad Holocaust thrust upon millions of your chosen ones?

Where were you? Where was your compassion, Lord?

Your mercy, your graciousness unto your people, who were annihilated even on the spot.

When the children struggled against the fire, when the children were gassed, when they screamed at being torn from their mothers, when they stood naked, disbelief in their staring, frightened eyes, their tender little bodies wrapped in freezing cold and drenching rain, waiting for certain death, why did not the world burn and consume itself in the bloody laments of those doomed people? Why?

Why did the world suddenly become deaf to the anguish and bloodshed of so many millions?

Why were your benevolent ears closed to the death struggle of your people, O Lord? Did you not hear! Eyes and lips begged for mercy. Oh, the lips that prayed for hope. Lips which could barely frame the words, through spasms of pain, whispered prayers. Fearful hearts called your name. But you, Lord, were silent.

One shudders thinking, they knew their certain end, yet they prayed, they called upon you. Where, oh where were you God?

Over there in Heaven, high above, far from the brutal sordid world, the screams and the crackling of the flames, the gasps and gagging in the throats of the little ones, did these sights and sounds not reach you? Almighty, all-seeing God!

Auschwitz, Treblinka, Belzec!

You, the symbol of mercy, and you Lord were silent.

The gush and flow of blood was like the outpouring of a lush harvest. When the myriad throats choking on the gases fed them, piled themselves in heaps and mounds on the floors of the extermination chambers, children, such innocents, perished.

No thank you, Ruler of the world, that you spared my life.

But please God, give me an accounting for myself. Why, God, why?

I Thought I Told You This

I could never tell exactly when the stories would come, what would be the motivating force behind the sudden gush of information. The holidays seemed to be the time that evoked memories of home and family, but the stories about the camps did not fit into that same mold. Those stories could appear anytime, anywhere, with no apparent provocation. And I could never be prepared for what piece of information might be added, what horrible fact would suddenly be revealed. Just when I thought I had heard everything, a new detail would show up to stun me.

One day, when I was in my thirties and my mother was in her late fifties, we were walking together on Castor Avenue. I had left Josh with my father in the store so I could help my mother with packages we were taking to the post office. We were bundled up against the wind, and the sun was shining in the way that it does in winter, brilliant and deceptive, with a glare that made me squint as we crossed the street. Mom started telling me the following story just as we stepped off the curb. I stopped in the middle of the intersection and turned to ask if I was hearing her correctly.

One day in Birkenau, perhaps a year into my mother's incarceration there, she was watching a train come into the platform. New arrivals were being hurried out of the cars with the usual frenzy of activity that accompanied a transport. The chaos was purposeful, a Nazi strategy to confuse the prisoners and weaken their ability to respond to what would happen next. Most trains arrived at night or were not unloaded until it was dark, keeping the human contents inside in the heat or cold without water, light or information about where they were. Their cries for help reverberated in the barracks where the veteran prisoners lamented for the new arrivals. The lights on the train platform were blinding, especially to those who had been locked inside the dark cars with only small openings for light and air. The sharp commands, the barking dogs, the pushing and shoving, the attempts to stay with one's family all combined to produce a sense of dislocation and powerlessness. Mom didn't remember when this event occurred exactly, but she did remember that her sister was no longer alive. If the train platform extended into the camp allowing new transports to enter Birkenau directly, it must have been sometime after she had first come there, because Mom had walked into the camp with her transport in early 1943. Now the trains pulled into Birkenau directly, making the entire operation more efficient, speeding up the process of destruction. It was probably sometime in 1944, and it most likely involved a transport from Hungary. Where else were there Jews still alive to provide fuel for the ovens? In that summer, the Nazis killed over 400,000 Hungarian Jews in Auschwitz in just a few months, the last large Jewish population in Europe.

"From one of the cattle-cars a bride came out, dressed in a white wedding gown. I could not believe what I was seeing." Mom spoke in a flat, almost passionless voice, but with an obvious urgency. She stood on the corner as I turned to question her.

"What? Someone came to the trains from her wedding?"

"They must have taken her right from the shul (the Yiddish word for synagogue), or maybe from a party?"

"Mom, a bride?"

I stepped back onto the curb to be closer to her as she continued to talk. She told me that two thoughts went through her mind. The first was shock that people were still getting married. She did not realize there were people who either did not know about Birkenau or who had chosen to ignore what it might mean for them. Her whole world and her every thought were of this horrible place; she thought it was everyone else's as well, except of course for the Americans, who would soon come to rescue them, or so she believed.

Her second thought was that the young woman, the bride dressed all in white, could not understand where she had landed. My mother pitied her. My mother, standing there in rags, half-alive, covered with lice, had pity for this young woman who had dreamed of a future that began in a white wedding gown. Mom told me she had very little hope this girl would survive the selection. It was clear to her just by the way she was dressed that the girl was not hardened enough to endure what would surely be her fate should she be allowed to live.

In her stories about the camps, my mother always made a distinction between those who had a chance to survive the harsh conditions of Birkenau and those who could not possibly do so. The bride was a particular instance of this. How could someone who still believed in weddings, who had thought the war was not her fate, possibly accept and survive the reality of Auschwitz?

Mom often talked about the Greek girls who were brought to her barracks in the spring of 1943. Though Mom had only been in the camp for a few months, she was already a veteran. She understood the system, what it took to survive—a curriculum one mastered quickly or not at all. The Greek girls were brought from the island of Salonika where a Jewish community had flourished for more than two thousand years. Mom remembers they were still beautiful, not emaciated, and filthy like she and her fellow prisoners were. They could not understand the kapo's commands in German and could not communicate with the other prisoners, most of whom were Eastern European. Though the more seasoned inmates came from all over Europe and spoke many different languages, most of them also spoke or understood Yiddish as a common language. The Greek girls were unfamiliar with Yiddish; they spoke their native Greek or Ladino (a form of Judeo-Spanish that mixes Hebrew with traditional Spanish. It was spoken by Jews of Sephardic heritage, primarily those from Spain, North Africa, Greece, Turkey, and the Balkans.) The Greek girls suffered many beatings because of this, unable to respond to orders quickly and appropriately. In addition, they were not inured to the cold damp Polish weather, and many of them succumbed to sickness and disease during the cold winter of that year.

Mom often pointed out that those from privileged backgrounds could not endure the deprivation. She, having spent almost two years in the ghetto before being transported to Auschwitz, starving slowly, was able to endure more. It was almost the exact opposite of what one would believe to be the case, that the well-fed would have a greater ability to survive.

I asked why she had never told me that story about the bride before and she shrugged. She always replied in the same way, "I thought I told you this." So many stories over so many years. Why did it come up now, when we were crossing the street, on this particular day? She wasn't sure. Perhaps it was the way the sun was shining on us, or something about being together, just the two of us, that had brought the whole picture to mind. I did not realize that Mom had thought about the inmates and their survival in a more analytical way, even while she was suffering in the camps. Later, I found this in her writing:

"The backbone of the camp are the "musulmans," an anonymous mass, continuously renewed, and always identical, who march and labor in silence, the divine spark dead within them, already, too empty to really suffer, one hesitates to call them living, or hesitates to call their death, death in the face of which they have no fear, as they are too tired to understand.

Day by day, everyone felt his strength vanish, his desire to live melt away, his mind grow dim, and the cold so great, the hunger so concrete, and all the rest so unreal, that it did not seem possible that there could really exist any other world or time, other than our world of mud and our sterile and stagnant time, whose end we were by now approaching. For us, hours, days, months spilled out sluggishly, from the future into the past, always a valueless material, The future stood in front of us, grey, like an invisible barrier. For us history has stopped. We were like shadows broken by blows, whom the blows no longer hurt.

The tunes were few, the same ones every day, morning and evening, they lie engraven (sic) in our minds and will be the last thing that we will forget. They are the voice of the geometrical madness, of the resolution of others to destroy us first as humans, in order to kill us more slowly afterwards.

The concentration camp was a great machine to reduce us to beasts. We must not become beasts and so we must force ourselves to survive, to tell the story, to bear witness.

We are slaves, deprived of every right, exposed to every insult. Condemned to death, but we still possess one power, our hope, and we must defend it with all our strength, and so we help each other to remain alive, not to begin to die.

We know where we came from, the memories of the world outside crowd our sleeping and our waking hours. We become aware with amazement that we have forgotten nothing, every memory evoked that rises in front of us is painfully clear, but where we are going we do not know."

Though I know of homes where survivors never told their children anything about the past, I felt both blessed and at times terribly overburdened by the willingness of my parents to tell us what had occurred. My mother spoke about her experiences less frequently than my father, but she never refused to answer a question I might have. For this I am extremely grateful. Those whose parents kept secrets from them undoubtedly sensed that there was something dark and dangerous they were being shielded from. Not knowing, for me, would have been more frightening than any story my parents could possibly tell. Even though the stories horrified me, to have my mother or father relate them allowed me to realize that survival was possible, that life did indeed go on, that the heroes were just ordinary humans who experienced the same emotions as anyone else. It was this that encouraged me to share what had happened to them, precisely because the survivors were as good or as bad as anyone else, no more, no better, and yet....

"I thought I told you this" was a familiar phrase, one I heard until the last days of my mother's life. Sometimes when I watch her video testimony, I want to stop the tape to ask her about a detail I realize has escaped my understanding, but I cannot do that now. Even as I sat with my memo pad and pen in her hospice room trying to capture the last pieces of her story, I understood there was much that I would never know, and now that she is gone, there is no one left to ask.

My mother's stories formed and transformed me, whether on a first telling or when repeated. Each time I heard them, some tiny aspect struck me as if it were the first time. Sometimes it was my age at each time that was the critical difference, but other times it was that she added the season of the year in which the story took place or included some other detail that brought the story to life. Perhaps it was my eventual recognition what my mother had endured was forever seared into me. I may not have experienced all that she did, but through some transference I was permanently marked by her loss, her suffering and her survival. When I came to realize this, the recognition transformed the way I taught, the way I wrote, and the way I have lived my life.

Shabbos Candles

Before the sun drops too low on the horizon, I open the glass cabinet in my dining room and remove the silver menorah my parents brought from Germany. Its curves and sinuous twists make it difficult to clean, and each Friday evening I chastise myself for not having seen to the task before the Sabbath begins. The menorah has a history that demands my attention and care, yet I have once again put it away without polishing it or removing the built-up wax that prevents the thick white candles from sitting properly in their tin holders. This menorah has suffered its share of neglect. Many years ago, when we still lived in the apartment above the store, my mother surreptitiously tossed it into the trash because she was so frustrated with her inability to restore it to the shine it had when it was purchased. She hoped my father wouldn't notice that it was gone, at least not until the trash had been picked up and the menorah could not be found. My father, somehow sensing that something was amiss, retrieved it and scolded her for what she had done. I remember hearing the confrontation in the kitchen as he held the menorah in his hand, a look of disappointment and confusion on his face. How could she have done it? How could she have thrown away something they had spent their meager savings on?

Yes, they could afford to buy a new one now, but this one had special meaning. It was one of the few things they brought from the old world to the new—their past and future encased in a parcel carefully filled with a fancy tea set they never used, two down comforters that warmed our beds for many years and this silver Shabbat "lichter," purchased from a shop in Germany sometime before they were to leave for New York. These meager belongings, the sum of their worldly possessions, accompanied my father on the *USS General Hahn*, as he sailed to join my mother already in Brooklyn awaiting him at her uncle's home, to begin what would become the rest of their lives in America.

My father told me since my mother had not cared for it properly the menorah would be mine. I couldn't have been more than eight or nine when this happened, and I was not sure I was even interested in the object or understood what it represented. I knew throwing silver away seemed financially irresponsible, but I had no sense of what the menorah symbolized to my family. We were not observant Jews. We did not light candles every Shabbos as we had done when we lived in Brooklyn, or as I imagine had been done in my parents' childhood homes in Poland. The shoe store was open until 9:30 p.m. on Friday nights. It would have been hypocritical to begin the day of rest and then go back to work in the store. So, the menorah appeared only on the holidays of Rosh Hashanah and Pesach.

Each time it was needed, my mother would remember she had not polished it and there would be a scramble to retrieve it from where it was stashed away in a closet somewhere, and to give it a quick scrub and find the proper candles. Still, when it was lit, its holy light never failed to cast an enchanting glow—an aura that suggested what the menorah's past might have been. I would never know its provenance, what woman had once stood over it, her head covered, her hands curved toward her face, reciting the blessing that brought the Sabbath to her home. Had she survived the war? Or was this the only remaining remnant of a Jewish family I would never know?

When Jim and I married, my father gave me the menorah. He was passing on the responsibility of the Shabbos candles to me, but it signified much more than that. It was his way of blessing our new lives, of transferring the responsibility for the Yiddishkeit he treasured to our newly established home. Dad was aware we had decided to maintain a kosher home and he trusted that the menorah would never find its way into the trash again. He was right. Though we have other candlesticks we received as gifts, the *lichter* is the one I prefer. Though not imposing in design or weight, it exudes an unmistakable power. When I hold it in my hands, as I clean it or just place it on the table, I feel connected to the past. And though it never belonged to anyone in my family before my parents bought it, this menorah is clearly old enough to have brought the Sabbath to other families before it came to ours. For someone with a legacy of loss as long as mine, owning something from Europe's Jewish past is a way of connecting to a chain whose links have been almost completely broken.

The sun is setting. The challah is under the cover that Jim lovingly designed and that we both stitched in the first year of our marriage. The menorah sits at the center of our table. I do what Jewish women have done for thousands of years and light the candles for the Sabbath. Shabbat Shalom! The glow of the Sabbath fills the room. We hold hands and kiss to signal the start of a new week. For a moment the Sabbath peace descends on our household. Rather than feeling transcendence, I glance at the table and castigate myself.

I should have polished the menorah.

FREILICH'S

The House

of

Beautiful Shoes

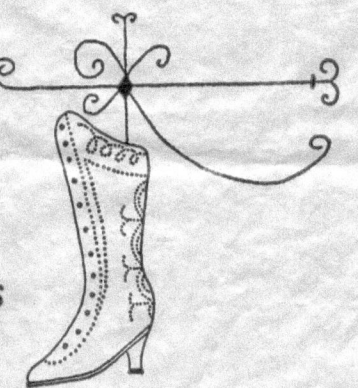

Dyeable Shoes Our Speciality

6637 CASTOR AVE.

PHILA., PA. 19149

FI 2-3770

Acknowledgements

A book is never finished; it may be published, but the work is never complete. There is as much left out as has been written. Choosing what to include is more difficult than any writing task.

I am indebted to those who read or listened to these stories as they took shape and who encouraged me to share them with the world. I know that my parents are "kvelling" over this accomplishment, although I am sure they would have many comments and plenty of corrections!

My sincere thanks

To my brother Harold Freilich, for wanting to hear my side of the story

To my sister-in-law Judith Wrubel, for persuading me these stories deserved a wider audience

To my friend Essie Abrahams-Goldberg, for her expertise and wisdom

To my friend Joan Saltzman for her encouragement

To Memoir Group (Bonnie Kay Marks, Gerry Schneeberg, Rina and Ivan Rosenberg. and that Essie woman again) for their suggestions

To Yiddish Club (Reli Gringlas, Alfred Stillman, Bebe Weiss, Rochelle Sauber, Joyce Bank and Mickey Eilberg) for their eager attention

To Jessie Williams Burns, for loving these stories when she didn't have to

To Andee Hochman, who planted the crazy idea that my stories should be published

To my daughter-in-law Sarah Newhouse, for providing the digital talent needed to preserve the pictures and documents

To my husband Jim Culbertson, for his loving and patient support – tech and otherwise

And finally to my son Joshua Culbertson, whose loving nature and boundless curiosity are the best reasons for attempting to preserve our past